Acclaim for
Still Going Strong:
Memoirs, Stories, and Poems
About Great Older Women

"This is a most enjoyable collection of pieces about women growing older. Some pieces are stories, true or fiction, some are essays, and some are poems. But all are about women growing older, and in many instances, at whatever age, still growing. This is what makes the book a pleasure to read. It is a heartwarming collection."

—Frances Sternhagen
Actress, currently in *Steel Magnolias*
on Broadway

"This anthology makes me look forward to getting older. A quick and enjoyable read, it passes my 'good book test'—I feel sorry when it ends. The characters are strong and realistic women who travel diverse life paths. They remain resilient and grow in response to the gains and losses that accompany aging. This book challenges our stereotypes of mature women, replacing ageist attitudes with images of women celebrating both independence and connection during the continuing process of self-discovery.

At times the women's personal portrayals are daringly honest, but also oddly reassuring. The challenges and inevitable declines of women in their second fifty years are more than offset by their developing power, self-determination, and wisdom. This book has the guts and candor to tell it like it is, announcing loud and clear that there is growth and joy in maturity. It describes and extends feminism in the third age, inviting women to define their own versions of successful aging."

—D.J. Shedlock, PhD
Associate Professor and Director,
Human Development Program,
Department of Psychology,
SUNY Oswego

"What a wonderful collection this is—poems and stories about and by mature women; poems and stories that illustrate and illuminate both the joys and the vicissitudes of the later years in women's lives. To read it is to laugh and it is to weep as you read. Most of all, it is to enjoy the wisdom, the humor, the passion, the wonders of being an 'older woman.' Janet Amalia Weinberg, you have created a wonderful volume. This eighty-plus-year-old woman thanks you."

—Rose Dobrof, DSW
Brookdale Professor of Gerontology,
Hunter College, City University of New York;
Editor, *Journal of Gerontology and Social Work*

Still Going Strong
Memoirs, Stories, and Poems
About Great Older Women

THE HAWORTH PRESS
Gerontology and Women
J. Dianne Garner, Editor

Still Going Strong
Memoirs, Stories, and Poems
About Great Older Women

Janet Amalia Weinberg, PhD
Editor

To Donna
Sister-writer and friend,
With love,
Sarah Shelby (p. 25)
1/29/06

The Haworth Press
New York • London • Oxford

For more information on this book or to order, visit
http://www.haworthpress.com/store/product.asp?sku=5591

or call 1-800-HAWORTH (800-429-6784) in the United States and Canada
or (607) 722-5857 outside the United States and Canada

or contact orders@HaworthPress.com

PUBLISHER'S NOTE
This book contains works of fiction and nonfiction. In works that are fiction, names, characters, places, and incidents either are the products of the author's imagination or are used fictitiously, and any resemblance to actual persons, living or dead, business establishements, events, or locales is entirely coincidental.

In works that are nonfiction, some identities and circumstances of individuals discussed have been changed to protect confidentiality.

The Haworth Press, Inc., 10 Alice Street, Binghamton, NY 13904-1580.

Cover design by Jennifer M. Gaska.

Library of Congress Cataloging-in-Publication Data

Still going strong : memoirs, stories, and poems about great older women.
    p. cm.
  ISBN-13: 978-0-7890-2870-9 (hc. : alk. paper)
  ISBN-10: 0-7890-2870-0 (hc. : alk. paper)
  ISBN-13: 978-0-7890-2871-6 (pbk. : alk. paper)
  ISBN-10: 0-7890-2871-9 (pbk. : alk. paper)
    1. Women—Literary collections. 2. American literature—Women authors. 3. Older women—Literary collections. 4. Old age—Literary collections. 5. Aging—Literary collections. 6. American literature. 7. Older women. I. Weinberg, Janet Amalia.

PS509.W6S75 2006
810.8'03522—dc22
                                                                    2005010639

In memory of my mother,
Elsa Cahn Weinberg

CONTENTS

STRENGTHS

CHALLENGES

JOYS

WHY THIS BOOK

We live in a culture that hates, fears, and makes fun of aging. In fact, our culture has been so concerned—some would say, obsessed—with the beauty and strength of youth, that it has not been able to see the beauty or strength of maturity. Most women accepted this attitude as the truth and were defined and diminished by it. Until now.

Women, myself included, are beginning to realize that our fifties, sixties, seventies, and perhaps even our eighties, could be some of the best years of our lives—if we withstand the prevailing negative view of aging. It is a big "if."

It is hard to age in a new way. I entered my later years with a surge of confidence, yet every time I expressed my new expansiveness, an inner voice warned, "You're too old." It was the enforcer of negative stereotypes such as the "old broad," "old hag," and "little old lady." That same voice speaks to many women my age. In one way or another, it tells us to shut down and back off from life.

Previous generations obeyed without question. Of course, there were always exceptions, those who ignored convention and thrived with age. My own mother grew radiant in her seventies and eighties, and to the end (she lived to ninety-one), was a beacon of compassion and joy. As more and more of us reject what our culture tells us about getting old, such exceptions could become the rule.

To speed this transformation, I put out a call for memoirs, stories, and poems, about women over fifty and asked my writing buddy and good friend, Margaret Karmazin, herself one of the new breed, to join me in writing an overview about the new type of older woman. (There's probably a new type of older man as well, but that's a subject for another book.)

The result is an anthology about vibrant, attractive women, aged fifty to ninety-seven, doing things typically considered young, facing some of the challenges of later life, and enjoying some of the benefits. Editing it gave me perspective on negative stereotypes of women over fifty and helped me feel better about aging. I hope reading it does the same.

Introduction

The New Older Woman

Janet Amalia Weinberg
Margaret Karmazin

We're a couple of older women. It took awhile for us to admit we were nearing the end of middle age and it took even longer to feel good about it. Like most people, we thought there was a border between middle and old age and that all the good stuff in life would stop once we reached it. At least, that's what we believed when we were younger. It's hard to say exactly when a woman crosses the line—it used to be around forty-five and now is somewhere between fifty and sixty-five—but we're both close enough to "the other side" to feel it loom large before us. To our surprise, it is not the dead-end, over-the-hill place we expected. In fact, it appears to be rich and rewarding and challenging and interesting—like any other stage of life.

What is defined as attractive and important depends on who is doing the defining. Until recently, young and middle-aged people dominated our culture and their interests and values set the standard for all. As a culture, we could see the physical contraction that develops with age but didn't have a clue about the inner or spiritual expansion that can also develop. A seventy-year-old woman may have overcome fears and obstacles and know the peace of fulfillment, but to eyes focused on achievements that matter in middle age, she looks "out of it," finished. She may radiate understanding and compassion, but to eyes obsessed with the beauty of youth, she is seen, if seen at all, as merely gray and wrinkled. Even when a mature woman was considered "attractive—for her age," she was being complimented for looking young. No wonder "old" was the last thing any woman wanted to be.

Women over fifty used to go along with our culture's youth-oriented view of them. They believed they really *were* unattractive and unimportant, too old to be passionate or fruitful. And they acted accordingly. They did not dance to throbbing music or kiss husbands or lovers in public because they thought it unseemly and feared people would snicker or sneer. They kept their voices low and their opinions to themselves because they thought they had nothing to say—nothing anyone cared to hear. Only young women had the right to enjoy and express the creative force, only young women were interesting and attractive.

But a liberating change is happening, a change as momentous as the liberation movements of the 1960s and 1970s. It brings respect for older people, appreciation for maturity, and the promise of a balanced culture.

People are living longer. Already, one in ten persons is a woman over sixty and the huge wave of aging baby boomers is just rolling in. Within the decade, fifty million Americans will be over sixty-five, the majority of them women. As the age wave builds, so does the influence of older adults. A growing number of books, movies, politicians, articles, magazines, and businesses cater to mature interests. And it's just the beginning.

Those of us now over fifty are different from previous generations; we have lived through social movements unlike anything our parents or grandparents experienced. The exercise craze and the rise of alternative medicine gave us personal responsibility for our health and fitness. The Human Potential movement encouraged us to value inner growth. The New Age movement taught us that beliefs—both positive and negative—become self-fulfilling prophecies. The Women's Movement raised our consciousness about demeaning cultural attitudes and helped us break free of them.

As a result, women are not only living longer but better. Many of us now over fifty are physically and fiscally stronger than our mothers and grandmothers, as well as more confident and independent. Our kids are grown, a lot of us are single, we are as comfortable in the world as we are at home, and we may have a third or more of our lives ahead of us. Old age for us will be different than it has ever been. We are a new type of older woman, a type that can enjoy and appreciate her stage of life.

Women today stay active longer. We may be in our fifties, sixties, and even seventies but we start careers, travel, have adventures, practice yoga, learn to belly dance and tango, write dissertations. We even enjoy sex and romance—and are not ashamed to admit it. Until recently, it was a given that older women were not sexy or sensual or even attractive. Now there are more and more films about romance in later life, our male partners take Viagra to keep up with us, and magazines are full of articles about mature sex. In short, women over fifty can enjoy the kind of aliveness once reserved for those younger.

At the same time, women can appreciate being older. Already, my generation is breaking free of traditional negative views of us—as we did when we were younger. Back then, with the help of the Women's Movement, we rejected attitudes that demeaned women and femaleness. Now we are challenging attitudes that demean *older* women and aging.

Take, for example, the fact that women generally stop being seen as sexual objects when they outgrow the bloom of youth. Our culture tells us this is a shattering loss but we don't have to buy that. Sure, it's a loss. But to an older woman who can appreciate her stage of life, it's also a gain: she doesn't have to endure unwelcome male attention anymore and is finally free to relate openly to men without being labeled a flirt. And what a luxury it can be to finally enjoy sex without having to deal with birth control or the pressures of children or a job.

Learning to see aging in a positive way is like exploring an unseen world. At times it can feel like groping in the dark, bumping into shapes that have no names. Terms such as "wisdom," "serenity," "post-menopausal zest," and "new freedom," are surfacing in articles and books, but as a culture, we're a long way from knowing what they really mean.

Personally, Margaret and I have bumped into moments of simply "being"—a state we longed for but rarely experienced when we were young. Back then, we were too busy trying to get somewhere and become something to enjoy or even tolerate such stillness.

What else? Sometimes when we're about to be drawn into one of our typical emotional upheavals, we suddenly recognize the scene and decide to pass it by. Such bursts of self-awareness did happen when we were younger but are more common now. After fifty or more years of replaying a psychological drama, it seems it can finally become boring.

Both of us experienced a major shift in our late fifties. I discovered the courage to do things I'd never done before and was propelled from my secluded mountain home into a new life in a new place with new people. Margaret was swept into a torrent of creativity. Not until we learned that other older women went through similar changes, did it occur to us that this surge of energy and freedom was typical for our age.

These glimpses of positive aspects of aging raise the possibility that women in their fifties and sixties and even beyond may not be *over* the proverbial hill, but at its *peak.* Previous generations of women may have known this but didn't talk about it. Or if they did, hardly anyone paid attention. Fortunately, women *are* talking about it now and people *are* beginning to listen, perhaps because there are so many of us.

Once into old age, we will face some of the greatest challenges of life—illness, loss, aloneness, and death. We will need courage and strength and humor. We will need each other. As products of our age-averse culture, it wouldn't hurt to have some good examples to guide and inspire us.

The women in this collection of stories, poems, and memoirs represent such guides. They are not Pollyannas who rave about how wonderful it is to get old, but mature women who are full of life, able to both meet the challenges of their age and enjoy the benefits.

The once common images of sidelined, depleted little old ladies are disappearing, and we women of age now hold the brush that paints the picture of our own futures.

STRENGTHS

If Love Comes to Me Again

Prartho M. Sereno

If love comes to me again
as a man with dark eyes,
and if he says to me
Open . . .
If he reaches toward me
when I'm afraid, turns
my face upward and asks,
Why hold back?
Maybe some day I'll decide
you're not my type. Couldn't you
love yourself through *that?*
Perhaps I will think, *I know things now*
that I didn't know then.
But love, in his tall hat
and lanky arms, in his infinite
pursuit of me, wipes out
the lie called memory
in a single glance.
If love comes to me again
as a drooling baby or that strange
woman in the mirror,
as a rock or a man,
and says *Open* . . .
This much I know:
every petal and thorn of me
will say yes.

Wild Life

Ruth Cash-Smith

I'm a certified couch potato from frozen Maine whose exercise consists of turning pages or stoking fires. I routinely squelch physical activity overtures; if an outdoor experience is unavoidable, I fret about bug bites, sprains, and dehydration. The only time I truly enjoy a hike is when I'm back on the couch with a heating pad, amazed by my body's ability to survive such rigors.

Imagine my reaction when my tan and fit friend Barb picks me up at the Tucson airport, prattling about the great time we'll have in two days when we join her "tennis ladies" for a walk. My joy at escaping a Down East winter fizzles and I launch into full protest: I'm over fifty, beset by numerous picayune health problems, and it's been years since I last broke a sweat. Striving for a nonjudgmental tone at such an idiotic proposal, I conclude, "You go. I'll stay here and read."

"Don't be silly, it's only eight-tenths of a mile," she says. "Besides, a couple of these women are in their eighties." Round One to Barb.

The next day I regroup, littering her kitchen counter with my various pills and inhalers. She doesn't bite. Over lunch I disclose my past altitude sickness attacks. Barb counters with how well I look, ignoring as only a true friend can my winter-white pudgy body.

That evening her nature-loving husband Mike tells me the Sonoran desert is unique in that it contains four of the six Life Zones, a geographic classification based on dominant plant species that was established by C. Hart Merriam about 100 years ago.

What this means, Mike enthuses, is that tomorrow when we leave Tucson at 3,000 feet (technically a desert scrub area), we'll pass through grassland (3,500 to 4,500 feet), oak/pine woodland (4,500 to

7,000 feet), and up to coniferous forest (6,000 plus in elevation) to reach the summit, where I can expect up to a thirty-degree temperature differential. Great, if I wanted to freeze my butt off I could have stayed put in Maine.

Hiking Day dawns and we're out of the house by 7 a.m. in an attempt to beat the desert sun. I pop two Tylenol. Just in case. . . .

At the parking lot we rendezvous with the nine "tennis ladies." During each introduction, I repeat, "I'm a flatlander coming from sea level."

"You'll do fine, dear," one svelte woman the color of toast assures me, lacing up her hiking boots. I notice then that I'm the only sneaker wearer in the crowd. "Perhaps we'll see some wild life," she adds, a cryptic comment that unnerves me further.

The tennis ladies are a tanned and fit bevy, mostly silver-haired with impeccable manicures, filled with high energy and daunting good spirits. The whole lot of them looks like they're barely old enough to join AARP. My spirits sink to hear they play tennis five days a week and hike together once a month.

After ensuring we all have sunscreen and hats, our trip leader, Rhoda, organizes car pools and we head north of Tucson to the Santa Catalina range, our destination Mt. Lemmon at 9,000 feet. I white-knuckle it in the backseat and refuse to look down at the steep drop-offs on the numerous switchbacks. Up, up, up we drive. As Barb points out the paloverde trees giving way to mesquite and yucca, I squeeze my eyes shut and offer up a fervent prayer that I'll live through this ordeal.

Thirty minutes later we are *still* climbing, past the manzanita with its red bark and the piñon pine. I feel like I'm mired in some blasted Discovery Channel episode! By now my terror is skittering worse than the gravel on the mountain road. If I break my leg, a rescue team will have to airlift me out. Or if I have an asthma attack, I'll choke to death on the ground, surrounded by the toned and shapely legs of the tennis ladies.

At last we reach the parking lot, our cars the only ones in the lot, which I interpret as a bad omen. I am devastated to learn that Barb got her wires crossed (or possibly outright lied to me); it's indeed eight-tenths of a mile—but that's just from the parking lot to the trailhead. The actual trail, Rhoda chirps, is five miles—the first half straight up.

My transparent offer to stay behind and keep an eye on the cars meets with uproarious laughter; I'm told mule deer, coati (whatever the hell that is), and badgers pose no threat to our vehicles.

Grudgingly, I plod along the Rose Canyon trail amid groups of chatting and giggling women when I discover I can move and speak at the same time, so I relax and take a break from catastrophizing long enough to puzzle over which woman is the eldest.

We hit a heavily rooted section of trail where loose pebbles demand we pay rapt attention to our footing. Next we inch our way up an extremely steep incline of sheer rock and clamber over three giant fallen ponderosa pines. By now I am panting, in part because of the unaccustomed exertion and in part because of panic. Will this sudden activity stir up stray blood clots? Is my will in order? Will my husband remember to give my emerald ring to my favorite niece? Will wild animals eat my carcass while the tennis ladies go for help?

As the morning wears on, my panic abates. Somewhat. The women slow their pace, encouraging or helping one another over the rough spots. The sun climbs higher and so do we. I'm sweating beneath my light jacket, although the alpine air is decidedly cool.

Mercifully, break time arrives and the women settle on rocks overlooking a stream, sharing M & Ms, wafer cookies, and orange sections. Just as my knees are stiffening up, we resume our hike. For the next two hours we walk. Up. It's hard to tell who's quaking more, the aspen or me.

At the summit, I prefer to drink in nature's beauty from terra firma, too terrified to join the others who are peering over the edge to Tucson, 6,000 feet below. A half-dozen cameras pop out of rucksacks and we mug shamelessly for group photos.

Once our visual documentation is complete, an incredible, inexplicable thing happens. Standing there atop Mt. Lemmon, we start swapping dirty jokes. One is more outrageous than the next and for fifteen minutes straight, we howl, whooping it up so much that we startle Steller's jays off their nests. Tears of laughter cascade down our faces and we cradle our aching sides.

By now the overhead sun is fierce, so we gobble our lunch, slather on more sunscreen, and head down. I chat at length with Fran, a peppy, petite woman who confides she's the oldest at eighty-five, a snowbird who drives herself and her husband west from New York every year to winter in Tucson.

Then Ruth, the sexy one, shows me her gold-glittered nails and mentions that she's eighty-three. Grinning mischievously, she mimics my dropped jaw.

The journey back goes fast as the hikers discuss the merits of long-term care insurance. Stock tips filter up and down the line and then a debate over how to avoid estate taxes breaks out.

Back at the cars, we linger, recounting the high points of our day. They apologize profusely for the lack of wildlife—no mountain lions, bears, or javelinas spotted today. A-okay by me. On the drive to Tucson, I don't close my eyes once, piping up from the backseat proudly and rather often, "I can't believe I did it!" Later, soaking away my aches in Barb's hot tub, I revel in the exotic sight of chain fruit cholla and centuries-old saguaro, their arms raised in a wave in the desert behind her house. Farther still are the four mountain ranges circling Tucson, one of them "ours."

Amazed by the Amazon

Sylvia Topp

Picture forty-seven assorted tourists squished into an eighteen-foot-square "floating store" on a riverbank in the middle of the Amazon jungle, squealing as they try to avoid giant water bugs and furry spiders that are fleeing a river oozing through the floorboards, while outside a torrential thunderstorm is pounding on the tin roof of their refuge, denying them any escape. In the middle of this squirming circle, their bravest companion is astounding and thrilling everyone by dancing the sexy "lambada" with Tristo, the cutest of the boatmen, both of them ankle deep in the sloshing water.

This scene was my initiation into an absurdly hilarious part of jungle life.

The store was built without a secure foundation because the river level changes hugely during the rainy season, sometimes rising forty feet. This system works perfectly well when it doesn't have to deal with some 6,000 extra pounds of human flesh taxing its floatability. The guides and storekeepers, who also had to suffer the bug invasion, behaved admirably. In a similar situation back home we'd have been refused entry, I'm sure, but here they not only smiled as they helped us all climb dripping into their shack, they even thought kindly to play some dance music on the old phonograph to liven up our stay, and didn't laugh too loudly at the few couples who were brave enough to awkwardly splash around the "dance floor."

At first, when I was offered a cheap ticket to Brazil, I thought about it awhile. I worried how a white vegetarian woman of a certain age who prefers to wear black and can't even dance before having a few drinks would fare in such a wild and sexy, meat-devouring, multi-colored country.

Before I turned fifty I would not have hesitated, although I might have been content to observe at the sidelines, to note and critique the antics of others, while taking no chances myself. But in the end, I decided that age has its responsibilities. I felt the urge to test myself, and although I was never brave enough to dance with Tristo, there were other times on the trip when I did myself proud.

We were a diverse group who made this Brazil connection—schoolteachers, sociologists, artists, businessmen, doctors, and dancers—and our ages ranged from seventeen to seventy-nine. We would never have found one another except for what we had in common: a desire to see the Amazon jungle before it disappeared.

After six days touring Rio and Salvador, we arrived in Manaus, the largest city in the Amazon region. There we boarded an *African Queen*-type wooden boat for the trip up river to the "peaceful but rustic tree-top lodge" we'd be staying in for three days, "surrounded by luxuriant rain forest."

This wondrous, evocative boat, with hammocks stretched randomly on the top deck and a wading pool in the rear, took four astounding sunset hours to reach our "hotel on stilts." And although it rocked mightily, and although I wasn't convinced I would never need the life jackets I couldn't find anyway, I refused to be afraid.

Okay, I was probably helped in this regard by the two delicious *caipirinhas* I sipped after watching each one being laboriously prepared by my first Amazonian contact, the patient boat bartender. First he chopped the limes by hand and squashed pieces in the bottom of the glass, then he carefully measured the sugar and mashed it in, then he located and added the ice, and finally he poured in the most important ingredient, the vodka-like liquor, *cashaca,* made from sugar cane.

It was dark when our boat squeezed through the final tributary, branches of unrecognizable trees slapping and scraping against its wooden sides. Our hotel lights dimly beckoned ahead, tiny sparks flickering high up in the dense dark jungle surrounding us.

We followed our guide up thirty steps from the landing and, twenty feet high in the air, we stumbled for five minutes along a two-foot-wide wooden pathway through the trees, another attempt at respect for the rising river of the rainy season. Very few, very dim lights were widely spaced to mark the way, and there were monkeys and coatis all over the place, curious and poking at our bags as we crept along in the dark. Some of the women screeched, but not me.

The hotel itself, the only one located in this huge area of the Amazon, was circular, with pie-shaped rooms leading off a central round hallway. The bedrooms had only a screen door, double-latched, as protection from the close and screeching jungle.

In the morning I woke with a monkey on my tiny veranda, his long arm completely through the hole he had patiently scratched in my screen door, valiantly reaching for my red underwear I'd dropped on the floor on the way into bed. I watched him quietly, and when his frustration overcame his desire, he swung joyfully next door and grabbed the mirror right out of my neighbor's hand as she stood on her veranda combing her hair.

After breakfast, many in our group were too monkey shy to leave the hotel, but I headed off with the adventurers. We dodged the playful animals on the high walkway back to the river's edge, then climbed into four long, thin, green, motorized "canoes" driven by four gorgeous, brown, muscular, Amazonian boatmen, each wearing a machete belt and little else. Every day they transported us up and down the various river "highways" searching out some "real Amazon life." We were relieved to find that the mosquito population was minimal, apparently due to the same chemical that darkens the water of the Rio Negro.

Since there weren't any towns nearby to visit, only simple wooden houses sparsely spaced along the river's edge, we unfortunately had limited contact with the local people. I got the impression earlier in Rio that big-city Brazilians think of Amazonians in the same way New Yorkers think of North Dakotans, say, Brazil being as geographically varied as the United States and very nearly as large. Although none of us could speak the local language, I found the natives I met gracious and congenial and intriguing. So apparently did a blonde Danish woman at the hotel who had fallen in love with a boat-man on her visit years before and had never returned home.

I felt awkward and obtrusive in our daily trespassing, even though our guide tried hard to convince us that we were always welcome to snoop around. One day trip took us to a typical small latticework wooden hut, with a palm-leaf-thatched roof, that appeared to have only one room in it, about twelve by eighteen feet. As with most of the houses we saw as we passed by in our canoes, it was built well off the ground on stilts and situated on the highest piece of land available.

As far as I could figure, this simple structure was home for all the people we saw during this visit—the two shy, lovely preteenage girls serenely scrubbing the laundry in the river, the three sweet young boys who followed us everywhere smiling all the way, the patient young mother, nursing a naked child, who affably accepted any candy or money that was pressed into her hands and smiled politely for all photographs, the two men who loped into the house from the jungle, bellowing as they banged their machetes against everything near enough to hit, and the creased old woman who sat inside gazing wistfully out the window. Although all of them were barefoot, none seemed the least bit bothered by the small brown ants that were busily biting at my sandaled feet. One man showed us his prize—a twenty-foot-long dried anaconda snakeskin, which I couldn't help but find fascinating. A couple from Minnesota excitedly purchased it even though they feared it was illegal to import skins back home.

"I can't imagine how anyone could stand this life of just doing nothing," a busy businessman confided to me, somehow forgetting that, without city conveniences, just "living" would take up all their time: growing and harvesting food, grinding grains, washing clothes and dishes by hand in the river, sewing with the same hard black palm needles that they used as poison darts to shoot birds, and fishing for every dinner, not to mention the hours and hours spent every day in jungle shelters enduring the exceedingly tedious process of turning poisonous, earth-covered manioc roots into edible white flour, and later paddling it up river to town, on the first lap of its amazing journey to our local grocery stores.

Night seemed to be the best time to search for alligators. I managed to get into Tristo's boat and he turned out to be best at this as he was at everything else. That afternoon we had all cheered when, with two of our boats hopelessly stuck in the weeds, Tristo stripped dramatically to his bikini, dove into the shallow marshes, and swam gloriously from boat to boat, pulling the grass out of the engines and freeing them. We even talked of "discovering" him for Hollywood.

To find an alligator, Tristo perched on the bow of the boat and shone an intensely bright light quickly along each shore of the river. When he spotted something no other eye could see, he directed the helmsman to that location, reached over the edge of the boat, and, presto, produced a four-foot-long baby alligator that had been too soundly sleeping. While Tristo held its fierce jaw closed and its thrashing tail still, he invited us to pat its white underbelly. Most of the others were reluctant, but I stroked it for a long time. It was amazingly soft. And I knew that even a baby alligator could bite your hand off.

The highlight of these three days was the piranha fishing. At first I wasn't going to go, but the guide assured me that any caught fish would be thrown back. Besides, this trip included a swim afterward.

We sat in our boats in shallow rushes at the edge of the river under the scalding sun for a long time, being outwitted by fish easily nibbling off the bait which was tied with thread to the end of simple tree-branch fishing poles. But eventually the artist from New York surprised everyone by somehow mastering the knack of wiggling the fishing stick just right, and he caught two piranhas. Once, his finger got a little bloody before the guide rescued him. Each time, our boatman held the small, flat fish tightly while forcing its mouth open to reveal its renowned, tiny, saw-edged teeth.

After about an hour of these minor successes in the treacherous sun, most of the boaters were ready to return to the hotel. "But what about the swimming?" I shocked everyone by asking. "Are you kidding?" they laughed. "Didn't you see their teeth?"

So the major test of the Amazon quickly became: who among us would be brazen enough to swim near the piranhas?

In the end, I was one of only seven, and by far the oldest, who were hot enough and undaunted. We amazed our companions by deciding to believe the guide's assurance that piranhas always stay in the shallow shore water and would never venture to the middle of the river, at least not more than one at a time.

One by one we flopped over the side of the boat and had the great fun of seeing our white skin turn cola color under the water that gives the Rio Negro its name. We were refreshed while the timid stayed scorched. And not a single one of us got bitten.

I surprised myself by falling in love with Brazil. But how could I resist a whole country of people who don't pay taxes, ignore traffic lights, have no idea how to capitalize on tourists, hug their kids, are cheerful, friendly, kind, handsome, and sexy, and who just recently made it illegal for a man to kill his wife?

My final Amazonian ordeal, not counting the tiny lumps that continued to decorate my ankles for weeks afterward, came on the flight home. The pilot startled me by adding his own twist to the routine landing announcement: "Ladies and gentlemen, please take you seats and fasten your seatbelts as there is the possibility of some casualties."

I panicked before I could laugh. But of course the true possible casualty will be if I never get to visit Brazil again.

The Growing Season

Nell Coburn Medcalfe

To Claire Koller, who continues to teach us so much about art and about living.

I join Pete under the big oak where the breeze is cool and the orchids hang from their baskets in a blaze of purple and lavender. He sprawls in his lawn chair, relaxed as an old cat, the business section of *The Miami Herald* spread across his middle. His face, still handsome at seventy-five, reflects his satisfaction with retirement and with the world. I kiss him, plop down in a chair next to him.

"How was the exhibit?" he asks.

"Wonderful. Especially Claire's watercolor. Gorgeous. Almost erotic."

"Erotic? Claire?" Pete flashes me his most wicked grin. "She's pushing ninety. What's she painting these days? Nudes?"

"Orchids. Huge, in-your-face, voluptuous orchids."

"Ah." Pete nods. A native South Floridian, he appreciates the sensual quality of tropical plants, especially orchids with their dazzling hues, fleshy leaves, and delicately veined petals. I look up at ours, wishing they could bloom like this year-round. Pete reads my thoughts, reminds me orchids need time off to rest and prepare for their next flowering. "Besides," he says, "if they always looked like this, we wouldn't appreciate them so much."

"True." Lulled by his voice, I lean back in my chair and close my eyes, tired after another good day.

I had joined friends from my weekly book discussion group to visit the gallery where the paintings, most of them botanical watercolors by female artists, were on display. We missed Claire, who had flown off to Alaska for a wedding. As we viewed the lovely, light-filled creations, I smiled at our reflections in the picture glass and thought *Aren't we wonderful!* Ten or so women in our seventies and eighties, glad to be alive, gazing with Zen-like concentration at the art before us. We stand slim and pencil straight. We walk with purposeful strides and possess minds as quick and buoyant as our steps. We wear happy colors and even happier faces and though we no longer can pass for fifty, some of us may never have looked so good.

I believe we look this way because we are in the midst of a rich growing season. With the freedom and fearlessness that come at our stage of life, we greet our lives with gusto, opening ourselves to new experiences every chance we get. We seek knowledge with the restlessness and zeal of children, learning different ways to paint, write, read, think, and be. Having met only after we retired and our children were grown, we find ourselves bound together by our creative lives and our admiration of Wharton, Nabokov, Piercy, and Plath rather than old judgments and loyalties. We like and respect one another for the persons we are now.

For me, living in the now has been a lovely by-product of growing old. I used to live my life looking forward: when I grow up, when I marry, when I have children, when they grow up, when I have the leisure to *really* write, when the mortgage is paid off. Even deep into my fifties, when Pete and I cared for our ailing, confused mothers while struggling with the problems of our own aging, I focused on an elusive afterward that promised something better, neglecting valued relationships and missing precious moments.

At a neighborhood pub where Pete and I sometimes go for a beer before dinner, a sign over the bar reads: FREE DRINKS TOMORROW. When unwary customers come in, read the sign, and show up the next evening for their free drinks, Hector, the bartender, tells them, "Look again, *amigos*. The sign says 'tomorrow.' This is today."

Of course I keep my eye on the future, for I intend to have one. Practical matters like estate planning, long-term health insurance selection, living wills, and personal finance all need to be addressed and regularly updated. Lucky for me, Pete, and John, our friendly stockbroker, have taught me much about making good, conservative investments for the long haul and I, mostly an optimist, plan on a very long haul.

But like a diet, optimism can be hard to stick to. Now and then at night, while Pete snores softly next to me, Future slips into the bedroom. "Silly you," she hisses. "Have you forgotten?" She's suggesting I'll end up like my mother, who spent her last years trapped in the dark unknown of an Alzheimer's-type dementia with its concomitant doctors, hospitals, rages, and nightmare nursing home scenes.

What helps is to remember Claire and the other women in the book group who have passed their eightieth birthdays. Talk about role models. Week after week they show up, steadfast in their devotion to good literature and to our teacher, who will turn eighty-seven next month. Absenteeism is practically nil; if they fail to show up, it's usually because there's a conflict with their travels or other commitments, rarely because they are ill. If they have medical problems, they don't talk about them. They drive zippy little imports, dine well, and laugh in great, lusty roars in defiance of Future's smirking countenance. Knowing this gives me such hope and healing that the ugly images of pain and dementia burn off like mist at midmorning.

It helps, too, to remind myself that I've always been a late bloomer. Much to my embarrassment, I entered puberty long after my friends. I had my two babies later than was customary for that era and graduated from college when they both were in high school. I received my master's degree just three weeks before my fiftieth birthday and was thrilled to debut as a published writer at sixty-five. Maybe decrepitude will come late as well.

I find little seductive about the past; no silken voices tempt me to turn my thoughts backward. When I do cast a nostalgic glance over my shoulder, chances are I've had a dream about my mother. I wake up stunned by longing, not for the symbiosis of childhood or her end-of-life bewilderment, but for the lovely long interlude when we were both adults and the best of friends.

When vestiges of guilt catch me off guard, Past, infinitely kinder than Future, whispers, "It's okay. You meant well. Chill." If her words fail to comfort and my ego hangs low like a dead palm frond, I work on my poems, for it is in my poetry that my best self is revealed.

I read somewhere that as people grow older, the locus coeruleus, the part of the brain that responds to stress, loses cells. Another perk of growing old. This might explain why, though I don't hesitate to speak my mind, I am less bitchy than I used to be, less inclined to panic when confronted with difficult or dangerous situations. With the pace of my life slower now, I find miracles in the mundane: the blue jay swooping alongside my Explorer to reach his ravenous nestlings; the astonishing, orderly crowd of tiny ants circling a drop of mango jam on the kitchen counter; the beautiful child spinning away from her friends to explode into a sinewy, exuberant dance. Never did I imagine such elegance existed in the world.

I do not delude myself that the best is yet to come. The loss of friends and loved ones will devastate me and already, the body is starting to betray: fatigue, arthritis, and a host of other sly rebel forces including lymphoma threaten sabotage from within. I detect in my daughters, both in their forties, a solicitousness toward me that was not there before and it terrifies me. Later, well-intentioned strangers will address me in voices decibels louder than required, call me by my first name when I do not wish it, and care less for who I am than for how well I behave. I wish we humans could emulate orchids, which continue to grow as long as they are alive, and when growth ceases, just dry up and blow away.

"How old would you be if you didn't know how old you was?" asked baseball legend Satchel Paige. Only when I spot my reflection in a shop window or in the merciless mirrors at Bloomingdale's do I remember my chronology. It's always a shock. For even when I don't feel so wonderful, there resides in me an everlasting spring, an ageless psyche, a healthy and vivacious young woman who's awaiting her next adventure.

Besides, it's difficult to feel old in this part of the country where the earth is rich and yielding and always, always warm. Month after month, endless varieties of flowers erupt in full blossom, in colors and proportions which are almost indecent. Like Claire's erotic orchids. Unlike T.S. Eliot and his gloomy take on April, I find the signs of youth and renewal profoundly reassuring. And time seems to stop here under the oak tree with Pete, who has been my lover and friend all these decades, ready to love and gather me up when I need love and gathering.

Pete fetches a couple of beers from the kitchen and we drink them right out of the cans. He holds up his newspaper.

"While you were out, John called to tell us about a tax-exempt bond. It's triple-A rated and yields a pretty good interest."

"But you've been stressing growth investments as a hedge against inflation," I say.

"I know, but inflation isn't much of a threat right now." He shakes his newspaper at me. "Anyway, we're at the age when our portfolio should lean heavily toward income investments."

"When is the bond callable?" I ask.

"It isn't. It's escrowed to maturity."

"When does it mature?"

"Not till 2022." His voice drops. "That's pretty far out. Better to stay shorter term, I guess." He sighs into the lavender-tinged dusk, fixes his eyes on someplace I can't see. "Hell, we'll be gone before it's redeemed."

Speak for yourself, I think. But oh, my beloved, I pray with all my heart that we are both escrowed to maturity and that together we'll hobble out to our chairs under this old tree and pop a couple of cold ones.

"Buy it," I say.

Coming of Age

Elayne Clift

In the fifties,
coming of age
meant
calendar secrets
and coded events
that gave you a
reason to be cranky
(PMS).
Girls were demure
and "girls" were
forever, and
if they knew
what was good for them,
girls never let on
how really smart they were.
Most important of all,
they never, ever
said what they thought.
Just played the game,
Front seat, and back,
and believed that
sloppy French kisses
were something to be
endured, for the sake of
a Saturday night.

Back then,
fast was for cars, guys,
and for doing the twist,
while slow was for dancing
to Johnny Mathis,
and they were the
only two speeds you knew.

In our fifties,
coming of age
means
unbounded energy
and post-menopausal
zest that gives us a
reason to rejoice
(PMZ).
Women are women,
and man, we're good!
And another thing:
We know how smart we are.
We tell it like it is.
And we've got your number, Bubba.
Yeah.
We dress smart,
(no more stilettos)
we work smart,
and we don't go in
for games at the
watering hole.
Saturday is just
Another day,
fast is how time flies
when we're havin' fun,
slow is for savoring
CDs with a good Chardonnay,
alone, or with a chosen chum,

and in between
are the magic moments,
and myriad possibilities
of who we are,
while we keep on
coming of age.

Forces

Sarah Getty

Polly Maynard was a saint; I always said so. It's been a year since she died, so she must be getting used to heaven by now. I wonder whether the saints know everything, the way God does. I mean, does Polly look down at me and say to herself, "Now, what is Grace up to? I thought she was going to marry Jack!?" Jack is Polly's husband, or used to be. I was the widow next door, and it's true that I had designs on him. But things don't always happen the way we think they will. There are forces at work.

I started studying these forces last year, when Polly was still with us. She hardly ever got up; she lay most of the day on the couch by the patio doors. I was reading about the streams of energy that flow along certain lines on the earth, and I was glad to see that Polly's couch was oriented north and south, because that is the way anyone's bed should be in order to get the benefits of the forces. After all, think of the hours you spend lying there, even if you're well. With the bed aligned right, the forces can run through you while you rest and clear out the negative energy and so on.

Now you're probably saying to yourself, "This is one of those kooks from California talking," but I assure you I am *not* from California. I didn't even want to move out here when Stanley retired from the U., but his heart was set on it. I am a perfectly lucid old lady from Ames, Iowa. I read Jane Austen and I attend St. Barbara's Episcopal Church down on El Camino. However, I have lived long enough to know that there are more things in heaven and earth than our philosophy has dreamed of.

I used to visit Polly every Wednesday afternoon after square dancing and every Sunday after church. Actually, I saw her just about every day, but on Wednesday and Sunday we'd have a real visit. I had a strict rule about that. For a time, on Sundays, I would just ride home with Jack after church, but I gave that up the week I realized that during church I had been praying for Polly's death. There are certain things a Christian simply is not allowed. I told Jack I needed the exercise, and, though I can drive myself, I walked to church and back even if it was raining. It was my penance.

I was so in love with Jack I couldn't see straight. I had hoped that Polly didn't know it, but she wasn't one of those simple-minded saints. One Wednesday I was sitting with her—the patio doors were open and that heavenly air was bringing in the smell of Jack's roses and just a hint of the ocean off on the horizon. I was telling her about the square dancing that morning; how Matty Waterhouse, brazenly pretending she had a blister, held onto Jack's arm and leaned over and showed her bosom to all and sundry while she took off her shoe. Matty, who dolls herself up like the Mother of Frankenstein's Bride, used to make me ragged with jealousy.

I remember how Polly laughed, carefully, as if it might hurt her. Then she looked straight at me. Her blue eyes were so bright those last weeks—I never knew whether it was from the pain or the painkillers. "I'm sorry she was holding onto Jack when she did it, Grace," she said. "That must have irked you, feeling about him the way you do."

Well. Though I knew Polly loved me like a sister, it was hard to know just how to answer that. I blushed until my eyes watered, and finally said something like "I just can't stand it when some birdbrain like Matty goes after him."

"Grace," she said, "I want to say this." Her face took on that lit-up look, like a shell with the sun on it, that made me certain she was leaving us. "I'm glad you love Jack. It comforts me to think of the two of you . . . together."

She was too tactful, you see, to say "after I'm dead," or even "when I'm gone." She wouldn't call attention to herself like that. Nevertheless, I was so flustered I blurted out, "But Jack doesn't think of me that way!" I don't know, really, whether I was defending his virtue or complaining. But it was true: although I have always attracted my share of compliments, he never gave me a look that wasn't on the up-and-up.

"Oh, don't be *modest,*" she said. Like many saints, she was lukewarm on the conventional virtues. "Jack's preoccupied now," she went on. She looked down at her thin little hands. She even pushed a sleeve up to look at her wrist, which was like a bone. "But he thinks the world of you. You'll be a great comfort to him. I like to think of that."

"Well, good," was all I could manage. It didn't seem right to deny anything, in light of what she'd said. In my embarrassment I fell to straightening the shawl that covered her—a gorgeous embroidered thing I got for her when Stanley and I went to Spain in 1978. Then, just to make my agony complete, Jack came in with a bunch of yellow roses. He is a tall man with a beautiful head of white hair, and as for the state of his body—let's just say that in jeans and a cowboy shirt Jack makes Ronald Reagan look like Willard Scott. He has that "Let me handle this" style that some Western men carry off so well. As soon as he came in and stood there, with the roses glowing in his hands, you could feel the energy coming out of him, filling up the room.

"Polly Anne," he said. "What do you think that tank's for—a doorstop?" He hardly saw me, which was a mercy. He went straight over to the couch, handing me the roses as he went by. "Could you find a vase for those, Gracie?" Then he was fiddling with Polly's breathing tube. "Oxygen's not doing you any good inside the tank, woman!"

Polly said, "Darling, I don't really need it when I'm not even sitting up. I can breathe okay."

"Okay's not good enough. You need pure oxygen for your red cells. You can't fight this thing without red cells."

He kept trying to stick the tube into her nose and she kept moving her head. That didn't seem like something you should watch, so I got up quickly and went into the kitchen with the flowers. "Let me do it *myself,*" she said, and when I came back with the roses in a Monterey Jade bowl she was lying there with the tube taped to her cheek. Jack looked grimly satisfied, like John Wayne after he's cleared out a nest of varmints.

"Doc Kraler says breathe oxygen, you breathe oxygen. Problem and solution, simple as that." Polly patted his hand and sneaked a little look at me. Jack knew how bad she was, but he couldn't always admit it. He was used to being the one who made things happen. And when you were with him you felt he could do it—just shrivel the cancer with his willpower.

I put the flowers on the coffee table and Polly exclaimed as if she hadn't ever seen a rose before. Jack told her there were plenty more where those came from. Then he noticed me. "So Amazing Grace," he said. Jack isn't one to let an old joke die peacefully. "Feet recovered yet?"

I explained to Polly, "I was complaining to Jack about the number of ways men manage to hurt my feet when we're dancing. Charlie Phillips steps on you—you remember—and Ralph sort of abrades the side of your foot when you swing, and Howard what's-his-name kicks my instep every time. If I could draw I'd make an illustrated catalogue. A Kama Sutra of foot abuse."

Polly chuckled at that, and Jack squinted at me and went "huh" the way he does when he doesn't know what you're talking about. Jack can't stand to be on the outside of anything but, bless his soul, he's just not the best-read man you've ever met.

Polly said, "Poor Grace. I hope you got to dance with Ernie McIntyre today. I don't think his feet even touch the ground. Like dancing with Fred Astaire, I always thought."

"Oh, Ernie," I said. "Isn't he a cupcake? He was my partner twice. But the trouble with square dancing is that you keep switching around. I just wanted to drag him out of the square and make him waltz with me."

Polly was patting Jack's hand again, to make up for our praising another man. But that's the way people always talk about Ernie: he's just a man that everybody loves. And he's short enough to match up when you take hold of him; I don't care for dancing with my nose on somebody's middle shirt button. Ernie and his wife, Laura, were the presidents of the Square Dance Club. You should have seen them together, like a pair of little dolls. And dance! They once won second prize, I believe it was, in a West Coast Ballroom Championship. With your glasses off you might take them for college kids, they were so trim and peppy.

"Huh," said Jack. "If Ernie stepped on your foot, you wouldn't even feel it. Little runt can't weigh more that eighty pounds." But he was just pretending to be jealous, flirting with us.

Just then we heard a siren, an ambulance coming down El Camino, turning into the entrance to the Village, and starting to wind around the hill. The place is laid out in concentric levels, like Dante's Paradise; our two houses—the Maynards' and mine, a unit with a common wall—are right at the top. We sat there and followed the wailing sound. I seemed almost to see the ambulance climbing—I have these flashes sometimes, like second sight. It's quite a common gift, actually. But when the siren stopped on the level below us, I couldn't quite tell where it was.

"O'Malleys'?" guessed Polly. "Cora Kneeland?" I said. "Maybe Fred Primack's heart," said Jack, and that seemed to settle it. Polly put her hand on the phone, but Jack stopped her. "Leave it to the grapevine, honey. We'll hear soon enough."

Suddenly the situation was too much for me—the implications, if you know what I mean. You hear sirens around here night and day; you might even get used to them. But sitting there with Polly, I was afraid I might break down and disturb the positive energy that Jack was giving out.

"Goodness!" I said, getting up, "It's time for my yoga program!" I gave Polly a kiss, and then I had to kiss Jack. It was something I went through every visit. That time it was worse than usual, with Polly watching and our conversation still running in my head. His cheek smelled of a shaving lotion unfortunately named "Chaps," which I had learned almost to like for his sake.

During my yoga program I microwaved a leftover chimichanga from Taco Bell and had my dinner. It isn't true that you have to *do* the yoga exercises while the show is on. The main thing is to absorb the energy that Lilias, the teacher, or Yogin, projects through the TV. I always sit right up close to the set and eat while I'm watching. It only stands to reason that the energy is penetrating the food, too, so that I get a double dose. There is nothing about this that a Christian can't recognize and respect. I stand firmly with those who believe that all religions are tapping into the same great set of forces.

Now, if you're of a scientific turn of mind you will no doubt discount everything I say about the forces, because no one has weighed one yet. Jack, for instance, would have said "baloney" if I tried to explain them. But doubt has no effect on facts. The forces exist, and I hope that, in time, you will become more broad-minded, as I have. For Jack, I fear, it is too late. He is a product of his time, when people were afraid of "crazy notions." But nowadays these ideas are becoming quite common. One of my granddaughters even gave me a sweatshirt last Christmas that says, "The Force Be With You" on it. I wear it sometimes when I'm gardening and also when I do my yoga exercises. I *do* do my yoga, you see, but not when Lilias's program is on. That seems quite straightforward to me, although some people find it hard to understand.

While I ate, I could also see out into the yard, and into Jack's patio, where he was talking to Jorge, the head yardman, about his roses. I was sitting behind my big split-leaf philodendron, so I wasn't afraid that he could see me watching. Jorge was measuring out fertilizer, and Jack hung right over his shoulder while he mixed it up and fed it to the plants. He pretended he was just being friendly, but I knew, and Jorge knew, that Jack was there to make sure he did it right. Jack got fanatical about those roses last year; it was like he was trying to force them into bloom.

During the evening news, I got a phone call. It was Laura, Ernie McIntyre's wife, calling about refreshments for next week's square dancing. I said of course I'd bring something, as long as I didn't have to bake it, and then she asked if I had heard about Fred Primack.

"Oh, no!" I said. "Is that who the ambulance was for?"

"Yes, but it's not so bad as they thought. Marie said he's feeling fine now and they're just going to keep him in the hospital overnight. He had a little chest pain, and she didn't even wait for his pill to act before she called them. She's so nervous, you know."

"Well, better safe than sorry, Laura." I was remembering Stanley's last heart attack, three years before, and my chimichanga was sitting poorly. I steadied myself by staring at the Hopi God's eye on the wall above my sink. "We have to look after these menfolks." *Menfolks* is a word I would never use on my own, but you develop certain ways of talking in a place like this.

After we hung up it occurred to me that Laura would make a fine wife for Jack after Polly died. She had a lot of backbone. She was healthy, except for a little blood pressure, and she was well organized; Jack would like that. Of course, the trouble was, she was married, and Ernie had the constitution of a mule. It was silly even to think of it, but I had a way of doing that: running down lists of women Jack might marry and thinking what I'd do if he did. If he married Elizabeth Cunningham, for instance, I'd simply have to dig up my hibiscus and move. If he married Matty Waterhouse I'd kill him. I wouldn't kill her, though; I'd make her live on and on, tormented by grief and desire.

Before I went to bed that night, I went out to the edge of my yard, where the hill falls away to the next level in a steep bank covered with ice plants. I looked down over the roofs of Buena Vista Village, and across the valley and way out to the ocean. I could actually see it, a fragment of glass reflecting moonlight out on the horizon. I liked to think of all that was going on there—the whales singing to one another and the dolphins quoting Plato and even the sharks, who can't help it if they're hungry. I looked at the Maynards' house. The moon was full enough to show the different colors of the roses along the patio. There was one light on in the house, in the bedroom. I couldn't help wondering what they did—whether Polly was strong enough to make love at all. She had said to me once that she was getting too sick to be a woman. That would be the worst, I think, to lose your husband that way, while you were still alive. Some people imagine it's the normal thing, but don't you believe it.

So I went to my own bed, missing Stanley terribly, but filled with longing for Jack. We had had twin beds, and after Stanley died I had his moved out to the porch, as an extra for when my children visit. But my bed should have been shifted too. It was aligned exactly wrong, with the head to the east wall, under my collection of Japanese fans, and the foot to the west. I sometimes indulged myself, at bedtime, in a fantasy about how I would get it turned around. I would ask Jack to help me move it. Then when we were grappling with the bed I would—well, the details varied from one time to another, but I'm sure you can guess the outcome.

These were not mere airy fancies, you understand. They were my entire sex life, except for the occasional fantasy featuring one of the yardmen. Having been an avid reader since the age of six, I'm quite skilled at bringing imaginary scenes to life. Afterward, of course, I felt guilty about Polly. Waiting for somone's wife to die is bad enough, but one sees so much of it around here; it's nature's way, I suppose. Wanting to have Jack right now, rehearsing it in my mind, was another matter. Before I slept, I would say a prayer asking God to forgive me and to make Polly go into a miraculous remission.

That night I lay there for a long time waiting for sleep. I could feel the lines of force running crosswise through the room; it was like lying in a canoe being bumped and jostled by sideways waves. Even in my sleep I was uncomfortable; I kept coming half awake and thinking, "I must get this boat turned tomorrow" and dropping off again. And there was a siren. It seemed to go on a long time, winding around and around our hill. I thought I was probably dreaming it. I also dreamed about Jack. He was with me in the boat, strapping Polly's oxygen tank to my back; he wanted me to go scuba diving off the long pier on Mariposa Beach. He said there were beautiful flowers down there, hidden among the rocks, and I should bring some up for Polly. I kept telling him that the tank was too heavy, it would pull me down and drown me. But he wouldn't listen, and then I was cold and sinking, with the weight on my back like a stone. . . .

The phone woke me before eight the next morning—too early to be anything but bad news. My heart was beating hard even before I heard Polly's voice saying, "Grace, I have something sad to tell you. Very sad. Are you sitting down?"

"Lying," I said. I thought, *My God, something's happened to Jack; this is my punishment.*

"Ann Brentano just called us. You know—the McIntyres' neighbor. Laura had a stroke during the night. Maybe you heard the ambulance? She died at four this morning. I knew you'd want to know."

"Laura McIntyre? But I just talked to her last night!"

"Yes, apparently she was fine when she went to bed. It was just—sudden. It's hard to believe."

But I could tell that Polly believed it easily. She spoke patiently, like a grown-up talking to a child. And she was right. Living here in Buena Vista is like waiting in a big airline terminal with a crowd of people on standby. We should be prepared, but every sudden departure is a shock.

I got dressed and went out to feel the sun warm up the morning. Dewdrops, tiny rainbow flashes in the grass, winked and dried away while I stood there. I could almost hear Jack's roses opening, popping like fireworks, pinwheels and puffs of color. It was clear to me that the world must be full of positive forces, to counteract whatever could erase Laura McIntyre overnight. I said a little prayer for Laura and asked God to sustain Ernie in his loss. Then I had a quick breakfast and went on down to the McIntyres' house.

As I expected, there were widows everywhere. Elizabeth Cunningham arrived when I did, carrying a casserole. Ann Brentano came to the door and let us in. Cora Reynolds and the unbearable Matty Waterhouse were in the kitchen and Violet Pfeifer was in the living room on the phone. Poor Ernie wasn't home, he was somewhere dealing with "arrangements."

I went into the kitchen, where Cora and Matty were arguing about which casserole to freeze and which to put into the fridge. The countertop—the yellow and blue tiles that Laura had picked out herself at the factory in Oaxaca—was covered with food. Cakes, pies, casseroles, Tupperware, baking pans wrapped in foil. Every one an offering from a widow. You might wonder how they got that cooking done so early in the day, but believe me, they have their ways. You see, a retirement community is like a medieval manor: there are three distinct social classes. At the top are the widowers, the pampered few. In the middle are the couples, the doughty villagers. At the bottom are the widows, the serfs. Excellent women in their own right, but desperate. And when someone as popular and healthy as Ernie is suddenly elevated to widower status, there is a stampede not unlike the opening up of Oklahoma to homesteaders in April of 1889.

Mind you, I'm not saying that this state of affairs is right. I myself abhor the idea that a woman has to have a man to validate her. I'm in total agreement with the feminist movement on that score. At this point in my life, I'd spent two years grieving for my dear Stanley and four years of contented independence and useful activity with the occasional date for comic relief. And, of course, my unfortunate crush on Jack. But that was only a matter of attraction—I never felt that snagging him would raise my social status or make me a better person. I like to think I have more self-respect than that. And I cook just as little as I can, so I wasn't about to show up on Ernie's doorstep with paella.

"My 'hacienda cheese-and-chili casserole' can*not* be frozen," Matty was saying. "It would decompose. I'll heat it up for Ernie tonight and he can finish it for lunch tomorrow." I noticed that her hair had changed color since the day before; instead of blue, it had a sort of pinkish cast, like old-fashioned peach ice cream.

"But Matty," Cora remonstrated. "He'll need something more substantial tonight. And chilies are terribly hard on a person's stomach who's under stress. He should have something, oh, like a nice lamb stew." She put her plump little hand, with all its turquoise rings, on the Tupperware container labeled "Cora Reynolds." The label, you understand, was just so Ernie could return the container to the right person.

The two of them gave me a glance, then went back to their argument, like two major powers ignoring a third-world country. And they were right, I had no status in the kitchen. I went back into the hall and down to the bedroom, by way of the linen closet. It was too early to clear out Laura's clothes; that would have to wait for Ernie's permission. But I have a little service I perform on these occasions: I change the sheets. It helps to distance the memory of that last awful night. And a fresh pillowcase, to my mind, is always a promise of better things to come.

I must admit it satisfied my curiosity to see the McIntyres' bedroom (I suspect that everyone who reads a lot is, at heart, a snoop). Their bed was huge; you could imagine them having to search for each other, like the couple in that limerick who ended up foot to head.

The headboard had a built-in bookcase, with Laura's mysteries and Ernie's "real books," the kind he says they don't write anymore. On the walls were some Mexican hangings and the usual pictures of grandchildren. Laura's dresser was rather a mess—drawers left open and scarves and bracelets and lipsticks jumbled about. I straightened it up and dusted it with a Kleenex, hoping someone would do the same for me if I went suddenly and other women descended on my house.

The sheets I had chosen were a nice, soothing blue. I hoped they would remind Ernie of the sky—the infinite, in the light of which our sorrows are so small. Laura's pillowcase smelled nicely of some cologne or night cream. It made me pause, but then I went ahead and stripped it off. As far as I could figure out, the bed was oriented diagonally to the lines of force. I decided to speak to Ernie about it at some more appropriate time.

As I loaded the bed linen into the washing machine, I could hear Matty insisting in the kitchen, "The chilies are *very* mild, and cheese is an excellent source of protein." I thought I might become rude if I saw her again, so I sneaked out of the house by the utility room door.

Two days later, it seemed everyone who was left alive in Buena Vista was at the funeral—Laura and Ernie were so beloved, and I think we all felt the need to kind of cluster together for comfort. At one point, just when Father Snyder was saying, "Thou knowest, Lord, the secrets of our hearts," it looked like Matty was going to get jostled right into the grave. But alas, she only swayed and regained her balance.

I turned to Jack then, just to see if he had noticed, and saw something rather shocking. He was watching the way some of the women made a point of moving up close to Ernie, patting his arm or offering a hanky. And the look on his face was—not jealous, exactly. Intrigued. Eager. Shrewd. In fairness, I knew that it had nothing to do with his devotion to Polly. It was just his natural ambition, his sense of what he had coming to him.

When it was all over, and Jack and I were walking to the car, Ernie caught up with us and thanked me for doing the flowers in the church—not those stiff things from the florist, but the real flowers, which I had arranged in silver bowls up on the altar. Matty was trailing after him, sniffling and dabbing at her face, as if she ever cared a thing about Laura.

"The roses were beautiful," Ernie said. He looked like he hadn't slept since Laura died, but there he was, just like Ernie, taking the trouble to thank me for the roses.

"You should thank Jack, actually," I said. "I took them from his yard."

It was a sort of confession, for Jack hadn't been too pleased with me when he saw the state of his rose bushes that morning. I explained to him that there are priorities, and the earth yields her increase for the good of all, but he couldn't see it. Now he was walking along next to Matty, giving her his handkerchief, asking if she had a ride back to the Village.

"Why, how sweet of you," she bleated. "I'm so upset I didn't even think about how I'd get back." It was a blatant lie, but I didn't much mind, she looked such a fright with her mascara dripping down into her wrinkles.

Jack helped Matty into his long white Lincoln as if *she* were the bereaved one. While he walked around to the driver's side she got out her compact and went to work on her face. I gave Ernie's hand a squeeze and got into the backseat. He waved as we pulled away; I could see that he was relieved that the funeral was over. He would probably feel unburdened and a little numb for a few days, wading in the shallows of grief. Next week, or the next, the breakers would come crashing in.

I thought of him, alone in his big bed, and I wished I had put on other sheets, not that cold blue. Then I had the most amazing flash— I saw the bedroom, and the bed, and Ernie, and *myself*, right in there with him. And I knew that I wasn't just imagining it, because the sheets were different. They were sheets I've never seen before, sheets from the future, with a zigzag pattern in earth tones, like a mountain range. You could have knocked me over with a feather.

I realized then that Jack was talking, reminding me about Polly's radiation treatment. He was taking her to the hospital that afternoon, and she would stay overnight. As usual, we'd arranged that I would make his dinner.

"Why, Jack, you should have told me," Matty said. "I have an extra casserole at home, and you know Grace just *hates* to cook."

"Oh, well"—Jack gave his Shucks, Ma'am chuckle. "She cooks for *me*. I mean, she's no fancy chef, but she's reliable. Aren't you Gracie?" This meant he'd forgiven me about the roses, but somehow I didn't warm to it.

"So, Grace," Jack laid his arm along the top of the seat and talked slant-wise back at me. "I figure I'll be home from the hospital about 6:15, ready to put on the feedbag. Okay?"

Well, I just felt like laughing. But I didn't. I said, "Certainly." I have always prided myself on my good manners. Then I sat back and gave my attention to the passing scene, for I felt as if scales had fallen from my eyes. We passed the Taco Bell, the Mission Bank with its blazing pyracantha, two boys in "Gang Green" T-shirts riding skateboards. After a minute Matty said, "Then you must let me give you brunch tomorrow, Jack, before you pick up Polly. There's nothing worse than having breakfast alone, when you're not—" she took a touching little breath—"used to it."

"Why, thanks, Matty. That's real kind of you. But, say—a gal like you should be able to have company for any old breakfast she chooses." There was that cowboy grin, and Matty smiled back at him, her mourning for Laura quite forgotten. They both looked extremely handsome, I must say, like contest winners: America's Senior Sweethearts.

After Jack dropped me off, I went right to my bedroom. I needed a nap in the worst way. But before I could rest, I had to get things straight. I squatted down at the end of the bed and took hold of the footboard. I only had to lift it enough to slide my little Persian prayer rug under one foot, then the other foot. Then I just pulled on the rug, duckwalking backward, using my leg muscles and not straining my back, the way Lilias tells us. In the middle I had to straighten up and move the nightstand and the wastebasket out of the way and push a bit on the headboard. A few minutes later I had a north-south bed, stretched right along the wall. It made the room so much bigger, there was almost enough space to form up a square and dance.

I got into bed, lined myself up and did my yoga relaxation exercise. Soon I could feel it—the energy was coming in at the top of my head and running right through my body and out my toes. It was like those little rivers that cut across the beach, the freshwater gliding so clear, flowing and flowing into the sea but never running out.

To me a nap means an hour, but that afternoon I slept on and on. When I woke up a shaft of late sunlight was shining from the living room window right into my bedroom door. I lay there awhile just looking at the dust motes dancing in the air. I felt fine—I could tell that the forces had cleared out some of my negative energy already.

When I made myself look at the clock, it read 5:30. I put on my jeans and sneakers and my "The Force Be With You" sweatshirt, I got a Celeste Pizza for One out of the freezer, and took the key to Jack's house off the hook by the door. The air outside was like a margarita—cool and sweet with that little rim of salt. I went in the back way, past the roses. They looked like they had been strung with Christmas bulbs glowing red, yellow, and orange. But those were the buds; I left a lot of them on every bush.

The Maynards' house was hot—they always kept the thermostat up for Polly. She had folded the Spanish shawl at the foot of her couch. An empty oxygen tank was lying there like a faithful dog, waiting for someone who might never return.

I put the pizza on top of the stove with a note: "Dear Jack, Hope all went well at the hospital. I've turned on the oven. Take this out of the box and heat it for twelve minutes. You should think about getting a microwave. They're awfully handy, Love to Polly." I signed it Grace, like what you say before dinner. Then I drove down to the Villa Napoli for a really good Italian meal. Naturally, I had to pass Ernie's house as I wound my way down the hill. But I didn't stop. I knew I could leave things to forces larger than my own.

The Same Old Kiss

Janet Amalia Weinberg

Long fingers of light reached through the lace curtains and touched the rocking chair, the worn braided rug, the cat curled in the corner. Richard, a stooped, graying man with kind eyes, moved through the shimmering shafts, set the tea things down, and joined his wife, Margaret, on the sofa.

Her legs were propped on the ottoman, as usual, with an afghan tucked around them. She couldn't walk well anymore, but her mind was agile and her smile, quick and cheery.

"Mmm," she murmured, her small face tilting with delight, "spearmint. Just what I wanted. And it's perfect with the spice cookies."

He waved her off. "Aw, you're just easy to please."

They sat and sipped their tea, content to not talk.

Suddenly, there was a commotion outside: scuffling steps, giggles, the squeak of the porch swing.

"Yeah, but I bet you don't know what people do when they kiss." The voice of Karen, their eleven-year-old granddaughter, slipped in through the open window.

"Anybody knows that." Her sister Mary's voice swelled with an eight-year-old's bravado. "They put their mouths together."

Richard winked at Margaret. "Shh," he whispered, "we might learn something."

Karen took a tube of tinted ChapStick from her pocket—she wasn't allowed to wear real lipstick yet—and meticulously smeared her lips.

"Bet you don't know what they do next."

"Do too." Mary stuck her chin out and glared defiantly. Karen may have had more than her share of good looks, but Mary had a heap of spunk. "They push their lips hard and move them around."

Karen blotted her mouth like the older girls do. "What else?"

"What do you mean, 'What else?'"

"I mean, what else?"

"If you're so smart, you tell *me*."

"I don't know if I should. . . ." Karen hesitated a tantalizing moment then whipped out the secret. "They stick their tongues in each other's mouths."

Mary made a face as if she'd swallowed a worm. "I don't believe you."

"It's true."

"How do *you* know?"

"I just know."

"Ah!" Mary gasped. "You did it with Tommy!"

The swing stopped abruptly and tipped them forward.

"Did not!"

"You did!" Finally, Mary had something on Karen. "I'm gonna tell."

"If you do, I'll never speak to you again. Ever!"

Mary folded her arms on her chest and kicked at the floor. The swing jolted back, forward, back, forward, back. She gave her sister a quick sideways glance. "Do Mommy and Daddy do it?"

"Maybe."

"What about Grandpop and Granny?"

Karen shrugged. "Bet they don't. I mean, how could they stand it after so many years? The same old kiss over and over and over."

A giggle bubbled out of Mary. "Can't you just see Grandpop, with the hair growing in his nose, grabbing Granny and sticking his tongue in her mouth?"

Karen's half of the swing shuddered. "That's so gross!"

"Know what else?"

"I don't want to know."

But Mary told her anyway. "Granny's got false teeth."

"So?"

"So, what if they fall out when his tongue is in there licking around?"

It was more than Karen could bear. She jumped up. "Come on, let's go get our bikes."

"I'll beat you to the barn," Mary yelled, racing ahead.

Inside the house, Richard turned to his wife and placed his hand over hers. "It's not as bad as all that, is it?"

"*I* never thought so. Besides"—light twinkled in her eyes—"my teeth may get loose but they *never* fall out."

"Mmm," Richard put on a look of grave concern. "Maybe we ought to check that out."

He took her in his arms and drew her close. She laid her cheek on his shoulder. She felt safe in his arms. She'd always felt safe there. Then their lips met. . . .

Long ago, she had tried to tell Richard how it felt: "It's as if something opens up and we're in a whole other place, like a field that goes on and on forever. Only it's not really a field. And we're not even you and me anymore. It's hard to fit into words, but we're more like two ends of a single string or like mirrors looking into each other. Know what I mean?"

"You mean like swimming in the ocean of the heart."

"That's it!" She'd liked the image. "You've got such a way of putting things."

And now they were there again, swimming in the ocean of the heart. They swayed slowly, buoyed by boundless being. There was no ground to stand on, no walls to contain them, nothing to hold onto but each other. . . . It was the same old kiss.

The Woman with Curious Hands

Edith A. Cheitman

Is the paint wet?
How deep is the crack in that glass?
Do the roots of this damn weed go down forever?
Is the iron hot enough for linen?

She has a curious woman's hands:
Band-Aids, sometimes paint, a few scars;
Dirt under ragged fingernails in summer.

Has he muscle here?
Is he supple there?
What would happen if . . .

Her hands are a pair of curious kittens.
Eyes open in her palms.
Hands of a beekeeper
Minding the hives for honey
No matter how often she has been stung.

Scary Movies

Jo Ann Heydron

My great-grandson James, who's flunking chemistry and cutting English, has to come straight home from school until his grades improve—that's what his mother says. She's asked me to spend the afternoons here with him, and so I have been, for a week now.

Ruthie's a realist. She's not looking for a Christmas-special, extended-family miracle. She hopes that James and I, he sixteen and I eighty-three, will get along well enough that I'll decide to move in. Ruthie's in banking and was just promoted to vice president. She'll need to travel now, a week or two each month.

James's chin clears the top of the refrigerator. He's holding the door open. He grew tall early, but until very recently had a twelve-year-old's high, squeaky voice. Ruthie tells me that other boys used to call late at night and ask for James in his own key, then laugh and hang up.

He unzips a grimy backpack and rakes food into it: two cartons of yogurt, two cans of Sprite, some unwrapped slices of bread. Wherever he's going there must be a food shortage.

"It's not like you can stop me from leaving, Grandma," says James.

That's all right. I understand. Your family gives you life then squeezes it right back out of you. And the less family you have, the more you expect from each member, the weightier each one becomes. All the family James has is Ruthie and me. When I was James's age, all I had was my big sister, Lydia. I was so hard up for people to love me that I made the biggest mistake of my life, at sixteen. School is the least of James's problems.

I look down at my swollen ankles, black orthopedic shoes. "You're right, James. How could I stop you?"

"I'll be back by dark," he says. It's still daylight savings time here in California. Dark is late. "Before Mom gets home." He raises his eyebrows.

Ruthie takes a class on Wednesday nights, but I don't think entering into a conspiracy with James will help him any. "Where are you going?"

Now he lifts his chin the way he does with Ruthie when he's about to explode.

"John's renting a movie."

Is that all? I was sure there was a girl. I don't much care for James's new friend John, though. "Watch it here."

"It's a Freddy movie."

James knows I hate that trash—girls in their brassieres meeting up with big knives. "Go on then. But if you're planning on watching a movie tomorrow, you better watch it here."

John, James. Men's names are plain, like suit coats off the rack, but the men themselves are handmade, by God and their families, the same as women are. I can't say that I've had much to do with the making of James—although for years he and Ruthie have lived just a few miles away.

Like Ruthie, I was in banking. I worked hard all my life, and by the time James was little, I was retired and rushing around taking trips, cruises, as fancy as I could afford. I suppose I still wanted to show Arboretum—the town in North Texas where I grew up, about the size of a pin when I lived there, smaller now—that I was more than the mark it left on me. Not that Arboretum was looking.

My first horror film was *Dracula,* with Bela Lugosi. I saw it in 1931, a pretty scary year whether you went to the movies or not. I lived with Lydia then, who had just married George Lindsay, only after making him promise that I could stay with them until I finished high school.

We were as jittery as babies walking home from the theater that midnight, but George, maybe because he was older than we were or because he came from a family that had a little money—George didn't get scared. That's what I thought then. He had some play and humor left in him, too. He carried a big, heavy flashlight wrapped in black sheet metal that could have been a weapon, and he threw its beam in great arcs across our path, up into the trees, into the mouths of the irrigation ditches that lined the road.

"Point that thing where we're stepping, George," Lydia said. Arboretum is an oven in the summer, and she was wearing a flowered, sleeveless dress. I remember how the slender muscles of her arms reached down as cleanly as a statue's, how her breasts seemed to float under the cotton print, free of the underthings that were supposed to contain them. Lydia believed she could speak her mind to her husband.

I was watching the beam and tripped on a rock that had been kicked up by a car.

"See?" Lydia said.

"Clara likes my little show. Don't you, Clara?"

"Never mind that," said Lydia, taking my hand.

That dark road leading west out of town didn't feel real to me, the oil rigs in the distance, the knee-high corn I knew to be in the near fields. If Count Dracula and his three gauzy wives had climbed out of one of those muddy ditches, if he had twirled his cape around me until, like Mina in the movie, I disappeared, I don't believe I would have been surprised.

It was 1 a.m. before we got home to our tiny rented house. I lay down on my bed in the front room and left the lamp beside me burning. I don't have the words to describe how terrified I was then, the sickening wait to have the life drained out of me, the conviction that every creak of that old house was a coffin lid opening—or how my own would sound closing. It must have been 3 a.m. before I slept, and this is how I woke: I felt a sharp bite on my neck, sat up, hit my head on the wall. The light had been turned off, and George whispered out of the dark, "Clara, honey, I'm truly sorry. I didn't mean to scare you so bad."

James is not home by dark, and Ruthie, who unfortunately decided to skip class and come straight home, is fit to be tied.

Ruthie's not actually my granddaughter: my grandson never bothered to marry her. That didn't surprise me much. His dad, my boy Luke, is on his fifth wife. All these generations, all this mess. And Ruthie's family? A mess of a different kind. That James left today is not my fault, but I begin to feel it's my problem.

In her black wool suit and stocking feet, waistless already at forty, Ruthie skates up and down the kitchen. James comes in at nine.

"Where have you been?" she demands.

"Playing basketball at the park."

He's told such a smart lie that Ruthie doesn't notice there isn't a drop of sweat on him. A week or two ago, she had a call from the basketball coach at the high school, who said he hoped James would go out for the team this year. He has talent, the coach said. When Ruthie asked James what his thoughts were, he said, "Team sports don't appeal to me." Ruthie said, "What does, James? Anything?"

Ruthie hesitates only for a moment. "Did you have to play until nine? Honey, don't you have any *concept* of the future? Your life isn't going to start later, when you're eighteen or twenty-one. It's already rolling. It is in *motion,* James."

He looks at me. I raise a hand to cover my smile. Ruthie is out of her mind if she thinks anything she can say will make James abandon the red blur of today's desires for the crisp black-and-white of some textbook future.

George lay down beside me after the bite. He must have known I'd let him, that I needed to be sure it really *was* him. "Clara," he said, "it was a stupid joke. I'll just stay here with you awhile until you're feeling better and can go back to sleep. That's the least I can do."

Oh, he only went so far with me that first night. I know I remember that part right. Even cocksure George didn't have the brass to join with his wife's sister when the wife herself was thirty feet away. And if he pressed up against me, if he sighed, well, I pretended to be sleeping.

Lydia and I had been separated as little girls, you see, after our mother died of influenza and our father wandered off. She was seven then; I was five. We became the project of the local Baptist church. I was taken in by the Gulley family, Lydia by the Lindsays. That's when George first met her. He was seventeen. She was an elegant little thing, he said after he'd married her, a diamond already, not even in the rough.

After two years Daddy stopped contributing to our keep. If we'd been boys, those first families might have claimed us, the lust for sons so strong that most people didn't bother to hide it. But we were not boys, so we were passed on, to separate houses again. In all those years we never lacked for shelter, although we were hard-pressed to feel grateful, to nurse any warm feelings at all, since Baptist logic or family need might at any time pick us up and set us down somewhere else.

The people I lived with the longest—almost three years—were the Franklins, and the last year I was there Lydia moved to a house down the street from theirs. My sister and I had always met up daily at school, where I was her shadow and, so far as I could make myself, her copy. But now we could knock on each other's doors and maybe sometimes be invited in. Better even, we could walk to and from school together, be sisters one hour a day no matter what. We felt like the Baptists had done us a big favor although it was probably just a coincidence that we ended up so close.

Not too long before I left the Franklins, I overheard Mrs. Franklin ask her husband, "Can't Clara stay? She's nearly thirteen and a worker if she doesn't get off the track, if you remind her what she's doing. And there's something in her that's starting to feel like mine."

Starting? If in three years Peggy Franklin hadn't done more than *start* to love me, I couldn't see how anyone ever would, except Lydia.

Mr. Franklin said in return, "Clara's growing like a weed. We can't feed her anymore, and we sure can't keep her in dresses."

Here's something else that didn't happen that first night with George: I didn't stop believing I was safe and start thinking I was in danger again. I couldn't.

The next afternoon I find myself watching *Scream* with James and John. It feels funny to see a horror movie in the middle of the day. Are you cheating if you know you won't have to walk down a dark hall afterward, climb into a cold bed?

"He rented it," James says, tilting his head at John.

"This is a very complicated film," says John in an important voice. He is James's opposite, short and squat, frizzy hair sticking out all over his head.

"The killer could be anybody," James explains. "Everyone's a suspect. That's what makes this movie so good. Don't worry, Grandma. It's a whole lot better than Freddy movies. And it's funny, too. It makes fun of horror movies at the same time that it is one."

Some blonde girl is alone at night in a big house in the country, about to watch a horror movie herself. I hope the man threatening her on the phone is just trying to scare her. "Have you boys seen this already?"

"Sure. Three times," says John.

"Twice," says James, a little sheepish now.

"Have you ever seen *Dracula*?" I ask them both. In *Dracula* you know right away who the bad guy is. The problem for Lucy is that her friends don't believe in vampires soon enough to save her.

"Which *Dracula*?" James asks. He narrows his eyes at John, warning him, I suppose, to be nice.

John says, "Do you mean the old one with the bats flapping on strings and the dude who keeps saying to everyone, 'I am Count Draaaac-u-la,' like that was as cool as being James Bond. That one?"

Why does James like this John? He's fleshy, coarse, rude.

In no time the little blonde is hanging from a tree with her guts spilling out. Some other girl must be the heroine of this movie.

James says, "Don't watch this, Grandma, if it's going to spook you."

I stay put. Someone should know what's filling up James's head. It's soon obvious who the heroine is. Her boyfriend's trying to talk her into sleeping with him.

"What a selfish asshole!" says James. "I mean her mother's only been dead a year!" The mother was murdered. The kids in this movie don't have a soul to take care of them. "Don't you think he could be patient a little longer, Grandma?"

John snorts.

"Your friend seems to have an opinion on this subject," I say.

"No, he doesn't." James glares at John, who makes a kissing noise.

I think hard at the heroine, *Don't you give in; don't you sleep with that boy.*

I slept on a cot in Lydia's kitchen after that first night, behind a door that locked, telling her she deserved a real sitting room with no beds in it. I was careful never to go anywhere by myself with George, but I knew he was watching for opportunities. On a wet and windy night that winter, Lydia herself, pregnant by then, sent George to pick me up at the bank. I worked there after school, inking in figures in big account books with marbled covers.

When I saw my brother-in-law looking in the bank window at 6 p.m., I said to Mr. Coates, the accounts manager, "I think I'll stay and finish up the month-end posting. I can lock the door behind me when I leave."

Mr. Coates narrowed his eyes. He didn't trust a soul. "Isn't that George Lindsay out there, come to drive you home? You all better get going before this wind blows any harder."

Did you ever see one of those old Fords, how big the backseats were, like a settee you and half the neighborhood could fit on? George parked the Ford out at the county park and right away he said, "Clara, I know you want to get into that backseat with me."

That was brilliant. George chose exactly the words most likely to sway me. I judged myself harshly then. You do that when you're cared for by someone different nearly every year. When you act bad they can't remember how good you used to be. They only begin to believe you'll be good again, that it's your nature to be good, and then it's time to leave.

I was wearing Lydia's blouse. She'd pulled it out of her closet that morning when nothing of mine was clean. Not that one, I said; it's practically brand new. More reason, said Lydia, not to leave it hanging here all by its lonesome. George reached right down the neck of that blouse and popped off the top button. I opened the car door quick and bumped my head backing out of it.

It was raining hard, and as I stood there getting soaked, I was thinking not of how much choice in the matter I might or might not have, but that Lydia had her own sitting room and brand-new dishes and George all spruced up to walk into church beside her, swaggering slow and lovely, as if there weren't a person alive looking in any other direction but his. All I had was a cot in the kitchen. I suppose I knew that most of the good things in life would wait up for me, that they couldn't outrun me if I kept a steady pace, but some were already out of the frame: a mother and father, a face and figure like Lydia's. I watched George's headlight beams shine up the rain drops and tried to make out what lay beyond in the dark. Then, after all Lydia had done for me, I climbed into the backseat.

We came home late, and George told Lydia we'd stayed in town for dinner because driving looked too dangerous. It was true that the wind could twist through Archer County hard enough to pick your car right up. I held my breath while Lydia gazed out the window to see how bad the weather was on this particular night. She turned back and stared at George and me hard, then shrugged and went into the kitchen to put away what she could save of the dinner she'd cooked.

George did the lying that time, but later on I took my turn. Lying is such an easy thing to do. It doesn't seem fair to blame people for it.

I'm trying to finish up on the toilet before James gets home from school. I have to sit up straight so my back won't hurt, and stand up carefully. At my place there's a counter next to the toilet I can hold onto. Here the only thing near enough to grab is a towel rack already half unscrewed from the wall.

Yesterday, by the middle of *Scream,* which, by the way, is not one bit funny, I wanted to run, not only from the TV, but right out of the house. I felt like the murderer was after me. But I kept watching. I had to know who the killer was. Then, the moment his identity was revealed, I felt fine. I realized I'd been working a puzzle all along, and there it was, all put together, the killer planted right in the middle. I'd never been in danger. That must be the point of horror movies, why James likes them.

Ruthie asked me again last night what I thought about moving in. She says she's at the end of her rope, but she says that all the time. I like my apartment, my privacy, driving my little red Camry across town to get here.

James is just through the front door when I come out of the bathroom. He hasn't been to school today, unless they're selling liquor there now.

"Lie down quick," I say.

Drinking wasn't on Ruthie's laundry list of James's problems. I'm guessing this is something new. The minute he's horizontal on his bed, his gorge rises. I grab the wastebasket by his desk.

"Honey, honey," I say.

"Do you have to tell Mom?"

I think about that in the bathroom as I run hot water on a washcloth and wring it out. If Ruthie wants me to live here, surely she expects me to take some responsibility. But since George, I haven't wanted anything to do with keeping secrets, that feeling of being crowded out of your life by what you can't say.

"This girl you like," I ask, giving James a second to wipe his face. "Is she in some kind of trouble?"

He turns his face to the wall. He may be crying. "Grandma, there's no girl."

"What is it, then? What's wrong?"

"Nothing's wrong!" A second later, just before his eyes close, he adds, "I'd tell you, Grandma, but you don't want to know."

George had work that winter surveying land for new oil drilling. The oil business had slowed down but not collapsed, and George worked on contract. He got paid when there was a piece of land to be marked off, and not paid when there wasn't, so he was a bargain.

He tried hard to arrange his day so he could swing by the bank at the end of it. He told Lydia he did this to save me walking home. And he told me the same thing, as if I didn't understand that there would be a half-hour stop off the road somewhere.

All that winter, green as a cucumber and then just plain white, pregnant Lydia kept moving, fat and skinny at the same time, lumbering from one task to the next. She found things to do you wouldn't think a girl under twenty would even know about. She flushed the kitchen pipes and wrapped the joints before the first freeze. Our house didn't have a basement, so she dug a sort of root cellar out in the yard, lined it with wood scraps and nailed together a cover for it.

Was doing all that work just another way of taking care of me, of showing me how to behave? Or was she trying to make both George and me see what mean and ugly things we were compared to her? I don't know which, still. It's possible she knew about us early, even right from the start. In 1931 I couldn't have told you which side George parted his hair on, what brand of whiskey he liked best. There was a way in which you didn't know men then, even the ones you lay down with. But up until then I thought I knew Lydia.

One evening when we came in, she was sitting out on the back stoop in the cold, and all she would say to me was this: "You get dinner, Clara. I'll be damned if I'm going to stand up in front of that stove tonight to feed the pair of you."

I tell Ruthie that James, still passed out, is studying for a chemistry test. *Valences, oxidation, equilibrium.* I never graduated high school, yet I've remembered these words for going on seventy years. I admit I'm a little fuzzy about their meanings.

I order Chinese for dinner. "I've never been much of a cook, Ruthie. You wouldn't expect me to cook, would you?"

"Clara, we need *you*. That's all." She shrugs and yawns, then smiles. She's embarrassed, I guess, to seem sleepy at a moment like this. "I know that's a lot."

I suppose Ruthie needs a little mothering, too. Who doesn't?

"Clara, you'll be my midwife," Lydia told me when she was more than eight months gone. George stood beside her in the kitchen. He wouldn't look at me.

"Don't be stupid," I said. We could have had a doctor attend the birth. We had enough money to pay one, just barely, and even if we didn't, we could have asked George's folks. At the very least there were women in town who would come when a doctor wouldn't.

Lydia said to us, "I can't have anyone from town in this house."

George stepped backward then, out the kitchen door, raising his chin at me as it swung closed, as if to say that he wasn't admitting to anything, that all along it had been my fault, me, Clara the temptress.

I find James staring out the dining room window at my car in the driveway. His shoulders are hunched. His hands hang limp. I sit down at the head of the table. Does James belong to me, and me to him, in any way that counts?

"You'd like to get in that car and keep going, wouldn't you?" I say.

He turns toward me. "Yeah, you want to loan it to me?"

"No. Have a seat, James. I want to talk to you."

"Oh, boy," he says, but he sits down.

"The thing about secrets, honey," I say, "is that sooner or later they get you into trouble. And if whoever you're keeping the secret from figures it out before you tell her, it's worse."

"You haven't figured anything out, Grandma!"

Do I have what it takes to see this through? James's secret, whatever it is, is big. I sense his breathlessness, the thinning out of the James that remains around what he's hiding.

"You haven't figured it out, have you, Grandma?"

The doorbell rings. We both go into the front room. It's John at the door. He looks worse than James, face red, eyes swollen. What is going on?

"Grandma?" James warns.

I back up a few feet, then decide to hold my ground.

"Let me in, James," John says.

"No, I told you."

"Let me in!"

"Let him in, honey," I say. I'm going to get to the bottom of this.

James hisses out a warning. I step forward a little, try to think what on earth I might do to put a scare into them.

John puts one hand on James's chest and gives him a mighty push, sends my great-grandson stumbling back into the entryway. He falls against the door of the closet there, bumps his head pretty hard.

"That's enough!" I say as loudly as I can. I don't command a lot of volume.

James finds his balance. John crosses the threshold.

But John doesn't mean to hurt James again. He puts his hands on James's cheeks. John's bulk, his carnality, seem suddenly to lighten as he stands on his toes, pulls James's head gently forward, and brings their faces together.

"I'm sorry, James," John says softly. "I love you. I am so, so sorry."

Other girls would have witnessed births in the course of family life, but I'd been kept apart in the houses I grew up in. I never went into the birth room or sat in the kitchen while preparations were made. Still, somehow I knew what I needed and rounded it up: something to cover the bed, swaddling for the newborn, sharp scissors to cut the cord and thread to tie it with. But setting these things on a high shelf in the kitchen didn't make me ready.

I sat beside Lydia through the first hours of her labor, followed my sister's wandering stare, the arching of her back, listened to her exhausted cries for George, who rocked his body back and forth on a straight chair in the living room, his eyes shut tight and two fingers shoved in his ears, scared out of his wits at last. I thought Lydia was breathing too fast, that her heart was pounding too hard, that she might die. I feared the blood that would come, Lydia's torn flesh, some awful wound in the child that I wouldn't have the courage to touch.

The last hours went on too long. Near the end I ran in and out of the birth room, talking to myself, crying. When the baby finally slid onto the bed, I watched from the doorway. In the unheated bedroom, it lay still and blue.

How long was it before I moved to the bed, wrapped the baby in the towels I'd warmed by the kitchen stove, tied off and cut the cord? It can't have been very long, for the baby lived. He breathed, coughed up mucus, breathed again. That was Luke born that day, Lydia's child, although I raised him.

She cried out, "I'm cold, Clara. Get me some blankets. I feel like I'm freezing to death."

"Just a minute," I said, staring down at the child, at his pinkening skin, his blinking eyes. There was plenty of George there.

"Clara, please!" Lydia wailed. So I gave Luke to Lydia and covered them both. I remember the moment when the tiny heft of the baby shifted to my sister, how cheated I felt.

Lydia died two weeks later of puerperal fever—infection—probably because I wasn't careful enough when I touched her, when I cleaned her up. There was never any question of George and me marrying. He couldn't stand the sight of me after Lydia was dead. I didn't want anything to do with him either, or with men in general. By the time I got hungry for them again, they were all off fighting the war.

There was a minute, a day, a week, when I wanted to give Luke away, too—to George, George's parents, anyone, just as Lydia and I had been given away. But before a month had passed, Luke belonged to me, and I to him. That was lucky, because Aboretum didn't want anything to do with us by then, George and me and the baby. They'd figured us out, or someone told them. Maybe, in my sorrow, *I* told them.

Some changes are going to have to be made in this house—in the bathroom, for starters.

Tonight Ruthie calls from New York. She's coming home tomorrow. James holds his breath while I take my turn talking to her.

"Thanks for not telling her," he says when we've hung up.

I can't see much of George in James, except around the chin, but sometimes I recognize Lydia in him, in his kindness.

"You'll tell your mother when you're ready, I guess."

I hope I'm doing the right thing.

The Canarsie Rose

Mike Lipstock

In 1931 I was eleven. Grandma was ninety-three. It was the Depression and she lived with us in a cold-water tenement five floors up. She was bent, wrinkled, and only one tooth was left in her mouth. But, boy, she had a thousand years of magic stored in her head. And to a kid like me she knew everything. She had all kinds of powders and colored liquids in her room, and when she mixed them up and we slugged them down, no one ever got sick.

She refused to learn English. When I asked her why, she'd shrug and say in Yiddish, "English won't help when the Cossacks come. They'll still break our heads."

"But Grandma, this is America; we don't have Cossacks here."

She'd stare at me for a moment and then mumble, "Cossacks are everywhere."

"You know," Mom said one day, "Grandma was once very famous."

"What for, Ma?"

"She grew a rose and it was beautiful. It was six inches wide and white like the top of milk. It was so famous that two men from the Czar even came to look. They gave her a paper and it was such an honor that the rabbi himself read it to us from the *shul*."

"Was it like a medal, Ma?"

"Yeah, some medal. A week later the Cossacks came riding through the *shtetl* breaking our heads and tearing the rose to pieces. Right after that we were all on a boat sailing for America."

The story of the rose bugged me and I begged Pop to find her another. Where we lived a blade of grass was considered a plant. A rosebush? Unheard of. Leave it to Pop. A week later he lugged a pot up five flights and handed Grandma a tiny new rosebush. She immediately sifted the soil in her hands and nodded with pleasure. After gently placing it on the fire escape, she kissed Pop on both cheeks and cried.

That summer I could see why the Czar sent his men to give her a prize. She fed and rubbed her rose with different concoctions. Even the thorns became her friends. The bush grew sturdy and when a bud finally appeared, she nurtured it like another child. At night she would sit near the fire escape and speak tenderly to it in Slavish, Polish, Romanish, and a few more that I didn't understand. In the beginning of July, six souls crouched on the fire escape, dizzy with excitement, watching as the huge bud unfolded its creamy white petals. She had grown a perfect white rose.

Not long after that Pop gave us some good news. The bunch of us, me, my two sisters, Grandma, Mom, and Pop were moving to Brooklyn. To a section called Canarsie out in the boondocks. Around us were miles of farmland stretching into the distance.

We were homesteading in a part of Brooklyn that was like the plains of Iowa and Kansas. Flat rolling land, green with eggplant, zucchini, and tomatoes growing everywhere. Grandma took one look and started to cry. Ninety-three and she had finally discovered America.

The house came with a backyard and Pop started a vegetable garden. Mom planted hollyhocks and some other stuff but the centerpiece was the rosebushes, Grandma's private preserve. That summer she planted six in different colors: reds, pinks, peach, and her creamy white that was going to look like the top of the milk. They bloomed and were gorgeous. But still, Grandma wasn't satisfied.

"I need a horse," she said. "Not just a horse, a special horse."

"For what, Grandma?"

"With the right horse I can use the manure for the rose."

"Isn't all horse manure the same, Grandma?"

"What are you, *meshugah*? There are hundreds of qualities and I need the best!"

So Mom and I were always on the lookout for the right kind of horse manure. We carried a shovel and filled bag after bag. They all

failed Grandma's acid test. Like a fine-wine sniffer, she would pulver-
ize the manure in her hand, take a whiff, and proclaim our fertilizer as
no good. Poor Grandma, she was looking for the perfect bouquet.

And then one day we had a big surprise, new neighbors moved in
next door. They arrived with a big horse and wagon that said
"Borden's Milk" on the side. Grandma and Mom were at Bill and
Grace Hart's door the minute the furniture was inside. They carried a
big welcome basket filled with Jewish goodies: *humentashin, strudel,*
even the *rugalach* that I was counting on eating that night. The Harts
were Irish and their brogue was as foreign to Grandma as the man in
the moon. The gesture, though, brought tears to the old milkman's
eyes. His horse, Buck, and the Borden's wagon were still at the curb
and when Grandma looked him over . . . she swooned!

"You see that horse?" she said. "He has a gold *toches*. When he
kvetshes, diamonds will come out."

"How do you know, Grandma?"

"How do I know, boychick? With a horse like that, the Czar gave
me a medal."

Bill was a kindred spirit in his love for flowers and never failed to
leave a bag of fertilizer at our front door with two quarts of milk. By
now they were old pals with a friendship based on shrugs, grimaces,
and red and blue liquids that they both shared. With the mixture of
Grandma's voodoo and Bill's manure they were developing gargan-
tuan flowers and rosebuds as big as a fist.

Just when he was needed most, Buck developed a severe case of
constipation. No more diamonds were tumbling out. It was a crisis,
and in a few days the Borden Milk Company sent a replacement, a
horse called Nick. I thought Nick was great, but Grandma pined
away for Buck. More bad news. Bill told us Buck had three days to get
well or he'd be turned into dog food.

"Murderers!" Grandma screamed. She was positive the Cossacks
were out to get her new rose.

"Not this time, boychick!"

The next day Bill took Grandma and me to the Borden stable and
we got ready for the cure. A gallon of prunes, plums, and other stuff
from her arsenal of medications produced nothing but a little wind.

This was much worse than Grandma expected. That night, we slept in the barn with Buck and toward dawn we watched as the old magician started her incantations. Bill was hypnotized. She was calling forth the same spirits that his sainted mother invoked when he was a boy. He crossed himself a couple of times and we watched as Grandma whipped out a Star of David and swung it in front of Buck three times. . . . Nothing, not even a little gas. But she was biding her time. When the sun rose in the east, she made her big move.

"Boychick," she shouted, "what we need is a tub full of *smetteneh*. You understand? *Smetteneh!*"

"What do you need sour cream for, Grandma?"

"Don't ask, just get it."

So Bill and Pop got a ton of sour cream and ladled it into Buck's trough. Not just plain sour cream but stuff that Grandma fortified with royal blue broth. That horse, Buck, lapped up the sour cream like an old Galitziana (member of a neighboring Jewish tribe) licking his chops. Suddenly there was an explosion that almost blew off the rafters and caused the other horses to stampede out of Borden's front gate. Fertilizer came pouring out of Buck like water from a burst dam. Fertilizer so rich in enzymes and proteins that it revolutionized Canarsie farms forever. A teaspoon of Buck's manure now accomplished what fifty pounds of ordinary fertilizer did before. Grandma and her blue sour cream had produced a new strain that created monsters in the garden. Cantaloupes as big as basketballs, dahlias as big as your head, and roses . . . oh boy! What roses!

The Canarsie Chamber of Commerce and Brooklyn Botanical Gardens awarded Grandma and Bill its highest honor for their creamy white rose. This new strain was even given a Latin name: *"Buckitus Smettenitus."*

When she accepted her medal, Grandma leaned over and whispered in my ear, "Boychick, maybe this time the Cossacks won't come."

At Canio's

Karen Blomain

Elbowing in beside a woman
I choose a book and wait
Savoring the anonymous moment
As the room fills for my reading.

Over my shoulder, I notice her
Moving the page away from her face.
"Middle-aged glasses," I smile
and hand her mine.

While I'm reading I notice
Her amid the others, leaning forward
The way we were taught
To better please and hear.

I look up at the room full of women
And wonder who has lost a breast
A husband? Who goes home to silence?
Whose kids don't call?

When I read, "My Last Period"
They titter, smile, yes, I've said it
For them. For me. Except for Canio
Dear man who listens with the heart's ear,

The men in the room, two, fidget.
Later one will engage me about poetry

His, and the other, new-smitten
And wearing a peacock suit, eager to show

His love how women's lib and fond
Of verse he is. I'm a tiresome woman
Amen, as his eyes rove the shelves behind me
And she clutches his arm, the prize

She'd won and must guard.
He'll want it all glossed over. Blood
And stain whited out of her poems. No pain
He's not felt harder. Glad to hear my own voice

I read on, glad I own my own life. Later
The guy poet ambushes me, playfully questions
Whether I think women writers
Are essentially different from men.

Nepal Through Bifocals

Sonja Johansen

The water buffaloes, fifteen or so large bony animals, plodded determinedly toward me. I was new in the village and more than a little nervous. I moved well off the dirt road. The animals seemed oblivious to anything or anyone in their path. Ready to jump, I watched them go past. Then I watched in amazement as three small children with sticks followed, herding these ungainly creatures to their daytime dinner pasture.

I was a Peace Corps volunteer, age sixty-six by the time my group's training was finished and each of us had been sent to a separate village. Since I was the only Westerner in my village, I provoked astonishment, hilarity, and bemusement at times—as when I first tried eating rice with my fingers or served as a dance student for a four-year-old instructor. (He was very agile and seemed to enjoy our lessons; certainly the rest of his family did.) I also attracted a lot of attention. Children followed me calling out, "Good morning," regardless of whether it was morning, noon, or night. Those with more advanced language skills would add, "How old are you?"

My own language skills were minuscule. I had been assigned to teach math (in Nepali) using Nepali textbooks. I was a major source of entertainment to my students, high school girls for whom I was also a female role model. I spent considerable class time with my nose in a Nepali-English dictionary. I justified this as "Showing Them How to Do Research." We actually spent more time teaching one another songs and dances, which I justified as "Cultural Exchange," one of the three goals of Peace Corps.

A memorable test of my Nepali language came on a jeep ride to the nearest bazaar. (An outdoor shopping mall with street vendors selling vegetables, bananas, tangerines, mangoes, and with sacred cows walking freely about.) I was the only Westerner in the back of the jeep, in which fifteen or so people were stuffed (though not pig piled; everyone sat on something or someone for the forty-five minute ride). They talked about me. "Where did she come from?" "Pragatinagar." "Where is she going?" "Narayangadt" (the bazaar). "What is she doing here?" "I don't know." "How old do you think she is?" "Oh, at least 100." I sat deadpan. The conversation veered to another topic. When we reached Narayangadt, I climbed over the other passengers, got off the jeep, turned to them, and said in perfect unaccented Nepali, "No, I'm only sixty-seven years old." My audience reacted with good humor.

Language was not the only difficulty. Class sizes of sixty high school girls made it impossible to give individual attention, check homework, prevent cheating, or learn individual names. Teachers conducted roll call by numbers, not names. These things bothered me. All students, of all ages, need to know that someone cares about them and that they are not anonymous.

I had better luck with my twelve ninth-grade computer students who were selected by the headsir (headmaster) as top-of-the-class. All of them prepared their résumés (yes!) on the computer. Since the printer I had rented was not working, I took the résumés to Kathmandu on a diskette, printed them, and mailed them to the village. The girls later told me they had never received a letter before.

The Nepalis I met during my two years were good-natured and friendly. My headsir at first did not believe I would fully appreciate the cold-water outdoor showers (I heated water in a pail instead), the lack of central heating in winter (I sat reading in the evenings wearing my down sleeping bag), the poisonous snakes in summer (I never visited the shack in the backyard after dark), the nonpotable water (I boiled and filtered always), the lack of telephones, refrigerators, washing machines, TVs, copiers, computers, hair dryers, and the frequent lack of electricity. But I did manage a year in the village, with improvisation. Peace Corps calls it "Flexibility."

My first Christmas in the village came one month after I was posted there. I put on my red sari, with some help from my landlady so it would not unwind when I walked. In class, I told the girls, in Nepali, my prepared story about the baby born in a barn and the three kings from Asia following a star, and we sang "Deck the Halls" . . . fa la la la la. Then I went to the village chairman's house for the special Christmas dinner they had prepared so I wouldn't miss my family. It was chow mein.

After a year in the village, I was transferred to Kathmandu to work with the Nepal Health Research Council but I maintained contact with my friends in the village and visited them periodically. During my second year, the village chairman and I developed two grant proposals that resulted in computer training for "my" girls and installation of a computer which I bought in Kathmandu and transported to the village in a jeep. Because of Peace Corps emphasis on sustainability, the village had to pay part of the cost, and arrange for ongoing maintenance if needed. I was happy to see the girls take to the computer so eagerly, and to make arrangements to continue training one another. In a country where women have been undervalued and have not had opportunities for education and employment, this was surely "Career Exploration."

A trek in the Annapurna region was exhilarating. I went with three Nepali friends. We took the bus from our village in the agricultural terai region to the city of Pokhara in the hills, and stayed overnight with a relative. That evening people came to hang out in our front yard. One man had made recordings of Nepali songs. Since I am a church organist and choir director in the States, I knew quite a few songs myself. He sang one Nepali song, accompanied by a guitar, then it was my turn to sing an American song, then another man sang, then I, and so on. We collected quite a crowd of mostly men; the women were home cooking dinner. I was given a cassette of their songs. One of the men, an engineering student named Gokul, accompanied us the next day on our climb. He cut classes. Maybe he thought we three women needed protection. We protected *him*.

I had been told the trail up to the village of Ghandruk was easy. One person said, "Can you walk three hours? Then no problem." After seven hours of climbing, often on stone steps, dodging porters in flip-flops and mules on the trail, we arrived. My friend Bidya (age thirty-one) located and negotiated a hotel room for the four of us. She and Sapana (age twenty-one) were as tired as I was. Gokul, being male, could not even discuss being tired. That evening, we sang.

The next day, with pouring rain outside, we ate, did some singing in the hotel, walked around the visitor center of the Annapurna Conservation Area, talked to a few villagers, slipped on wet rocks, and went to bed early.

On day three we headed down the trail, thigh muscles soon screaming from the descent. The highlight for me came partway down, when a very old wrinkled Nepali man watched me wobbling down the steps. He called to me, and with a huge smile and very kind eyes gave me his walking stick. It made all the difference.

The same cast, without Gokul, went to the Royal Chitwan National Park. We took a jeep, then a bus, southwest to the village of Megauli near the Indian border, hired a guide for the next day's excursion into the park, and stayed overnight with another relative. That evening we dropped in at a health post staffed by a visiting British physician who gave us Earl Grey tea, a Beethoven concert on her CD player, and conversation *in English*.

Early the next day we hiked into the park. The terrain was flat, open scrub brush at first. After fording the Rapti River several times on foot and crossing it in a poled canoe ferry, we came to a medium-dense jungle. There were lots of hiding places for Royal Bengal tigers, one-horned rhinoceros, cobras, and other animals I did not care to meet, unprotected and on foot as we were. I remembered the guidebook cautioned against jungle walks and recommended riding safely, if uncomfortably, on the back of an elephant. Too late.

We reached one of the visitor centers where some staff of this very large park lived, and where tented and stilted lodge rooms had been constructed for rich visitors. We avoided the crocodiles in the river and rested on a bench in the elephant area, watching elephants bring large loads of grasses back to their enclosures for dinner.

On the way out of the park, we paused at the main visitor center to appreciate a one-horned rhino staring motionless at us from across a small gully, a short distance away. We had been told that rhinos move very quickly and could be upon us in seconds. I located the nearest hiding place and prepared to run, of course with camera in hand.

Half an hour later, the rhino crashed off down the gully, in the direction of the dirt track we would need to take to get home. After waiting a decent interval, during which the park men informed us that fresh tiger prints had been spotted nearby, we made a nervous and quiet retreat. That's when I remembered the guidebook suggested wearing jungle-colored clothes. We were dressed in the usual brightly colored Nepali style. I consoled myself with the thought: one tiger can't eat all four of us.

We got home very late, very tired, but alive.

The next day we hitchhiked back to town and got a ride with an ambulance. It was transporting a teenage boy whose arm had been broken in an encounter with a domesticated water buffalo. Wild water buffaloes are aggressive, but you also have to be careful of tamed ones, as they are very large.

At one point, my friends in the village told me they had cried because word had reached them that I had broken my leg. I did fall off a mountain in Bhutan but several months later, when I visited my village again (limping, but happy to see them), there was a heartwarming celebration.

Nothing else untoward happened to me personally, although the Maoist rebels intensified their violence and, by the time my stay in Nepal ended, they controlled about a third of the country and caused many deaths. Scheduled elections could not be held because of safety issues, the king took over the government, and uncertainty hovered over the country.

Overall, my two years of Peace Corps service was somewhat of an emotional rollercoaster ride. On the downside were sad stories about girl trafficking (selling unwanted girls to Indian brothels), government corruption, wild elephant attacks destroying crops, reverse killings (if you hit someone with your truck or bus and injure them, you should back up and run over them to be sure they are dead so your company does not have to pay long-term medical expenses). Also, there were my personal experiences of massive general strikes *(bandh)* against the government, which closed schools and businesses, and of leech bites that kept bleeding due to the injected anticoagulant.

On the upside were the Himalayan trails and scenery, the music and dancing, the warm friendships and memorable people, the colorful Buddhist and Hindu festivals, and the respectful way I was treated. In Nepal, age is honored and I, at age sixty-seven, was always given the best, sometimes only, chair. Once, a bed with five people assigned to it was vacated so I could have it alone while the five slept on the floor.

I am now back in the United States. I sit and smile at the memories. I still don't understand rebirth and reincarnation but I like the Buddhist emphasis on happiness rather than guilt, and now believe that meat is not a necessary part of the diet.

Returning to the United States was a major adjustment, due partly to the materialism here. Are hair dryers and kitchen scissors really necessary? How would I explain that to my Nepali friends? I know we all think and behave the way we have learned but I am distressed by the games I see people playing: flirting, elections, money. My Nepali friends would not understand the need for manipulation and games.

Eventually, I hope I am able to reconcile my thinking about the two extremely different cultures but all in all, the experience was a blast. Try it!

The Palace of Physical Culture

Valerie Miner

I love to watch naked women. I would enjoy men, too, but they're not allowed into the ladies' locker room. Watching is the best part of each day at the Y. Of course, the glance must be discreet; you don't want people thinking you have designs on them or the handbags they leave behind when they shower. Actually, most women are curious: comparing, contrasting, worrying, admiring. In this reunion of exiles, long separated by civilized attire, I decide that naked assembly promotes democracy because, after all, most of us have the same basic equipment. We stare at ourselves, at what we might become, at what we once were: big bottoms, little bottoms, pregnant bellies, surgical scars, buff thighs, silvery stretch marks, shaved legs, hairy armpits, tattoos, bunions, pink nipples, red nipples, brown nipples, pierced nipples.

My dear brother gave me a summer pass to the Y this June when I turned fifty. A complicated present. Yes, I'd been planning to exercise as soon as I found time, but was he saying I looked fat? Did he notice the way my leg stiffened after sitting through a long movie? Was this a use-it-or-lose-it ultimatum? No, honestly, he insisted. He worked out himself and just thought I'd *enjoy* it. What a thoughtful gift. Maybe he wanted me to live longer.

By July, whenever I enter the locker room, I anticipate the familiar, curiously welcoming potpourri of disinfectant, sweat, moisturizer, deodorant, and talcum powder. Today I spot Mrs. Hanson slowly rolling support nylons over the amazingly irregular shape of her left knee. I hold my greeting until she has pulled the pantyhose to her waist.

"So, how's the new hip?" (A macabre question, I would have thought a month ago, but now it seems as natural as the frequently asked, "What's your pulse rate?")

"Good, good," the old woman nods with pleasure. "I got through all the kicking and treading."

I savor the smell of Mrs. Hanson's apple-mint soap.

"And the waterjacks. All of it," she says beaming.

On first encounter, Mrs. Hanson is an oddly diaphanous figure: wispy halo of curls atop white, bulky shoulders; thighs and hips like so much loosely packed ricotta cheese; breasts sagging like the flesh of a plucked turkey. Who assigned me a locker across from this enormous old woman? She's hardly what I consider a fitness muse. For a while, I am annoyed by the whole Senior Aqua Class who usurp bench space, noise space, shower space in midday, when joggers and weightlifters need to slip in and out over tight lunch breaks. Can't the water birds reschedule for three in the afternoon? Or is that nap time, prime canasta hour, the perfect part of the day for a sloe gin fizz and a little virtual sex? In truth, I grow petulant.

Then I study the naked Mrs. Hanson. Dignity is the only word for her movement in the nobly earned flesh of those pale arms and legs. Her walk is light and graceful, despite a limp, which I soon understand is from her second hip replacement. I've learned a lot about Mrs. Hanson this month, about how she still goes ice fishing on Lake Minnetonka in February, about how she lives alone, but likes to visit the "elderly ladies" at a nearby retirement home, about how she plans to be walking perfectly by September, so she can visit her grandson in San Francisco for her eightieth birthday. Usually, we have a long chat, but right now Mrs. Hanson is hurrying off to "take an old dear to the doctor."

Today's class is "Stretch and Strengthen." Surrounded by the studio mirrors—glass and human—I enjoy the initial deep breathing and arm raising, but soon feel like a cartoon of a decrepit ballerina. Fifty years old, what am I doing here? As a child, I thought fifty was ancient. I remember telling myself that there would be no point in visiting the library after fifty, because I'd be almost dead, anyway. Now, I am head of a branch library and go to the gym every lunch hour.

At first this class looks easy—swinging pink baby weights back and forth, up and down. I sign up to swell my self-confidence and because I like the Salsa music.

Within two weeks, I am using the green, three-pound weights. Once, on a double espresso day, the macha five pounders.

A new instructor stares at me.

"The lady in the back row," she calls, "don't *swing* your weights. Concentrate on lifting and lowering. To the beat."

Today's music is speedy rap.

"That's it," she says. "You can feel it now. Lift and lower. You've almost got it."

Almost?

My arms are sore. Sweat pearls on my forehead. My coif is losing its fure. Smelly, wet hair drips around my headband in humiliating strings.

"Just eight more," exhorts Brunhilda-the-Brawny.

Defiantly, I pause to sip water.

"Just seven more," she cajoles in that cheerful-earful voice, effortlessly pumping her own ten-pound weights. "Seven. That's it. Six. Come on, five. . . ."

Whenever I skip a workout, I feel that old childhood remorse about missing Sunday mass. And when I keep my new exercise schedule, I imagine the sacrament of penance erasing sins of sloth and gluttony. Sick, I know this is sick, the transfer of Catholic schoolgirl guilt into menopausal health guilt. But first I'll deal with the body, then I'll tackle the bad attitude.

Marta, the "Otter," and her mother, Rosa, are laughing in the locker room when I return, exhausted from class. Luckily, it's never hard to hold up my end of the conversation with Marta, who eagerly keeps me apprised of her progress on the Otter Swim Team.

This nimble six-year-old has the taut, androgynous shape of an archer's bow and—while she casually surveys the older bodies as if she's shopping for a puberty outfit—Marta tells me that having mastered the crawl, she will learn to dive this week.

Quiet, self-contained Rosa is her daughter's mirror image. Lean and dark as Marta, but virtually silent each afternoon as she helps Marta into her striped yellow suit and purple cap. At the moment, Rosa has retreated to the corner studying a computer science text.

"Mama is going to be a business executive," Marta tells me.

Rosa rolls her wise, twenty-five-year-old eyes. "Graduation. An office job maybe."

Since June, I've discovered much about Marta and a little about her mother, such as although Rosa grew up in Cuba, she never learned to swim. Now, every day, she wilts in the chlorinated steam on the bleachers, peering as her daughter bobs in the big pool. I cannot imagine how, as a single mother, Rosa manages to work as a janitor, attend junior college, and escort Marta to the gym, but I get the impression that Rosa and Marta believe swimming is as important as eating.

In early August, I begin a Circuit Class, which my brother warns, is only for serious exercisers. I understand why, within five minutes, when we commence a gruesome rota of one-minute ordeals: push-ups, weighted butterfly lifts, star jumps, bicep curls, step straddles, and tricep hinges. Our respite after seven of these in-place routines is to sprint back and forth across the gym five times. Then we continue the torture circuit on the other side of the room—squats, back curls, double crunches. . . . The single pleasure here is the vibrant beat of reggae music.

Despite the virtues of this invigorating workout, I find my glance wandering toward the fashion show. Toward the plump blonde in black lace exercise brassiere and striped pedal pushers. The young Islamic woman performing jumping jacks in baggy sweatshirt and black scarf. Isn't she baking in there? Then there's the brave, solitary man in his veteran university shorts and threadbare T-shirt. Concentrate, I scold myself, Zen into an alternative state. Attitude. You in your body. You are your body.

When I return from Circuit Class, a pouting Marta stands by the locker, dripping from her yellow stripes onto the floor.

My first thought is not about this little one, but about Mrs. Hanson, whom I haven't seen yesterday or today. Is she okay? It's too early for her San Francisco trip, right?

Soon, Marta's sullenness fills the room.

"What's up?" I ask.

"Nothing," Marta mutters, wringing the purple rubber swim cap in her strong little hands.

Marta's mother shrugs and returns to her heavy textbook.

"Didn't you have a good swim today?" I try again.

Silence.

Suddenly, I remember. "Did you make it? Did you swim from one end of the pool to the other without stopping?"

Head down, Marta glowers at her turquoise toenails.

"Answer the lady," instructs Rosa gently.

"Stupid!" exclaims Marta. "What's the point of getting all the way across? You just have to swim back."

Grinning, Rosa encourages, "It's the next stage in learning."

"You can't talk," Marta snaps. "You won't even stick your foot in the water!"

Often I am given free reminders like this that I would flunk motherhood. How will she answer?

Rosa is spared because a tall, red-haired woman has just appeared from the shower, a white towel around her waist. We are all surprised by the left side of her chest, by the long red scar, the missing breast. Marta moves forward for a better look. Rosa and I glance away, maturely pretending to busy ourselves with important thoughts. Marta continues to stare and when I turn back, the woman has noticed Marta. She bends down to the little girl and winks. Marta puts her hand over her heart and winks back. They both break into wide smiles.

It is the last day of August and I am leaning on the registration desk renewing my membership, when Mrs. Hanson hobbles up behind me to sign in.

"Hello! I was worried," I say hectically, then note the cane. "Oh! Are you okay? What happened?"

A little fall, she explains, as we walk gingerly together toward the locker room. I hold the door open, wincing at her ragged gait. She'll never make it to San Francisco at this rate.

"Your grandson," I ask. "Did you visit him?"

Deftly, she slips into her water-bird suit. "Well," she sighs, "there's good news and bad news."

I hate this expression, but have never heard it uttered with Mrs. Hanson's charming fortitude.

"The bad news, of course, is the fall. I had to postpone my visit until December."

I nod, waiting.

"The good news is that he's taking me down to Disneyland for Christmas!"

"How wonderful," I say, that and a few other empty phrases, as she proceeds purposefully with her cane toward the pool.

My favorite class is step aerobics. Maybe because the teacher plays Aretha and Bonnie Raitt and Patti La Belle. Never before have I felt graceful. Yet here I accomplish knee lifts, hamstring curls, side leg lifts, V-steps, diagonals, L-steps, repeater knees, side lunges, back lunges, and turn steps. Before joining the gym, I lived in my head, which seemed roomy enough, with space for yesterday, today, and tomorrow, but I couldn't go back to residing there full-time. Not now that I've located all these bones and muscles, some of which I know by nickname: abs, glutes, pecs, lats.

While my classmates' speed and strength can be amazing, the most impressive folks are the rubber people. I watch agog as they stand up straight, bend at the waist, and place their palms on the floor. Some women sit on the mat, hold their legs wide apart and put their arms flat on the ground between their knees. Then there are the neck stretchers. How do they get their ears to touch their erect shoulders? You'd think a librarian's head would be heavy enough to cooperate with gravity. I'll never be Ms. Pretzel, but I am pretty good at the stand-on-one-foot-and-bend-the-other-back-to-your-bottom routine. My balance is improving and I enjoy the pull on my "quad" as I now fondly call it.

After all that fancy stepping, I deserve a long shower. Melting under the hot water, silently humming a new Queen Latifah song, I am blissfully alone, but surrounded by other women washing and shaving, by mothers cleaning children's ears, teenagers shouting gossip to one another over the noise of the pipes. Showering is the simple, perfect pleasure. *Paradiso.* Ah, divine heat massages new, old muscles; cleansing water sprays away the dregs of menstruation, the sweat of anxiety and exercise. I shampoo my gray-blonde hair and feel face, shoulders, body growing relaxed and alert. A sudden image of Mom in middle age—emphysema, arthritis, migraine headaches, complete set of ill-fitting dentures. Did such a memory provoke my brother's birthday gift?

"Hi!"

A small voice interrupts the drying of my ten exceedingly clean toes.

"Hi, yourself," I say. "How's it going?"

Marta waits expectantly. Finally I look up, notice Rosa standing beside her in a glossy red swimsuit.

"You?" I ask.

Marta answers for her mother. "She promised."

Rosa renders her characteristic shrug.

"She promised once I made it across the pool, she would come swimming."

"I said," Rosa corrects her nervously, "I would stick my *foot* in the water.

I begin to congratulate her, to say something motivating, and then realize I can't say anything at all because I am on the verge of tears.

Rosa saves me, "Eh, I figure, at my age, it's about time."

The Painter at Ninety-One

Edythe Haendel Schwartz

Her eyes fatigue.
Ghosts dance around the rods and cones,
wash halos over reds and blues
as if the dazzle of an ordinary day
were singed. On the easel, flecks of
paint blink on and off like fireflies
in haze. Split vision's usual,
a trick the body plays in age, and yet
she hungers for an image,
marvels that Matisse,
too ill to paint, cut papers,
fuchsia, pink, and green,
collaged improvisations, rhythm, jazz.

She squeezes colors on the glass,
cerulean blue, the hue of ocean water
near her childhood home, and ochre
like the glint on ripe tomatoes,
as though her eyes remember how to harness light.
Fingers bent as winter twigs,
she works the yellow into crimson,
gilds the grasses of a meadow tangerine,
and shapes a woman standing at an easel,
holding brush to air.

Encounter in Milan

SuzAnne C. Cole

Accompanying my husband on a business trip to Milan had sounded good back home in Houston, but now that we were here, I wasn't particularly happy. We were not having the romantic interlude I had fantasized as just the tonic our thirty-five-year, empty-nest marriage needed. In fact, I hardly saw him as business meetings and dinners occupied him every day and most evenings. Still, I consider myself a fairly independent traveler, able to get along alone in a strange city when necessary, so rather than stay in our tiny, spartan room, order room service, watch CNN, and have a pity party, I took myself off every morning to explore the city.

That day I had chosen to tour the museums located in the *Castello Sforzesco*. For my husband's convenience, we were staying at a business hotel in an office park on the far outskirts of Milan; to sightsee in the city, I had to walk a couple of miles to the end of the subway line and then ride to the central plaza surrounding the *Duomo,* the great cathedral called "the navel of Milan." From there I walked through elegant shopping galleries, marveling as usual at the svelte, chic Milanese women, bitterly comparing and criticizing my own "mature" figure. No wonder the romance in our marriage seemed to have disappeared.

Reaching the *Castello,* I explored its many museums, going through art galleries, rooms of applied art and stringed instruments, and a surprisingly good, if somewhat out of place, exhibit of aborigine art from western Australia. Even though none of the museums had English guidebooks and I have no Italian, I still enjoyed myself. Looking at my map after leaving what I thought was the last museum, I noticed there was also an archaeological museum on the grounds, so I decided to give it a quick look before heading for the park behind the *Castello* to enjoy the mild February sun.

Walking around the courtyard, I had just decided which door marked the museum's entrance when an attractive, young Italian, with long, straight, dark hair and dark eyes behind dark-framed glasses, casually dressed in jeans, sweater, wool jacket, and bright muffler, noticed me studying the sign on the door. He said, in the first English I had heard all day, "This is the archaeological museum."

"Great, that's where I want to be," I said; he held the door for me, and we began to chat as we walked down two flights of stairs together.

The museum was dim and its rooms unoccupied except for an occasional dozing guard. Since the young man's English was so good, I asked him a few questions about the exhibits; he in turn told me that he was from Florence and was in Milan playing tourist while his wife, who was in Congress, was attending meetings. He asked what I was doing in Milan, and I said I too was accompanying my spouse on business. By then we had also exchanged first names—his was Marco.

The cases of broken pottery and bits of bone were not holding my interest, so, longing for the bright day outside, I told Marco good-bye, saying I had had enough museums for one day. I was a bit surprised when he followed me up the stairs and outside, but it was not until we walked into the courtyard, and he reached for my hand, holding it as he gently swung our arms in unison, that I realized he was trying to pick me up.

For a moment or two, I flirted with the idea—what harm in spending the afternoon exploring this lovely city with a bilingual guide? Who would know or care? Wouldn't it be nice to have lunch in one of those charming *trattorias* with a companion, instead of my usual solitary sandwich on a park bench?

But prudence firmly squashed my budding fantasy; after all, this young man seemed hardly older than our eldest son. I withdrew my hand from his grasp as a lie quickly sprang forth—"Marco, I'm so sorry, but I'm meeting my husband in thirty minutes." He looked so forlorn I almost changed my mind, but instead, I went quickly and briskly on, "Have you seen the Australian aborigine exhibit yet?"

"No."

"Then let me show you where it is. I saw it earlier today and I think you'll really like it." Quickly I walked him to the entrance, smiling to myself as I remembered the very attractive, young blonde Australian woman staffing the exhibit who had been so kind to me earlier in the day.

"Ciao, Marco, and *gratzie*."

"Ciao, SuzAnne," he said as he leaned forward and kissed me sweetly on both cheeks. Straightening my shoulders and pulling in my stomach, I walked away feeling years younger and much more attractive. At a stall outside the *Castello* gates I bought my husband a bright wool muffler.

Texts

Mary M. Brown

We spend our years as a tale that is told.

Psalms 90:9

Over the past seventeen years I've become addicted to my thirty-mile weekday commute from Anderson, Indiana, to Indiana Wesleyan University, where I work—addicted to beginning and ending the daylight hours with wheels in motion and the moving landscape, with unconscious observations of the bean crops, the highway repair crews, and the farmers' market near Summitville.

My husband laments the time I must spend on the road, but his concern, like Thoreau's warning that one cannot waste time "without injuring eternity," seems irrelevant to me. Time, I'm convinced, is nothing but God's little sleight of hand, a divine ploy to keep us weak-spirited mortals interested and engaged in eternity. It's the illusion of life's real mystery—its endlessness, beginninglessness, its middlessness—another one of God's little now-you-see-it, now-you-don'ts.

Unlike me, my friend, Marj Elder, who keeps an office next to mine, would rather walk than drive. Marj is eighty-one and still teaches half time at Indiana Wesleyan. For her, a day in which she has to get in her car and drive the half mile or so from her house on Nebraska Street in Marion to the parking lot next to our office building is a bad day—or at least an unsettling one—a day of heavy rain, ice, or snow or of a flare-up of her vertigo, a day when the walk seems more threatening than the drive. Those days Marj gets into her '76 Impala, which she bought new and which now registers just over 76,000

85

miles, and drives to work to lead her seminar in Hawthorne or Melville or Twain, classes students still remember after twenty-five, thirty years. There was a time, Marj says, not long ago, when her exercise bike had more miles on it than her car. She had let Andrew, an adolescent boy who visits her regularly with his family, ride the bike for the last "mile" and watch the odometer turn over one hundred thousand miles before she replaced the bike with a new one.

After fifty years of walking to her office at IWU, Marj still often arrives with her fists full of treasure—in the autumn, fallen leaves that have a singular coloration, a particularity that delights her and motivates her to pick them up in wonder like a child picks up shells on the beach. Occasionally I find the leaves laid dearly on my desk with a note: "See what I found on my walk to work!" or "Never found one quite like this, have you?"

Marj has a better understanding of the relationship between time and eternity than I will ever have. And I suspect if she had an afternoon or two to spend with Stephen Hawking, she might give him pause and plant in him an urge to begin a major revision of *A Brief History of Time*. Marj says she hopes to live long enough to see the confirmation of a theory she's long held. She believes that one day she will hear the voice of her beloved Hawthorne—that sound waves produced years, centuries, ago are still suspended in the air we breathe in the twenty-first century, jammed together like clothes in a closet, and that we are just waiting for someone to develop the technology that will rematerialize, individuate, and identify those sounds.

Marj cares little about the scientific process. What she dreams of is the experience of hearing words spoken before the advent of mechanically recorded sound—the singular textured utterances of men and women of experience, wisdom, and faith—not only of Hawthorne, but also of Emily Dickinson and Edward Taylor. And perhaps, in another part of the world, of Abraham, Isaac, and Jacob—maybe even of Christ himself, although I have never heard Marj make that specific wish. What Marj imagines, I think, is not time travel but travel altogether *outside* of time. The idea would not be so outlandish to Hawking, I suspect, but the look in Marj's eyes when she talks about the possibilities might move—perhaps even enlighten—the most noted physicist since Einstein.

But Marj may never have the time to spend an afternoon with Hawking. She devotes at least a half day every week (and often more) to her excursions with Avis, a research librarian some fifteen years younger than Marj, retired from IWU. The two of them search for books—for themselves and for anyone who wants to place an "order." Marj catalogs the requests—for Nancy Drew mysteries, first editions of Dickens, collections of Ansel Adams photographs, seventeenth-century sermons—on 3" × 5" cards that she totes with her to used book stores, library sales, and antique shops. She scans the shelves, digs in boxes, and talks to the bookstore owners, all of whom she knows intimately.

Marj and Avis are looking for a few books for me—ten or twelve (I've lost count, but Marj and Avis know) Shakespearean plays, small maroon volumes to complete the American Book Company set of Shakespeare's works that I bought ten years ago, and for the few Edith Wharton works I do not yet own in hardback. Several years ago they unearthed a book I loved and reread as an adolescent—*Sink the Basket,* whose author's name, Sally Knapp, I did not remember and never would have recognized. I had checked out the book from the Holy Cross Lutheran Grade School Library so many times during my fourth grade year that when I reread it recently in my late forties, I encountered no surprises, only memories.

Of course Marj got a deal on that book—at least ten percent off the price ($2.50) penciled in the top right corner of the first blank page of the book. She passes the discount on to me and to her other "clients," refusing to take even a small finder's fee or money for her time or gas. She knows that some of the books she hunts for might well be found on eBay or some other Internet marketplace, but she counts each book search she is commissioned as a privilege and a joy.

Occasionally, Marj can't resist and buys her*self* a book—a George McDonald novel or a new Kurt Vonnegut book or a volume of Frost's poems in a beautiful binding. She always hesitates a little now before she buys, knowing that most of the corners of her small house are full of books already, all neatly stacked or boxed, all catalogued, not only by author and title and date, but by how they were acquired—at what bookstore on what date for what price.

From my perspective, her collection is beautifully quirky. Some books she buys for the author, some for the content, some for the particular edition, some for the unusual binding, some for the history, some for some other literary or wholly personal intuition. She purges her collection periodically by giving pieces of it away to colleagues or students, bringing the volumes tenderly, unexpectedly to school and saying, "I just thought you probably would like this," or "You have more use for this than I do," or "Here, take this now so I don't have to will it to you." Marj, who never married, has spent more time with her books than most of us will ever spend with our spouses, takes better care of them, perhaps even loves them more.

For Marj, time is text. Minutes and hours are to be read or heard, reread and reheard, studied, absorbed, lived fully, and then perhaps relived and integrated into memories and understandings of other times. Beginnings and endings become indistinguishable and, anyway, irrelevant. Days are pages of print, the black on white that is bound and covered, contained and tamed only to remind us of what is bigger, boundless, and inscrutable. The ticks of the clock are to be attended to and treasured, but only as an incarnation of eternity. Text that has been read begins to exist other than on the page, joins in the human imagination with other texts, and assumes a singular vitality. Time, too, semiotically perpetuates beyond an appointed mortality and breathes another breath, a new life.

Marj would scoff at such philosophy—at an intellectually pretentious word like *semiotically* used to describe anything about her. Actually, she would never *scoff,* for that requires an attitude of superiority, an unkind judgment toward someone else. Instead, in the self-deprecating way of a woman simultaneously and paradoxically unaware of her wisdom and secure in it, she would remind me, as she has in the past when we were celebrating a student who was graduating *summa cum laude,* that yes, she too, "graduated with some Latin words" after her name: *in absentia.*

Do you understand her brand of wisdom? Do you see why I look to her as a kind of guide, think about her lessons as I drive the thirty miles to sit at a desk a wall away from hers, sometimes scattered with fallen leaves, or the Snoopy the Novelist cartoons she has clipped for me, or a copy of Charlotte Gilman's *Herland* that she thought quite interesting once, but didn't think she'd be reading again, and wondered if I didn't just want.

Unlike Marj, I won't be teaching at eighty-one—won't be making the commute north. Perhaps I'll be attending to my grandchildren as they begin raising children of their own. As much as I am now addicted to my regular drive, I have trouble enough imagining myself making the ritual pilgrimage after Marj is no longer a physical part of the destination. But I tell myself that perhaps by the time Marj dies some student of Stephen Hawking will have engineered a way to harvest sound waves. And I will ride in my car and casually, frequently, pull up the quiet, reverent, uniquely accented voice of Marj reading Frost's "The Oven Bird" or Thoreau's "I Am a Parcel of Vain Strivings Tied," a voice so transporting even the twenty-year-olds say they could listen to it forever.

Late Bloomer

Ruth Harriet Jacobs

Nonconforming
A few trees bloom in fall
And here I am in my seventies
Wonder age from Genesis
A wise, joyous old woman
Glorifying silver hair
Flaunting the large space
I occupy in this world
Laughing outrageously
Aging courageously
Giving to unorganized charities
Helping disorganized people
Listening to their troubles
Working to end war and violence
Praising God for dreams leading me
And letting me see again loved ones
No longer on this earth.

Seven Little Words

June Rossbach Bingham Birge

As an English major, with emphasis on writing, I was sensitized to the importance of the single word. Sometimes the word is a newly coined one, such as today's "interface"; sometimes it is one that has been given a wholly new meaning, such as today's "mouse." The latter recalls the time when I was hitchhiking across the country with my late husband, Jonathan Bingham, and we were offered a ride in a huge empty trailer truck. As we settled in its cabin, I asked the driver what he usually hauled. "Cats," he said. "Cats?" My vision of furry creatures must have communicated itself to him and Jonathan because they both laughed so hard they could hardly explain that "Caterpillar tractors" was what he had meant.

One word that has radically extended its meaning today is "old." Whereas formerly it implied a decrepit creature with cane or wheelchair, it now includes my "children" (who are grandparents and members of the AARP). This, in turn, points to the need for a new word to cover "grown children." But when I suggested "growns," I was greeted with groans.

It is therefore with diffidence that I suggest we adopt the following seven new, or newly adapted, words: "welderly," "frailderly," "tenergy," "peopled-out," "enjoyer," "adequatism" and finally, "altruicide."

A unique facet of our time is that in the developed countries, young parents are likely to have more grandparents than children. Because this shift is forcing more young and middle-aged people to work to support the old, it lays responsibility on us welderly (well-elderly) to stay as self-reliant as we can, and on the frailderly (frail elderly) to follow their doctors' orders as unforgetfully as they can. At the same time, the middle aged might be startled to hear that many of us welderly have more in common with them than we have to the frailderly.

Yet even the most buoyant of welderly must face new limitations to their tenergy (combined time and energy). For one thing, we easily get peopled-out. Descendants who come for lunch and stay until 5 p.m. or who arrive for self-instigated four-day visits with babies, have no inkling of the toxic fatigue that may strike their nonetheless adoring grandparents. For example, my afternoon nap has moved from the realm of luxury to that of necessity. And I am similarly forced into a new form of rationing: no longer, like the typical American, can I jam as much as possible into my day; instead, I am forced to choose between performing a duty, such as my volunteer work, or enjoying a pleasure, such as going to theater, or perhaps (oh joy!), having an uninterrupted stint of writing.

At the same time that modern medicine has provided us with a lagniappe of some thirty years, a figure equivalent to the entire life expectancy in the least-developed countries, our doctors are often baffled as to how to deal with us once we reach *un certain âge.* Some no longer bother to measure our cholesterol because no norm for us has been established. Others are learning (by trial and error) that our medications must come in far smaller dosages than before. A friend was recently given a double prescription, one for the drug, the other for the pillcutter.

Last summer, at a family reunion of twenty-nine of my direct descendants and their mates, a doubles match was arranged between my eighty-six-year-old husband, Bob Birge, and my eighty-two-year-old self, against the senior of my nine great-grandchildren, a jock of six, and his father, thirty-four. That morning the boy—who takes his tennis seriously—awakened his mother, "For this match, I should wear my whites," he said. And wear them he did (as did the other three). Our rallies were hilarious, and we ended up seven-all. As we walked off the court, I said to him, "You know, next year, you and your dad will be playing better, but Bob and I will be playing worse." He looked at me with amazement that anyone could sound so cheerful about a prospect that to him would spell disaster.

What I didn't try to explain to him was that although the skills of the welderly diminish, our enjoyer (capacity for pleasure) may grow. To observe one's own or someone else's enjoyer at work, the golf course is even better than the tennis court because distances, as well as scores, are measurable. Some welderly hit a long drive and complain all the way to the ball because it didn't go as far as it used to. Other welderly, with fewer remaining skills, are content if their club's "sweet spot" connects with the ball every so often. In the meantime, like Ferdinand the Bull, they take time to admire the beauty of the trees even as their ball nestles among them. Simply to be out in the air and able to take a full swing without pain or loss of balance fills them with the joy of their lately achieved adequatism (outgrown tendency toward perfectionism).

Lastly, in both senses, is altruicide, a form of suicide undertaken by a patient in part for the sake of family members. Many of these devoted descendants would be willing to care for their frailderly relative whose predictable deterioration would reduce her to a caricature of her former self, but the patient, while still competent, would literally rather be dead than impose that kind of burden. In today's world, where the lives of seniors are sometimes saved and sometimes interminably prolonged by doctors, to commit altruicide is no longer, as suicide was once considered to be, a blasphemous throwing back of the gift of life into the face of its Creator.

Instead, it seems to me to be but a thoughtful rejection of what the scientific community hath, rather absentmindedly, wrought. Certainly I am poignantly grateful to those of my clan who insist that they will cherish me in whatever my pitiable state, but what I hope and pray for is that they will feel not the slightest smidgin of guilt if I choose, after the doctors have ruled out depression as the cause of such a choice, to slip away on my own time.

Meanwhile, our language, fully alive, continues to offer us new ways to express what we, who are lucky enough to have enjoyers still at work, can only marvel at.

CHALLENGES

Old Broads

Karen Blomain

are everywhere
even here
turn around and look
yes you
look. They are doing
the broad
jump,
the dirty
bump and if you can't accept it,
get lost. Old broads
don't
care if you approve.
They've divorced
themselves from caring long ago
so
keep your dirty looks
your patronizing groans
your high and mighty eye
brows.
If you don't like our hair
what we wear
or when we wear
on you in grocery lines
taking too long to write a check

pick
a
melon. We don't care.
It's our time
and when yours comes, little sisters,
you'll be glad,
like always,
that we
were
here
first.

Gray Matters

Marsha Dubrow

> The color of truth is gray.
>
> André Gide

I have tried to grow gray gracefully ever since high school. But for decades, hue by hue, I've been tempted to hit the Miss Clairol bottle.

I began plucking my melanin-deficient tendrils while cramming for college finals. Weeding the errant gray matter was relaxing. But out, out damned strand worked no better for me than for Lady Macbeth. I stopped after a few years because the options were go bald or go white.

As my twenties turned, so did my hair color. Nowhere in *Hair* did they sing the praises of gray, far outside the psychedelic prism of the age of Aquarius. In the hippy-yippy era, I had biddy hair atop a go-go body.

Then, the second coming of feminism made me feel like Dr. Jekyll and Ms. Hyde, campaigning against sex-objectivity while traitorously fretting about my hair. Sisterhood was powerful and black was beautiful, but white hair was neither. Feminism, aided by pragmatism, helped my mantra become "Stay Gray." But I felt so young to be so platinum.

In my thirties, I had more gray than either of my parents, but at least I had escaped my family's propensity for early wrinkles and pudge. Most relatives had grayed late except for Grandmother, whose waist-length hair turned white during her escape on foot from revolutionary Russia with her eight-year-old son, my father.

So if graying wasn't due to my genes, maybe it was due to the stress of my jobs: reporting on presidential campaigns, scandals, and im-peachments—no wonder my color changed right through the turn of the century. While working as press secretary for U.S. Senator Bob Packwood before he left Congress due to a sexual harassment scandal, I had another profusion of gray. Then another while freelancing for a dozen years earning my living article by article, like a migrant worker paid gooseberry by gooseberry.

My hair's texture changed along with the color, coarser and coarser, expanding the definition of big hair even in my home state of Texas. One suitor termed it "Bride of Frankenstein" hair, after which I'd have sooner wed Frankenstein than this balding doctor.

Later, at my mother's burial in Houston, one of her best friends ex-claimed at the gravesite, "Marsha, you're so—gray!" Had I been as coarse as my hair, I would have replied, "And you're so—rude."

But not all comments are left-fisted compliments. In fact, the grayer I get, the more I get complimented. Sometimes people even ask whether I highlight, streak, or tint my hair. I thank them heartily and reply, "If I did, I wouldn't choose this shade." I particularly ap-preciate being called "prematurely gray" now that I am too mature to be prematurely anything except dead.

More solid praise has come from invitations to model at coiffure shows and bridal shows—always as mother of the bride, never a bride. But the best invitation was to participate in *Washingtonian's* cover story "Great Hair" a few years ago. They asked gingerly whether I would allow my hair to be colored. That was dying with impunity, so I gladly submitted.

With my tresses in dozens of tinfoil wrappers like antennas, I did resemble Mrs. Frankenstein. I switched my imagery to Venetian women in antiquity who coated their hair with horses' urine and sun-bathed to turn it Titian blonde. Instead of aiming for such "high-lights," I was getting "lowlights" to turn my salt and pepper back to pepper and salt.

For days, few people seemed to notice, so I wondered whether I should have chosen charcoal briquette rather than a pin-striped shade. But then my best friend said, "You look ten years younger." Only your best friend will tell you?

I have nothing against looking younger, but if I couldn't accept aging at this age, whenever could I? And if I gave in to the bottle, what might be next—Botox, HGH, DHEA, and other antiaging acronyms?

The only other time I tried to change my hair color, I was attempting to look older. While away at Girl Scout camp, I used Clorox to turn my nearly-black locks to Marilyn Monroe blonde. Her shade was as unobtainable for me as was her shape. My scalp turned red but my hair remained unchanged—and miraculously still attached to my head. I fulfilled the wrong part of the dumb-blonde stereotype. Had I lost my sanity to vanity?

Both attempts revealed that satisfying the temptation to dye was like consummating a fantasy; the reality was less rewarding than imagined.

So I let the lowlights grow out while I resumed trying to grow up and grow gray confidently. I have made myself appreciate each hue, and finally have decided I enjoy being a gray. It links me with a powerful sisterhood, complimenting each other on our gray badge of courage. A woman with dreadlocks resembling pillars of salt approached me on the street and said, "You go, girlfriend. We're gray and we're proud—and gorgeous." We smacked high fives.

More and more women are letting their hair go gray, while fewer men seem to. Ads for male-only hair products have proliferated like Viagra ads. One man I knew tried to regain his original hair color by ingesting so much zinc he poisoned himself. After hospital treatment, he recovered his health but not his original tint.

He hadn't read P.G. Wodehouse's quote, "There is only one cure for grey hair. It was invented by a Frenchman. It is called the guillotine."

I much prefer Robert Browning's view, "A common grayness silvers everything."

Katherine Banning:
Wife, Mother, Bank Robber

Melissa Lugo

Wakefield Gazette, July 12, 2005

90-YEAR-OLD WOMAN ROBS CHASE BANK!

On the afternoon of July 11, at 3:10 p.m., Katherine Banning, a ninety-year-old woman, is alleged to have robbed $500 from the Chase Bank in Wakefield. Banning was caught at 5 p.m. at Wendy's. The weapon used in the crime, an unloaded BB gun, was on her, but the $500 was nowhere to be found. When asked why he felt so threatened by an elderly woman with a toy gun, Henry Warnaby, the teller, explained: "I was afraid she'd really shoot me."

Banning spent the night in jail, and unless she confesses, will be held there until her trial. When asked why Banning was not allowed to return home, Captain Kirkland chuckled. "Because she'll cut and run," he said, "and I'm too old to be running after her in a high-speed chase."

Many people in Wakefield are shocked by Banning's alleged criminal behavior. Her neighbor, Mrs. Annie Selwyn, observed: "Katie was a good wife and is a good mother. She always helped out at church and her roses are just beautiful! Katie would never—she must have been sick . . . or confused."

Unfortunately Banning was unavailable for comment, so she could not offer her worried neighbors and friends an explanation. For now we are left only with Dr. Connelly's analysis: "Mrs. Banning was merely staring death in the face and affirming life."

Well, robbing banks is a strange way to affirm life. Let's just hope that other senior citizens in Wakefield don't follow Mrs. Banning's example.

*   *   *

July 11, 2005

The morning sun reaches its arms over the horizon and shines on the roof of the white house with green shutters, the one that faces east and sits on the corner of Willow Avenue, a quiet suburban street in a small town called Wakefield. As the sun pulls its fat body up, hand over hand, its rays slide down the roof and spill through the second-floor window, into the yellow bedroom, and onto the face of a woman, sleeping flat on her back in bed. The light seeps into the crevices around her mouth and in between her eyebrows; it pokes at strands of her thin white hair; it prods her sagging cheeks. Suddenly, her eyes pop open, squinty greenish-grays that gradually blink themselves into an alert pair of large almond-shaped eyes. She closes them again and groans.

"How many times have I told you to shut the blinds before you climb into bed? You always insist on leaving them open to see the sun-set, when I keep telling you that this window faces east." She opens her eyes again and glares at the mound next to her under the covers. "Jimmy?" She groans again, rolls her eyes. "I know you're awake, now get up and close that blind, will you? I've done it every single morning for sixty years and I won't do it again."

Never mind that I've said this every morning for sixty years, too, she thinks. "Fine, fine, have it your way; you always do. I'll do it." A mass of fleshy veins and thin bones swell under her skin as she clenches the edge of the bed. She twists and leans over the lump that is Jimmy and pulls the string of beads. With a metallic swish the blinds close, the sunlight evaporates. The sudden darkness feels cold; to warm up, she arranges her body against Jimmy's.

He is so still, she thinks. *I am not warm,* she thinks. Her lip trembles. "Jimmy?" she says in a small voice. She presses herself still closer to him, lays her cheek over his.

"Oh my God." She tries to roll him onto his back, but is not strong enough. The bones in her spindly hands feel as though they are about to snap.

"Why did you have to gain so much goddam weight? The doctor told you to lose weight, didn't he? And how many times did I tell you!" The tears are snaking down the creases of her face. "Oh God."

She cannot move him. She cannot even get up off the bed and call somebody because there is no strength left in her. Her body sags over his. She knows he is dead.

For a long time she can remember nothing, although she knows she is thinking. Then scraps of memories come to her. Jimmy eating cheesecake. Jimmy watching football and shouting for his beer, his dinner. Jimmy spanking the boys. Jimmy patting her cheek, telling her, "Kit-Kat, don't worry." Jimmy with his large hands on her body, making her moan with pleasure. Jimmy sitting in his big chair, hostile, silent, ignoring her. Jimmy looking for the sunset through the window that faces east.

Pain palms her heart with icy fingers and closes its fist. She gasps, believes she is having a heart attack. *I'm coming too, Jimmy,* she thinks. But the next breath comes, and the next. . . .

Now what to do?

She thinks of the rosebushes outside. She thinks of her boys who rarely visit. She thinks of her kitchen, her books, her TV, her neighbors, her nurse, Kyra, who comes at 11 a.m. every day and looks decidedly annoyed about it. She remembers that day when she went to the supermarket and the children were repulsed by her wrinkles and bulging veins, and the cashier, Lucy was her name, treated her as though she were senile, when all she was trying to do was make sure she'd gotten the right change.

Maybe there is nothing to do, she thinks.

The cold body of her husband repels her. She grits her teeth and forces her body away from him, to the opposite side of the bed.

I'm alive. Alive.

She slides her legs slowly over the bed until they droop off the side. Then she reaches for the bedpost and, inch by inch, pulls herself to her feet.

When Kyra lets herself in, Mrs. Banning is lounging on the couch stark naked except for the roses pinned onto her few remaining strands of hair. She shovels cheesecake into her mouth.

"Mrs. Banning!"

"My husband is dead."

"I'm sure he's just in bed, which is where you should be." Kyra is beginning to look annoyed.

"No. He's dead. And you're fired."

"Mrs. Banning—"

She smiles. "Call me Katherine."

Katherine stands and surveys the musty attic, taking in all the cobwebs of her life. Her wedding dress, packed away in a trunk. Boxes full of children's toys. Ragged furniture, which in her mind's eye still looks new. Her bow—she used to be on the archery team. Her coach called her eagle eye, said she could go on to the Olympics. But then she married, had kids, quietly unnotched her arrow, and laid down her bow.

She creaks across the worn wooden floor, picks up the bow. She likes the feel of it, her body remembers it and molds around it into the proper stance. She strings an imaginary arrow, tries to pull it back—but can't. She lowers the bow, looks at her right arm, sees for a moment the young arm, tanned, muscled. Then the tan pales and the muscles sink into the flab of old age. She falls to her knees, the bow clatters to the floor, and she cries for the woman in her head, the one smiling with the bow in her right hand, the trophy in her left, the arrows in the quiver on her back.

When her tears trickle to a sniffle, she grips the torn arm of the old couch and hoists herself to her feet. She raises her eyes and gasps, startled by the image of her naked self in a dusty mirror. Entranced, she wipes the dust away and stares at her body. With gentle fingers she explores the blotched, sagging flesh, first her protruding stomach, then her hanging breasts, then her double chin, her wrinkled face. The sags of her face gather together, heave upwards into a toothless grin. *My eyes are my same eyes when I smile,* she thinks. Her hand falls from her face and she cocks her head. *I wonder,* she thinks. Then she hobbles to the box marked JAMES JR'S & MICHAEL'S TOYS.

As Lenny pulls his cab up in front of Chase Bank, he swivels in his seat to face Katherine. She is wearing a low-cut black top, skin-tight black slacks, a long leather jacket, and knee-high black leather boots. A shoulder-length blonde wig perches on her balding scalp, on top of which sits a broad-brimmed black hat, tilted at a rakish angle, with red roses around the brim. Her eye makeup is smoky, sexy; her lips are bright red.

He bites his lip, runs a spotted hand through his unruly gray hair. "Are you sure you're all right?"

The red lips curl up at the ends, the long false eyelashes bat at him. "Of course I'm all right, Lenny darling," she purrs. "What makes you think otherwise?"

Lenny lowers his eyes. "Well, you look a little—well . . ."

"What, sexy? Bold? Outrageous?" She leans forward in her seat.

"Different." Lenny's eyes travel over her. He clears his throat, pulls his white beard.

She smiles, gets out of the car, and comes around to the driver's side window. Lenny lowers it, and she leans her elbows on the car door so that she is close enough to let him smell her perfume, to let him glance quickly at her low neckline.

"Different is very, very good, Len. You should drop by to visit when you're ready." She laughs. "Just don't wait too long, because I could drop dead any day now."

He gulps and lowers his eyes. She glances at her watch. "Wait here for me, I'll be right out. Keep the motor running." She strides into the bank.

Katherine surveys the tellers and picks the one on the far right, closest to the door. He is a middle-aged man, very average looking—everything on him is brown and midsized. His name tag reads: HENRY WARNABY. *I can break him,* she decides as she waits on line.

The man, two people behind her on the line, is tall, hulky, and dark-skinned. *Perfect,* she thinks. *In case I need back up.*

"How can I help you, ma'am?"

"You can help me by wiping that patronizing smile off your face, kid."

Warnaby's mouth hangs open for a moment, then his brows bunch up and his mouth turns down. "Now there's no reason to be rude, ma'am. I assure you I was just trying to be helpful."

"Oh, so now I'm not reasonable? I'm a crazy old bag?"

He rolls his eyes, mutters, "Not another one," and grabs the phone.

She reaches into the front of her slacks, feels the bulge of cold steel, whips it out, and under the cover of Jimmy's oversized jacket, points it at Warnaby.

He laughs. "You've got to be kidding." He picks up the phone.

"Put that phone down before I blow your brains out the back of your head. And keep your hands where I can see them before I shoot your fat fingers off, sonny."

A silly grin lingers on his face, but he keeps perfectly still. His eyes travel over her, sizing her up.

She has spent the morning watching Jimmy's favorite action movies—*Lethal Weapon, Predator, Rambo.* So her stance and her grip on the gun seem professional; the deadly look in her eyes is a perfect imitation of Rambo's when he is really pissed off. "I will not be ignored. I will not be laughed at. I am a woman to be reckoned with. You will respect me." Her hand tightens on the gun.

Warnaby hangs up the phone.

A surge of power flows through Katherine's arteries, filling them with new blood; she can feel her arm muscles bulge again.

"Now take it easy, ma'am—"

"Shut up." She passes him an envelope. "Put five hundred dollars in there."

He smothers a smile. "Five hundred dollars?!"

"Are you mocking me, kid? You want me to enjoy putting a few holes in your gut?"

His smile dissolves. "No ma'am. I'll have your five hundred dollars right away." He shoves a wad of cash into the envelope and passes it to her.

"Now you keep your mouth shut and your hands above the counter till I walk out of this bank. Or else. See that big guy standing behind me in line? Well he's packing an Uzi and he'll gun you down. He owes me a favor, and since he's been in and out of jail his whole life, he doesn't mind going back if he has to. So don't do anything stupid."

She slips the gun back into the waistline of her pants and walks to the exit. At the door she glances over her shoulder. Warnaby is helping the next customer on line. His hands are well above the counter and his eyes are glued to the big man in the line.

Outside, Katherine stops and tips her face up to the sun, reveling in the warmth on her skin, and the way it reaches inside and quickens her blood. Then she strolls to the cab and gets in. As the car pulls away from the curb, she hears the sound of police sirens, the screech of brakes.

Lenny glances in the rearview mirror and whistles. "Wow, what happened in there? Did one of us Wakefield geezers go and have heart trouble?"

"No, it was a younger man. He just had a little bit of a scare, that's all." She smiles brightly.

He smiles back. "You know, you look good. Really good." He scrunches his head down between his shoulders. "But then, you always did. I've always thought Jimmy was the luckiest guy." He looks into the rearview mirror. "You're crying!"

She sniffles, pulls out her handkerchief. "I didn't think anyone noticed."

"Sure, everybody loves you around here."

She dabs viciously at her eyes. "Yeah, well, what good was all that love? I never felt it."

"What do you mean?"

"It's phony, that's what I mean, a whole lot of words and hooey. Did anybody ever act on it? Do something daring, something really meaningful?"

She drills her eyes into the back of his head. "Did you?"

Lenny eases the car to a stop in front of a red light. "You're married."

"Who cares?"

"I do. You do."

"Let me tell you something, for your own good. You play by the rules, and you just let things happen to you, and all you end up with is a ninety-year-old body falling apart around you and a corpse sleeping in your bed." She shoves a twenty-dollar bill into the slot. "Stop here." She gets out, slams the door shut behind her.

Lenny shouts through the window, "Katie!" She turns to face him. But just as he is about to speak the light turns green, cars behind him start honking. His face twists. "I'm sorry," he says, and drives away.

Katherine shakes her head, shrugs, and lifts her chin. Then she strides up the block to Wendy's for a gooey greasy cheeseburger with everything on it and a strawberry milkshake to wash it down.

Katherine sits in the interrogation room at the Wakefield police station, facing the pudgy, graying Captain Chris Kirkland and the tall, dark-haired, intellectual-looking man the captain introduces as Dr. Connelly.

"A shrink." She chuckles. "Chris, you know I'm not crazy."

Captain Kirkland sighs. "I'd like to believe you're not, but with all due respect, so far today you left your husband dead in his bed without reporting it to anyone, scared your nurse by answering the front door stark naked, got yourself dressed in this getup, and robbed a bank with an unloaded BB gun, and then went and had a cheeseburger at Wendy's."

"I had a milkshake, too. It was strawberry." She laughs again.

He crosses his beefy arms over his belly. "This is not a joke. You are in serious trouble."

She rolls her eyes. "Oh please, who cares about locking up an old lady? Am I really such a menace to society?"

He circles her chair, like a wolf about to go in for the kill. "If you rob banks you are. People worked for that money, and you scared poor Henry out of his wits."

She bangs her fist on the table. "People in this town have more money than they know what to do with! And Henry will get over it, in fact he might be a nicer man because of it."

"What are you planning to do with the money?"

She shrugs. "Nothing."

"So why the hell did you take it?"

She grins. "Because I thought it would be fun, because I've never robbed a bank before, because I wanted to see if I could do it, because it was an adventure just for me." Her smile fades. "But mostly because people pay more attention to that money than they ever did, or ever will, to me." She leans back in her chair, puts her feet up on the table. "Those good enough reasons for you?"

"Put your feet down and try to act like a lady," he snaps.

"No!" She rounds her mouth around the word, drawing it out, enjoying its unfamiliar flavor. "No. I've spent my whole life acting like a lady, Chris. I want to be a woman now."

He changes tactics, uncrosses his arms, unclenches his fists, and sits across the table from her. His pale blue eyes are friendly and mocking as they peer over her black boots. "Well fine, you've had your little adventure, why don't you return the money now, like a good girl?"

She glares at him. "Don't belittle what I did. It was grand."

He stands up, pushes her feet off the table so that the high-heeled boots clatter to the floor. "Mrs. Banning, I'm warning you—"

She stands, jabs her bony finger at him. "You think you can threaten me, Captain? When you stare death in the face, suddenly powerful people don't seem like much. That's the beautiful thing about being ninety years old. You've got nothing to lose."

The captain draws his heavy black brows down, like a judge pronouncing the death sentence. "And your husband—did he have nothing to lose? Is that why you disregarded his death?"

Katherine tosses her head. "None of you knew what Jimmy meant to me. I can't explain it to you—you would have had to have lived in that house with him, been his wife for all these years. He was my life. And the same way people love and hate their life, that's the way it was with me and him. A struggle, but with good parts." She walks to the barred window, looks out with the yearning of a caged bird. "People want to live while they're alive, but I think that maybe, when it's finally the right time, maybe behind those closed eyelids they're relieved."

"So you were happy your husband died?"

She sighs heavily, turns to face him. "I was sad. I was very, very sad."

Captain Kirkland throws his hands up and snorts loudly. "I can't do anything with her."

Dr. Connelly, who has been standing in the shadowed corner silently watching, escorts Captain Kirkland to the door. "Why don't you leave me with her? I'll see what I can do." Dr. Connelly gestures to her chair, and Katherine walks slowly away from the window and eases herself into it.

She closes her eyes for a moment. Her body is so tired. She opens her eyes and trains them on Dr. Connelly, watches him walk toward her, seat himself in the chair across from her. She cocks her head. "You're very graceful for such a tall man. Are you a dancer?"

He looks startled for a moment, then smiles. "You're very observant. I did dance, once."

"I used to be an archer. I could have won a gold medal at the Olympics."

He studies her with velvety brown eyes. "Are gold medals guaranteed? I've seen plenty of top athletes miss them."

She shrugs. "Yeah, well, I could have tried."

"Why didn't you?"

She shrugs again. "I got pregnant."

"You could have gone back to it after you had the baby."

"I got married."

"So?"

"Jimmy didn't like it. James Junior needed me. Then I got pregnant again."

He smiles. "Well then they must have been more important to you than gold medals."

She sighs. "They were."

"Then you made the right choices. Why do you regret it?"

She gazes out the window. "There was nothing for me."

He touches her gnarled hands, folded on the table. "They were for you."

She draws her hands away. His skin feels too smooth to be touched by hers. "No, people can never belong to anyone. They can only agree to coexist. You have to have something else—a thing, an act, some secret knowledge."

He knits his brow. "Why couldn't you have that?"

"Because I didn't know I was supposed to have it!" She gestures wildly with her hands, flailing. "My mother never taught me that. All those years I was empty, and I didn't know why."

"So, you woke up . . . and robbed a bank."

They both laugh.

"Yeah," she says, "something like that."

He hands her a sheet of paper and a pen. "Well, how about you write something like that here, and sign it at the bottom, and maybe include a map to the hidden treasure, so that you can get out of here and have fun with the rest of your life now that you've finally got the secret knowledge?"

She studies him, checking the depths of his brown eyes to make sure he is not mocking her. When she finds the sincerity there, she takes the pen and paper. As Dr. Connelly heads toward the door, she says: "You're a nice shrink, but you should go back to dancing."

A week later Katherine is pruning her roses when the mailman, Fred, drives by. He looks a little afraid of her as she approaches with the shears, so she drops them in the grass and holds her hands up. "Don't worry, I've been taking my medication and I'm unarmed!"

Fred laughs heartily, whether with relief or humor Katherine isn't sure. "Good morning, Mrs. Banning. Your roses look great, as usual."

"Thank you."

He hands her the mail and drives on down the block. She goes to her rocking chair on the front porch and flips through her mail. She stops when she sees an envelope from Dr. Joel Connelly. She opens it and sees a copy of her confession, with a note from Joel on the bottom of the page.

CONFESSION OF KATHERINE BANNING:
WIFE, MOTHER, BANK ROBBER

It all started, I think, when I saw myself naked. I remember I was in the attic, and then I saw my body in the mirror and I jumped. Really scared myself—all those wrinkles and lumps and sags. But after I stared at it awhile, I kind of got used to it, and then I became fascinated. My body, after ninety years. I wanted to get to know it, all of it. I looked like an alien creature—yup, that's the best way to describe it. An alien creature that's different, but not horrible. I stood there and wondered about all the things I might want to do with this body.

When you get old, you get ugly in other people's eyes—I say "other people's eyes" rather your own because that's how you first notice it. It's like a twitch in their eyes they try to blink away, like an itch in a rude place they can't scratch in public. But after a while, they blink you away till you become invisible and they scratch their crotch right in your face. Too ugly to be looked at, too weak to be a threat, too damn boring to be noticed. That day in front of the mirror, I started to become interested in myself. I felt pretty. I felt interesting. I felt powerful.

So I went outside, stark naked, and cut some of my roses and twined them into my hair. I thought for sure my hair would fall out with the weight of the roses, but it didn't. I took that as a good sign.

So later that day I decided to rob a bank.

Crazy, you say? Well, wait till you hit ninety and realize you still want to live, that even though you're way past menopause you want another child, and that even though your breasts make tracks in the mud, you still want a lover, and that even though your hands shake, there are still things that you didn't get to do (like going to the Olympics and bringing home the gold), things you want to do, that you will do. Then, see what you're capable of. And you'll be perfectly sane. Senility, temporary insanity, it's all bull. Old folks know exactly what they're doing. One of the good parts about being an old fart is that you have a license to be loony tunes, to live the wild way you didn't have the balls for before. At ninety, you see, your dignity's gone the way of dirty diapers, and your life is heading the same way fast. You have nothing to lose except the moment, this moment; so you use it, you fill it up with everything you want, and that's what you hold onto, that's what's yours, the secret knowledge that bolsters you up even in the face of loneliness and humiliation, fear and death.

As for the five hundred dollars, it's stuffed in the boxers my dead husband's wearing. I figured that was the last place anyone would want to look. Happy hunting!

Katherine smiles at her own joke, happy all over again with her confession. Then she squints at the bottom of the page, at Joel's neat, loopy handwriting.

Dear Katherine,

I thought you might want to have a copy of your statement as a monument to your continuing quest for more secret knowledge. I also wanted to let you in on my secret knowledge. To find the hidden treasure, look under the loose slate on your front walkway.

Cordially, Joel Connelly

Katherine leaves her confession on the rocker, and goes to the loose slate. Stiffly, she bends to her knees, nudges up the slate, reaches under and pulls out a gold medallion.

"Oh my God." With trembling hands she turns the medal over, looks at the note taped onto the back.

I was an ice dancer, and my partner, Eileen, and I won this at the Winter Games. Then Eileen got pregnant, and we quit skating and got married. Eileen died of cancer last year; it's her that I miss, not skating; it's her that I want, not this gold medal. So I want you to have this, not because you deserve it, but because you deserve much more than this hunk of metal could have ever given you, and because you are much more than this thing could have made you. The thing, the act, the secret knowledge goes beyond this medal, and exists apart from it. The secret can be found anywhere, even within the bounds of an ordinary, unnoticed existence.

Katherine folds the note, puts it in her pants pocket. She cups the medal in her hands, measures the weight of it, runs her fingers over its texture, holds it up to the sun to see it shine. She brings it to her lips, kisses it. Then she nestles it back in its hole, covers it with dirt, and entombs it under the slate.

She gets to her feet and hobbles into her house to phone her sons. *And maybe I'll give Lenny a ring sometime, too,* she thinks as she reaches for the phone, dials James Junior's number. *Invite him over for coffee or*—she grins—*if he's lucky, a glass of red wine.* She imagines herself walking into Victoria's Secret and asking a saleslady for a lacy bra and—*what's that new thing they wear now?*—*oh yeah, a thong.* She laughs.

The phone rings and rings, but Katherine does not hang up the way she used to. *I will not be ignored.* While she waits, she remembers James Junior when he was five years old, when he had nightmares every night and wet the bed, screamed her name in the darkness. She smiles and feels his plump arms clinging to her desperately, his wet, shaking body.

Finally, a deep voice sighs, exasperated, into the phone. "Hello?"

"Hi, Jay-Jay! Just wanted to see how you were doing."

Tentatively, so that he sounds younger than he is, he asks, "Mom?"

"Yes." She nods emphatically. "Yes."

Blonde Jokes

Mary M. Brown

We discuss but do not know
whether to call it a globe or a dome,
but we *do* know there must be some trick
to removing it from the ceiling above your sink
so the burnt out bulb can be replaced.

We are not engineers.
How many blondes does it take
to change a light bulb?
How many PhDs?
We laugh out loud,
me on the ladder, you below.

You suspected yourself too old—
not to climb the ladder—
but to *presume* to climb it,
to dismantle the dome or the globe,
to balance the curtain rod, so ill-designed,
to swipe at the cobwebs
as one must in such a position,
to screw in the new bulb
and get back down, alone,
everything again intact
in the ordinary quiet of this home.

But today is not quite ordinary
and you are not alone.

You said you could hire this work out,
but I am here and somewhat younger
than you and have no scruples
about presuming.

And I am experienced in working
for nothing in the midst of joy
and feeling shamefully overpaid.

Forever Red

Janice Levy

"Promise me," Nana says, "when I get too sick to put on lipstick, you won't let anybody in. No visitors. You'll tell the nurses."

My grandmother packs her cosmetics as if tucking in children. "Wrinkle cream, cleansing gel, toner wash," she says, wrapping each in tissue paper. "Demi-matte makeup in 'Light Mist'? This one they gave for free so I should look like a ghost. My skin turns this color, you should pull the sheet over my head. Ten minutes, I'll be dead."

Nana hands me a list. "You should check I didn't forget. Lately, I don't remember."

"Moisture On-Call, nail protein, Turnaound Cream, alpha-hydroxy, Collagen Surge," I call out. "Facial Flex?"

My grandmother wiggles her lips. "Thirty muscles it works. It says on the label. I'll be thirty-two percent firmer in eight weeks, I should live so long."

"They're just doing some tests," I say. "You'll be out in a day or . . ."

"You get the jewelry; I spoke to the lawyer. It's written down." Nana whispers behind her hand. "I don't want You-Know-Who should touch nothing; you'll have to move fast. The good stuff on the top, behind the . . ."

"Nana," I drop the suitcase. "Enough."

"Believe me, it'll be enough. You'll keep a few pieces, sell the rest. Buy yourself something nice." She hands me a curling iron and points with her chin at the suitcase. "I changed lawyers. Rosenberg I never liked. His hair, that's the style—that grease? You could fry *latkes*."

Nana gives me a business card. "The new lawyer, Mr. Birnbaum, is a nice boy. I don't think he shaves yet. Our side never knew from such straight teeth, like they were painted. They're all capped," she whispers, "I asked."

My grandmother lines up lipsticks across her drawer like soldiers. "So you'll promise. About the lipstick. And the same thing with my hair, if I can't wash it. If you're dying they don't like to waste water."

"Nana, you're not going to die!"

My hands fly out of my lap like birds released from a cage. I watch them, as I had watched myself enter Nana's bedroom a thousand times before, posing in her makeup mirror lights, my hair in pink curlers, testing perfumes from a silver tray. When I was the flower girl at my father's wedding, she draped her pearls around my neck. "He's a good man," she said. "One day, God willing, he'll realize you-know-what about You-Know-Who." Then we wiped our tears and reapplied "our" lipstick shade, "Forever Red."

My grandmother looks beautiful, I think, backlit against the window, her white sundress blowing slightly, the sleeves full, her hair wispy, almost like an angel. I kiss her neck as I open the window.

"The doctors are just looking," I say.

"Looking shmooking," Nana says. "With your mother they also looked. Like she was a pincushion, all black and blue, such a look. You're lucky you don't remember." Her hands shake as she tightens her bottle of Shalimar. "Close the window. You could freeze to death, they'd find the body, you wouldn't even know.

"And another thing," she says, her voice muffled as she leans into her closet. "I need what to wear. Something with a little color. Maybe a scarf, the pearls. To frame my face. So I don't disappear."

Nana taps her foot. "And my sandals. With the open toe. In case my feet swell, I should have room in the coffin."

She pulls the skin back from her eyes. "This is how I used to look. You don't remember." She points to one of the photos tucked into the side of her mirror. My grandmother is wearing her temple suit with a slit up the side and a lace doily pinned to her hair. I am dressed as Queen Esther, my head tilted forward under a silver tiara. Nana had rouged my cheeks with a wet sponge and penciled a beauty mark on my chin. A young woman sits in a wheelchair, holding my hand, only her red lips showing under a broad-brimmed hat.

"I had good legs," Nana says. "Even the rabbi noticed."

"To tell you the truth, the doctors don't look so good—this one's coughing, another's scratching. I'll first get sick yet." Nana chews on ice chips, her voice hoarse.

I put another pillow behind her back and crank the hospital bed. She reaches for her brush. "Dr. Weissman's gay," Nana whispers, "I asked."

My grandmother unwraps the free samples of Christian Dior cosmetics I have brought. She sniffs the cologne and coughs. "Another one busy looking," she says. "What did you buy?"

I hand her a tube of lipstick. "Remember? They stopped making it. Then they brought it back. 'Forever Red,'" I whisper. "Everybody asked."

Mazurka

Pamela Uschuk

Blue as a plum, Alexi's face was bloated with the kind of surprise he often boasted he had seen on enemy faces when he dispatched them to the next world. Sixty years ago Maryá returned home from work to find her husband spread-eagle on the kitchen floor, his head and shoulders pointed to the oven as if he'd wanted to crawl inside. The kitchen reeked of gas and tasted like coins. It wasn't until she turned him over that she saw his face. Maryá thought she'd buried that memory years ago with her husband in River View Cemetery, but recently, Alexi began to drop by to annoy her, whispering an indecipherable language. Sometimes he dared to grasp her arm, to insist she go somewhere as he does now.

"Go away!" her torso twitches and she jerks awake. In its alcove, the clock chimes twice, her beloved walnut mantle clock with the ivory face and delicate gold filigree hands. The melody, a Viennese waltz, soothes her. It had been a wedding present from Alexi.

Maryá dabs at her burning eyes with a linen handkerchief, then surveys the rose couch, the lace curtains, the worn Oriental carpet, the color TV taking up one corner of the room with its maple cabinet. Nothing else.

"Not to the angels yet." Maryá yawns, and a belch escapes. She laughs aloud. "Or devils. No thank you, Mister."

In his bedroom, her second husband, Mike, snores. Leaning forward in her swivel rocker, she whispers, "Sleep, you old fool." She is angry because Mike started with whiskey first thing that morning. He lifted a shot and toasted her health before their breakfast of black coffee, rye toast, and boiled eggs. Outrageous.

Maryá lifts the heavy trifocals from her nose, wiping away tears, which make her look sad when she isn't. Since laser surgery for detached retinas, her eyes water so that the world swims past in a fishbowl of shifting light. Although she's dizzy, she doesn't complain. Maryá never counted on living beyond forty. Ninety-five was inconceivable, and when she imagines the number now, she feels giddy. Despite arthritis in her fingers and knees, stomach upsets, and the disturbing way her arms and legs fall asleep when she wants to use them, she laughs easily and often as a girl. The older she gets, the more humorous life seems. To bring back feeling, she taps her feet which have fallen asleep inside her black orthopedic shoes. If only she could have tap-danced with the great Mr. Gene Kelly.

Everything seems more humorous except for Alexi's visits. "Troublemaker. Why bother me?" Alexi floats toward the front door. Slim, fine-featured, he is as tidy as the white pearl clipped to his dark blue silk tie, handsome except for his ice black eyes which are as unpredictable as cats on a Halloween sidewalk.

A sudden tingling shivers across Maryá's forehead. When she grabs the arms of her chair, she sways to one side. A high wind drowns out all other noises. Her head falls backward, pulling her shoulders and chest through the chair while the room blinks red to electric black. There is no pain, just pressure in her temples as she sinks through silky curtains of darkness until the roaring stops.

"God, stop your joking," she laughs at the room that slowly reassembles. As she has since she was a girl, she wonders what God looks like. Is He blinding as sun on new snow? Does He have ears? Her cousin, Dmitri, was so strong her brother said he could lift a yoke of oxen, but his ears were so big that people made fun of him behind his back. When she was a child in Bohemia, Maryá believed God looked like her grandfather with wild bushy eyebrows and large peasant's hands. The priest and her mother told her that God was good and loved her. When she married Alexi, a strict Russian Orthodox, he said that God was cruel and punished all sin, which did not prevent Alexi from being a bootlegger and a murderer. After a priest ripped open her blouse in the vestry when she asked him for advice, Maryá stopped attending Catholic mass. Lately, she imagines God as the ocean, cool, deep, and shifting, an ocean who invents stories that are people's lives. She believes one of God's flaws is that He does not know how to invent proper endings. She sometimes wonders if grace is surviving God's creativity.

While Maryá's head buzzes, her heart palpitates like a captured wren's. Had she taken her heart medication with breakfast? Shrugging, she waits for the spell to pass. Dr. White said her arrhythmia was complicated by arteriosclerosis, and prescribed red capsules, but Maryá doesn't always take them. "No amount of pills can cure death," she giggled at the doctor, but he didn't think it was so funny.

She examines the watershed of puffy veins under the thin skin on her hands. She had scrubbed floors and wrung out laundry for countless wealthy women so she could feed her children. After Alexi died, the authorities threatened to take away her children, so she married Mike, Alexi's cousin, even though she was not in love with him.

The doorbell startles her. "Who now?" she hopes it isn't those women, Jehovah's Witnesses, dressed in fancy clothes who came to her door yesterday and asked, "Are you prepared to meet Jesus?" They left abruptly when she shooed them away, laughing, "I have trouble just to meet my lunch. I have no energy to meet Mr. Jesus Christ."

Gripping the chair arm, Maryá reaches for the cane that Mike bought her at Wal-Mart, then rocks herself up to her feet. Before she walks half the room, the bell rings again. By the time she unlatches the screen door, she is out of breath and doesn't recognize who is there.

"Grandma, I missed you!" The tall slim ghost with long dark hair slides through the door to hug Maryá. In one arm, she cradles a bouquet of daisies wrapped in green florist's paper. "These are for you. I didn't grow them, but they're pretty, don't you think?"

Maryá smiles as if she's just tried on a pair of shoes that fit perfectly. "So it's you. Anyá, I get so old I think you are another peddler! Two came yesterday to sell me Mr. Jesus Christ, himself. Outrageous. Come in and put the daisies in water, honey girl, in the kitchen. They are so beautiful."

"Be careful, Grandma," emitting a nervous waterfall of laughter, Ann takes Maryá's arm.

Nearly throwing herself off balance, Maryá shakes free. "Thanks no, sweet girl. I walk myself. When I am r-r—really r-r-really r-r-really," she rolls the r's as she would boiled eggs in her mouth, "old like Mike, then you help."

"You'll never be old, Grandma." Ann sighs, shifting the bouquet to her other arm. High strung and thin, she seems always in motion. A smile flashes across her serious face. "You are absolutely right, Gram. Women have to take care of ourselves."

"Thanks God I have my health." Maryá puffs, lowering carefully into the rocker. She smooths the faded skirt of her lilac housedress. "Where is that no good husband of yours?"

Without answering, Ann wheels and strides to the kitchen where she fusses, arranging the flowers in a blue glass vase. Afraid she has offended the girl, Maryá waits quietly until Ann returns and sits on the couch. Tentatively, Maryá pats Ann's arm. "You know your grandma jokes. Tom lets you come so far alone?"

"Lets me?" Ann snaps, running her nervous hands through her thick black hair. "Tom doesn't let me do anything. I do what I want."

"Honey girl, what is wrong?"

"Nothing. I mean, I'm sorry. Tom and I aren't exactly getting along. Not at all. I don't know what to do. I mean, like I do, but I don't." Ann's dark eyes glitter. She drums her manicured fingernails on the worn sofa. "I want a divorce."

"Dear girl, don't cry. Tell me." Maryá continues to pat Ann's arm. "My mama used to say that a woman's tears become the songs of birds."

"She must have meant vultures." Ann wipes her eyes with long delicate fingers that are almost clones of Maryá's. Her blue jeans rustle as she crosses her legs. "Don't say anything to Mom or Dad. Tom doesn't, like, want anyone to know. He says everything is fine. It's my imagination. I told him I want out. I mean, I've had it. Tom would be furious if he knew I'd come to dump my problems on you."

"Dump? Such things these days." When Maryá shakes her head, the room spins. Of all her grandchildren, she is fondest of Ann. Before

Ann married and moved to a city a hundred miles away, weekly she took Maryá shopping or to a movie. They chatted and giggled as if they were girlfriends, as if they had no end.

"Remember, Anyá, summers when you were little? You slept on the cot beside my bed . . ."

"And when I had a nightmare, you'd make me tell it. Then you sang until I fell asleep." She shifts in her seat and pushes back stray hairs that threaten her blue eyes. "I had so many nightmares."

"Now, you have another. So, tell me." Maryá watches a frown deepen Anyá's face. When she was thirty, Anya's age, she was married to Alexi. His eyes would turn hard as obsidian, his words click like bullets striking her when she contradicted him. His kisses ignited her chest, her stomach, her womb. Suddenly, he'd be furious over the look in her eyes or the way she smiled, and he'd slap her or pull her hair. One moment his beautiful body pressed into her, the next he screamed at her for daring to laugh.

"Dear girl, some years you care for your flowers and still they get sick and die," Marya rocks slowly back and forth. "Then, with no care, they bloom by themselves. Who can tell about love?"

"Tom's married to that stupid computer business. He leaves for work early and comes home late. All he talks about are programs, microchips, bytes. He hardly notices I'm alive. I don't know if I am alive. He never, I mean, never has time." Ann's words burst out, crashing into one another. "Know what I think? Another woman. I mean, I can feel it. I'm not stupid."

"No, really? Outrageous. I break him in half, like this!" Maryá grabs an imaginary twig and snaps it. "Did you ask?"

"I don't have to, Gram." Ann bites at her chapped lower lip. Even though she clears her throat, her voice breaks. "He can see I'm a wreck, but he doesn't care. He just walks away."

"Anyá, men aren't smart about such things. You must tell him what you feel." Maryá hears Mike cough in his sleep. She and he do not talk about their feelings. "Anyá, Anyá, it's hard to keep yourself warm in bed alone, but it is worse to sleep next to a stone."

Maybe it's Maryá's tone that makes Ann snicker. Maybe it is because Maryá laughs at her own joke. They both laugh hysterically until they have to wipe away tears.

"You should talk, Gram." Ann coughs, composing herself. "I notice you sleep alone."

"Mike sweats. He smells like a saloon floor!" Maryá protests. She leans close to Ann and winks. "Besides, he snooooores!"

"I hear. Since when did he start taking naps?"

"He drinks too much. Last night he hears on television about the space shuttle. The Russians build something, I forget, in the stars. His talk. He will go back to Rovno. Be a hero. The first old man in outer space! I hope they have whiskey in outer space." Maryá spreads her arms wide. This sends them into another fit of laughter.

Maryá's thoughts roam back to the wild Carpathian Mountains. Behind her mother, she hikes through the tall pine trees where they hunt mushrooms and herbs. Suddenly, they run through her father's steamy summer fields of barley, rye, and hops, until her mother sits down between the green rows and tells her the story of Baba Yaga, the witch who flies in an iron cauldron stirring up evil every night. Baba Yaga is finally defeated by a poor orphan girl with a magic wooden doll that had been given to her by her dying mother. Maryá is so frightened she clings to her mother's skirt. What would she do without her mother? Maryá touches her mother's face, flushed red by the sun, so clear there isn't a blemish, caresses the high cheekbones, looks deep in her mother's eyes the color of wet cornflowers.

Not long after that, during the worst year of her life, both her older brothers were killed in the Crimean War, and, just months later, her father died from pneumonia. Her mother's hair shocked white. Worse, she borrowed passage money to send the sixteen-year-old Maryá alone to America. Aboard ship, Maryá huddled with other women, frightened and seasick, on the miserable deck. She spoke no English. A cousin in New York with money was supposed to take care of her, to bring her mother over later, but that cousin turned out to be a short, overweight monster with oily brown hair and a scar splitting his lip who immediately sold her to a sweatshop in Philadelphia.

"Grandma?" Ann repeats, shaking her grandmother's arm.

Maryá opens her eyes and waves away shadows that have gathered in front of her face. "Honey girl, I'm sorry. I dream too much." Maryá's voice sounds like someone else's in her own ears. "Stay here with me tonight."

"I can't. I promised a friend . . ." Ann says, lowering her eyes.

"Life passes quickly, Anyá. You get old. And you talk to ghosts. Be careful how you treat living people and how living people treat you. When I come to this country, I am lonely. I miss my mother. She want me to be a lady. I found a rich man, but that did not make my heart laugh. . . ."

"I hear you. My heart stopped laughing a long time ago," Ann interrupts. She stares over her grandmother's head, then she bites at her thumbnail.

"When I come to this country, I roll cigars, day after day. Sixteen hours a day. Ten cents an hour." Maryá smiles. She reaches out and pulls Ann's thumb away from her mouth. "But, there is no time for dancing."

"One Saturday night, my friend, Lilianna and I, we go by ourselves to a carnival. We see poster on our street. There is a show in a big tent with lights and women who danced and sang. They were so pretty. There was a contest for local girls, and I love to sing so I try. Lilianna say, 'Maryá you get in big trouble for this.' But I win! I leave my room that night, and the carnival boss, he has a daughter my age, I forget her name, and he take me in. For a year, I sing and dance on a stage." Maryá leans her head to the side and hums.

"The night Alexi walks into the tent, I sing just for him. So handsome. A prince. He buys me real silk dresses, candy, flowers, outrageous hats. Only after we marry, I find out he is a hoodlum. A bootlegger. In the Purple Gang. Bloody murderers! He stacked whiskey behind my washtubs, in false steps he made to the attic, in the walls. When the police came, I am scared and I lie for Alexi. But they kept coming year after year so I stop talking at all."

"Did you love him, Gram?" Ann asks, worrying a strand of hair around her finger. She re-crosses her legs. "Daddy hates him."

"Love? Mr. Smarty Pants. Oh, Alexi could dance! Yes, fine like a racehorse. Love, yes, I love him so much I think it will kill me." Maryá's head drops to her chest. "Who is there, by the door?"

"What?" Ann asks, shaking her grandmother's shoulder. "Gram, are you all right?"

"Nothing, honey girl. Just remembering. Mike calls it moths." Crossing her hands in her lap, Maryá chuckles. "Moths flying in my head."

"Daddy says that when he was little his father would take him and Uncle Nick on whiskey runs. They'd hit the floor of the car when bullets began to fly. He said his father beat him. Why didn't you leave him?"

"Where I leave? No money. Three children I have." Maryá frowns. "I pray and pray for Alexi to change, honey. I tell you now the story of the one summer afternoon.

"Your father, he is fourteen. Alexi is off someplace with his gang. I don't know, he does not tell. So I take my boys and their two friends on the bus to a movie. I love movies, so dark and cool and cozy. We laugh and we eat popcorn. I know Alexi will be mad I spend money on movies for children. He doesn't believe in movies. But he is not home, and we see Mr. Errol Flynn who is a pirate with a kind heart. He falls in love with a lady pirate who has a sword and is as brave as he is. It is a good story.

"When we get off the bus, I see Alexi pace up and down like a bear on the porch. Even a block away, I see his thick black belt in his hand." Maryá wipes her eyes and picks up a glass of water from the end table. She sips slowly before she sets the glass down.

"Were you scared?" Ann leans forward, her chin propped up in her hand, elbow on her knee that is momentarily still.

"My stomach growl like a train! My heart hurts." Maryá puts her hand over her left breast, remembering that her hands wouldn't stop shaking. "I tell my boys to wait on the sidewalk. I send the friends home. I am scared. You bet your life, I am scared. I can smell Alexi. He is burning. His eyes are hard—how you say—staring at me like I am his terrible enemy. Outrageous. My ears ring like bells. All I think is that I don't want Alexi to hurt my boys.

"So, I walk to the front steps. Alexi slaps the belt on the inside of his hand so now I know he will hit me in front of the neighbors. He will hit me in front of my sons like he hits me when nobody sees. I am shaking so hard I trip over the milk bottles at the bottom of the steps and, before I think, I have a milk bottle in my hand and I break it over the porch rail. I am angry and running up the stairs, yelling, 'Now, things must change, Mister. Come, hit me now, Mister. I dare you, Mister.'"

Maryá's heart races as she sees the surprise turn to fear in Alexi's eyes. She watches him back away from her, hears the belt drop and the buckle clank as it hits the floor. The broken milk bottle gleams in her hand, slashing at him. She speaks slowly through clenched teeth. "Now things will change." It is then she knows she can kill him. With the jagged edges of the bottle aimed at his throat, the jagged edges of her fury, she backs him into the door.

"Wow, Gram. You're tough. What happened after that?" Ann sits up straight, her eyes wide. "Weren't you scared he'd kill you?"

"No, honey girl. I look in Alexi's eyes and they are dead and he goes into the house. He says nothing. He sits in his chair in the front room. When I come in, I see he is crying but so quiet I don't hear. I stare at him and I make our dinner and we eat with no words. He never hits me again. He does not hit my boys. Until the last day. No sir."

"Wow, you are something else." Ann looks at her grandmother as if she has become another person sitting in front of her. Her voice lowers until it is almost a whisper. "Awesome."

"Let us have tea. I am thirsty as a desert!" Maryá laughs. This time, Maryá accepts her granddaughter's arm as they walk to the kitchen. She keeps her eyes on the flowered carpet. It doesn't matter that it is blurry. She knows every stem and petal. When she was younger, she kept the house clean. It smelled of lilac toilet water and cooking food. Now a tinge of sweat and mildew, a sweet coppery smell disturbs her.

"Daisy, Daisy." In her strong alto, Maryá croons to the bouquet. She sits down at the pink Formica table. Afternoon sun butters the kitchen as Ann sets out teacups. The clock chimes four.

"Give me your answer, do." Ann joins in wistfully as she reaches for black tea on the shelf above the sink. With a wooden match, she lights the burner of the antiquated stove. "I'm half crazy . . ."

Turning to the window, Maryá points. "Look at the magnolia, Anyá. She blooms without me or anybody. So pretty, like a tree wearing seashells. The wren, she likes to sit in her branches. That tree is older than you. Alexi said it would never live this far north."

"Anyá! So, you come, hey?" Mike coughs as he walks in. He spits in the sink, then runs the tap and splashes cold water on his face. While he tucks his sleeveless white T-shirt into baggy gray trousers, he asks, "You drive so far? Where is Tom?"

"He's working, Grandpa, but he sends his greetings." Ann smiles furious as a salesman selling a new set of encyclopedias.

"He is a good man. Old woman, where you put my vodka?" Mike bends, rummaging in the cupboard behind Maryá until he straightens up, holding a brown quart of Canadian Club. "Who will toast with me?"

"We drink our tea, Mister." Although she smiles, Maryá declines, waving her hand as if to push away Mike's words.

"No, thank you, Grandpa. That stuff's too strong for me." Ann laughs, spooning loose tea in the metal tea ball. She snaps it shut and drops it into Maryá's ancient hand-painted ceramic pot, pours in boiling water, and closes the lid.

"*Horosho!*" In one long swallow Mike drains his glass. When he finishes, he grins at his wife. "Okay, see, I have only a little. For you."

Mike holds up the empty tumbler and replaces the bottle in the cupboard. "I go read the paper until the news comes on. You women talk. It's nice you visit, Anyá. Don't listen to your grandma. Drink some vodka. It makes your blood strong."

"Wait, Misha, take these. You have no lunch today." With effort, Maryá turns and lifts a sack of cookies from the counter behind her. He curls his lip but takes them, whistling as he walks briskly out of the room.

By the time Mike leaves, Ann has set out sugar, milk, and spoons.

"You like to dance, Anyá?" Maryá pours tea into Ann's cup.

"It's fun, but I can't keep up with the new ones." Ann shrugs, reaching for a sugar cube as she sits down opposite her grandmother. Popping the cube in her mouth, she sucks tea through it.

"I loved to dance. Loved to. You and Tom should dance." Maryá's blue eyes sparkle, recalling how she loved to dance the mazurka that Alexi taught her.

Maryá sighs deeply. Her words sound too far away. "We all suffer, man, woman, does it matter? Some people live to suffer; some see only their own wounds. Others live long enough they laugh at themselves, like me. My mama said to follow my heart. I believe that is what you must do."

"I'm sure you're right, Gram." Ann answers, raising her eyebrows. Her foot taps out its own nervous code beneath the table. She glances at her watch.

"Honey girl, I am just an old woman," Maryá reaches across the table for her granddaughter's hand, "but, listen, your heart knows what is right. You are like the rose. It blooms even after it frosts. Beautiful . . ."

"Not as beautiful as you." Ann blushes, holding her secrets behind her smile. "I have to leave soon, Gram, I'm sorry. I'm meeting someone."

Maryá's eyes burn. Letting go of Ann's hand, she rubs the lids and leans into the back of her chair. From a distance, she hears the clock chime five. She imagines the lacy hands moving like ballroom gloves around its calm ivory face. "I love that clock. Do you think there are clocks in heaven?" she asks. "Seventy-five years and still it keeps the time."

Like vases the two women sit in silence. Maryá drifts in a warm sea of late light, while Ann studies her grandmother's face as if it were a lost Babylonian scroll. Her nearly translucent forehead is framed by her thick gray hair. Her eyes dance back and forth under the delicate lids.

"I really do have to go, Gram." Ann clears her throat and squeezes her grandmother's hand. "I'll call tomorrow and I'll stop by before I leave town."

With great effort, Maryá focuses on Ann. She doesn't know where she is or what time of day or night it is. When it finally comes to her, she smiles. "Good-bye, dear girl. I will see you in the clouds when the wind stops."

Tilting her head, Ann opens her mouth to reply but nothing comes out. She rises, pushing back her chair with a squeak. After she walks around the table, she puts her slim arms around Maryá's solid shoulders and kisses her. "Gram, I could call my friend and cancel. I mean, I could stay overnight with you."

"No, Anyá," Maryá smiles and hugs her back. "You are young. Dance 'til your heart's content. I am happy to see you. Now, go."

Maryá doesn't hear Mike come into the room. Behind her, he stands, his hand on the back of her chair, watching her head nod.

"You awake, old woman? It was nice she come to see you. Anyá's a good girl." Mike touches her hair.

"Misha, how do we get so old?" Turning, she smooths a wrinkle in the clean white shirt Mike has put on against twilight's chill.

"Old? Lady, you come sit in the front room." Cautiously, he rests his hand on her shoulder. "Come, we talk and you feel better."

"My feet are like wood." Maryá stamps her shoes on the linoleum. Through the window, the sunset dyes the yellow walls peach.

"Here, I help you." Mike offers, lifting her to her feet. Comforted by the familiar odor of stale whiskey and tobacco, she leans against him as they walk. She recalls the times they strolled at nightfall around the neighborhood, greeting and exchanging gossip with neighbors. How she loved their stories.

When they reach the front room, she lowers herself carefully in her chair, while Mike tosses an afghan over her lap. As he walks to his chair, Maryá notices how loose his pants are, how they bag in the seat. Almost like a child's. She must remember to make him eat more. Tired from Ann's visit and the attempt to stay awake, she rests her eyes for just a minute.

She floats to the ceiling. She can smell Mike's cigarette smoke, then hears Alexi's laugh. He is young. She looks at her hands, firm and strong. Alexi and she are in the beautiful Philadelphia hotel room he has rented. Through the amber stained-glass window, light grows so intense she watches the black whiskers of his mustache move as he breathes. Alexi motions her closer with his white hands while lace curtains billow like parachutes in the warm breeze. Her heart pounds. Alexi removes his blue waistcoat and folds it on the bedstead. From its pocket, his engraved gold watch falls, slow as a feather onto the floor, where it breaks open, chiming every hour at once. "Why wait, my bird?" His question swallows the room.

Closer and closer, Alexi dances. Arms held wide, he twirls the mazurka, takes her hands and swings her. His breath smells like rain. "Forgive me," he pleads. "Sweet bird, forgive me."

Alexi's fingers are cool on her cheeks, the pressure of his body like air against hers. He laces his fingers into her long auburn hair, pulls back the long strands and kisses her.

"Oh, devil," she says, letting go his hands, "enough. Who can say what is to forgive?"

The clock chimes and Maryá's eyes open. She studies Mike as he reads the paper by the last rays of sunset. Smoke curls up from his cigarette. Her head turns to the daisies in the blue glass vase. Mike has placed them on top of the TV, where a cowboy gallops on a shining black horse away from the posse that chases him. The Shasta daisies are large and their petals so white they seem to be bioluminescent, as if they've captured tomorrow morning, throwing off an internal glow above the cowboy who's been taken captive in pictures that shift across the mute screen.

Year End Villanelle

Karen Blomain

As the year counts down in little breaths
We rehearse the world's refrain,
similar syllables woe or hope.
The choice is always ours.

Eager children place their shoes
in the path of three gifted kings
seeking a starlit cradle
As the year counts down in little breaths.

In work, law, politics, film and text,
the best, alas, doesn't always win.
Can we reject the risable?
Woe or hope. The choice is always ours.

The horizon purples against the seam
of sky lit by the weary wink
of twilit towns, night's vestibule
As the year counts down in little breaths.

The flow of tired soldiers engulfed
in wars, guns, street gangs,
mischief, mischance: apocryphal?
Woe or hope. The choice is always ours.

Certainty like youth and spring and peace at least
Distant as heaven. Will fear or prayer enable
As the year counts down in little breaths
Woe or hope? The choice is always ours.

Ride

Janet Amalia Weinberg

Minnie sat slumped on her porch swing, hating the bum leg that kept her from driving. She'd built up such an agitation that when the rumbling sound started, she thought it was in her.

Must be that fellow on the motorcycle, she decided, perking up. She'd seen him ride by before.

"He's like a wild horse racing the wind," she'd told her kid sister, Francis.

"Oh my," Francis had said with that sarcastic tone Minnie hated, "what fancy talk."

But Minnie got her back. "Least someone in this family has class."

They'd been bantering like that for sixty-seven years; it was more like ping-pong than war.

Suddenly there was the bike—sleek and black with a tail of dust. But something was wrong. It was skidding, careening to the side, way, way over to the side. . . .

For an instant it was two years earlier. Minnie was in her Chevy, spinning out of control, hurtling toward a tree. "Nooo!" she screamed.

There was a teeth-clenching screech, a sickening thump. Then deadly silence. . . .

She stood, stunned. Then, fast as her lame leg could go, Minnie hobbled to the road.

The fellow was sprawled face down in the dust. His bike was on its side over where it had gouged out her driveway. And Minnie's mailbox, which had stood erect for forty years, now leaned at a twisted angle.

"You all right?" She stooped to touch the man's shoulder. A skull and crossbones blazed red on his black leather jacket.

"Ohhh," he groaned, rolled over, and propped himself up with his arm.

"Careful." She gestured toward the shredded knee of his jeans. "Something might be broke."

He felt the knee, winced as he bent it. "Naw, I'm all right." Surveying the wreckage, he added bitterly, "If you call this all right."

Despite his lanky build and graying sideburns, he looked like a lost little boy, the way he sat on the ground and hung his head, holding his face in his hands. Minnie wanted to take him in her arms.

"Thank goodness," she said. "I thought you were a goner."

"Just let me sit awhile," he said.

She spotted the hawk tattoo on his neck and imagined what Francis would say: *He's trouble. Get in the house and lock the door.*

"I'll do no such thing," she said to the man. "If you can get up and walk, you're coming inside. If you can't, I'm calling a doctor." She was small and chunky—"like a lima bean with stick legs," her sister teased, but when she had a mind to, Minnie could talk as tough as any man.

He raised his head and smiled through a grimace of pain. "Guess I better do what the lady says." Slowly, he got to his feet and stood dazed, rubbing his knee. "My bike, . . ." he looked over at it as if it were a fallen friend, "I got to see to my bike."

"Leave it for now," she said with a don't-you-dare-argue-with-me tone.

"Hold on." He walked unsteadily to the bike and squatted down to check it out.

Minnie waited, her hands set disapprovingly on her hips.

He dragged the bike off the road and came back to where she stood. "I can fix it."

"Well you're not going to fix it now," she said, reclaiming her authority.

That pushiness of hers used to drive her son, Billy, crazy. In fact, it drove him away. But this man didn't seem to mind.

"Yes, ma'am." He smiled again and let her lead the way.

He washed and bandaged his knee then joined Minnie at the kitchen table, filling the room with the smell of gasoline and sweat and maleness.

She wagged her finger at him the moment he sat down. "You should've had a helmet on."

"Don't like 'em!" He scowled from under a ridge of dark eyebrows. "A guy could sure use one around you, though."

She scowled back and was about to tell him off when he let out a whoop.

"Ha! Had you going, didn't I?"

She shook her finger at him again and tried to mask her grin with a frown. This was the kind of man she wished her son had become.

"I'm Hawk," he said, waving his hand in a casual salute. It was a large, workman's hand that could probably build an engine or break a jaw.

"That your first name or your last?"

"It's my *only* name."

"Bet your mother didn't give you a name like that."

"Her?" His mouth contorted. "She didn't give me nothing."

Minnie could hear her Billy talking like that about her, tearing out chunks of her heart. . . . "I'm Minnie," she said abruptly.

He went on to brag about his Harley, a chopped, 900 Low Rider, and about hanging with a gang once. "Naw, not Hells Angels," he said, "but man, they were just as ugly."

Minnie was impressed. "My, that's really something."

He told her he was staying at the rooming house in town. "It's not bad—if you don't have to be there too long. And I never have to be *any*where too long," he said, as if that were something to be proud of.

When she asked what he did with himself he took a yellowed newspaper clipping from his wallet, carefully unfolded it, and reached it to her.

She could make out some people circling a huge tree and facing what looked like a crew of hard hats with chainsaws.

"That's me." He pointed at one of the figures in the circle, then leaned back as if expecting praise.

"Oh yeah?" She squinted at the picture. "What were you doing? Dancing?"

"Dancing?" He sounded hurt. "It took two thousand years to grow that there tree and they were going to chop it into matchsticks."

"So?"

"So I stopped 'em, the greedy bastards."

"Looks like those hard hats wanted to do you in."

"Damn right. But sometimes you got to take chances." He shrugged. "What good is life if you don't live it?"

"I won't argue with that. I was a daredevil myself in my day." Her eyes lit up at the thought of it. "You should have seen me galloping up and down these hills, me and my horse, King. What a time that was. . . ." Her voice faded.

"Now I can't even drive the car no more, not since my leg got smashed in that accident." She thought about the old Chevy. After her husband, Sam, died and Billy ran off, the Caprice had been her life.

"Mm-hm," Hawk mumbled, searching through his wallet again.

She went on anyway, talking more to herself than to him. "Now the car is stuck alone in the barn, I'm stuck alone in the house, and all the two of us can do is sit around and rust till we die."

"Get a load of this." He held out a photo across the table. "This here's my little darlin'."

Minnie leaned close to look at the laughing child in a sailor dress with a Raggedy Ann doll in her lap. "What a little sweetheart," she said and forgot about feeling sorry for herself.

Minnie called her sister as soon as he was gone.

"Guess what?!" She rushed on without waiting for a reply. "The fellow with the motorcycle was just here. His name is Hawk and he looks like that actor, Gary Cooper, and he's got his picture in the paper and he tore up my mailbox but he said he'd fix it, and—"

"For goodness sakes, Min," Francis's tone splashed cold on Minnie's excitement. "You're making a fool of yourself."

"I'd rather be a fool than a spoilsport like you," Minnie shot back. "You'd think I'd have learned by now not to tell *you* anything."

"What do you mean by that?"

"Remember when Mom said we were too little to go fishing by ourselves and we made a secret pact to go anyhow?"

"No."

"Well *I* do because you chickened out and ruined everything."

"Oh lord, that's got to be over sixty years ago."

"So?" Minnie threw the word at Francis. "You haven't changed."

"So?" Francis threw it back. "Neither have you."

Minnie sidestepped the charge. "Why thank you. That's the nicest thing you could have said to me." She'd won that round and enjoyed her triumph—but only for a moment. "Too bad it's not true."

"Now don't go feeling sorry for yourself again," said Francis.

"You don't know what it's like. You still got Harry to take care of and all those grandkids. What have I got?" Minnie made it sound as if her disappointments were all her sister's fault.

Francis snickered. "You got Hawk."

The next day, Hawk was back as promised. Minnie had on her dark green polyester pants and red and green cowboy shirt with mother-of-pearl snaps. She snapped and unsnapped the breast pocket, snapped and unsnapped it as she let him in. "Wasn't sure you'd come," she said.

She hadn't felt this charged up since that fellow, Harris, from the Senior Center surprised her with a kiss. She knew what Francis would say: Are you crazy? This fellow's no insurance man like Harris. He's a biker, a criminal for all you know. But then Francis never had any fun.

Hawk didn't talk much. Just fixed and reset the mailbox and said he'd be back to smooth out her driveway.

A few days later, Francis and Minnie were in the variety store in town when Hawk's little girl looked out at Minnie from one of the picture frames on sale there. In fact, that same little girl looked out at her from a whole row of frames.

Minnie felt her bones collapse. There was nothing left to hold her up. She grabbed a shelf to steady herself and examined the photo, hoping she was wrong but knowing she wasn't. The child was wearing a sailor dress and had a Raggedy Ann doll in her lap.

Francis rushed to help. "You okay?"

Minnie hated to tell her sister about the picture but was too upset to keep it to herself. "And don't go telling me I told you so," she said with as much bluster as she could manage.

"Well, I did, didn't I?" It was Francis's turn to gloat. "He probably made up *everything* he told you. It wouldn't surprise me one bit if . . ."

Minnie cut her off. "Take me home." Her leg was paining her something fierce and it was all she could do to limp back to the car. She should have had her cane but wouldn't be caught dead out in public with it and she could have leaned on her sister's arm but didn't want to give her the satisfaction.

As Francis drove, she patted Minnie's hand. "It's like with Billy, isn't it?"

Minnie snatched her hand away. "How can you say that? This fellow's not . . ." she hesitated, "not like Billy."

"I mean he lied to you, same as Billy."

"Hmph, that's for sure." After all this time, it still hurt to think about her son—not because he was nothing but a mild-mannered clerk who wrote poetry and liked to shop, though that was upsetting enough, but because he'd made up so many stories about girls and dates that when she finally found out he was homosexual, she felt totally betrayed.

Neither spoke till Francis stopped the car in front of Minnie's house.

"Min," she said gently, "maybe this biker fellow just needed you to like him."

Minnie rejected the idea. "Played me for a fool, is what he did."

"Maybe that's why Billy lied too."

"If I ever see the bastard again," Minnie snarled, "I'll rub his face in his lies."

But she didn't get around to it the next time she saw Hawk. Or the time after that.

I'll do it for sure today, Minnie told herself. Hawk was unjamming her kitchen window while she set the table with coffee and cookies—she'd made peanut butter puffs, the kind he especially liked.

He got the window sliding smoothly and put away his tools. "Want to know the name my folks stuck me with?" he asked when he joined her at the kitchen table.

"Sure."

"You won't laugh?"

"Promise."

He took a swig of coffee, plunked the cup on the table, and braced himself with a breath. "Ralph Waldo Ramirez. The Ramirez part's okay—my old man's from Mexico, but the rest of it." Hawk shook his head.

"Wasn't there some writer called Ralph Waldo Emerson?" Minnie asked.

"Yeah, that's who my old lady wanted me to be like." His mouth contorted the way it had the last time he'd mentioned his mother. "She hated how I turned out."

"That's terrible," Minnie said, wishing she could undo the hurt. "If you ask me, you turned out damned all right. It's not your fault your mother was too big a fool to see it."

He looked straight at Minnie as if trying to see if she meant what she'd said. Then he grinned and pulled out the yellowed news photo of the people and the tree. "I ever show you this?"

This was it, the perfect time to let him have it for lying to her. But she was seeing herself at that same table, scanning a column of As on her young Billy's report card and him with his big, eager eyes waiting for her to say how good he was. But she didn't give him that. She never did. "What's this?" she'd said, fixing on the C he'd gotten in gym. "Your As won't help you in the real world if you don't toughen up."

"You don't have to show me that picture," she told Hawk. "I knew what kind of man you were when I first saw you ride your bike."

"You did?" Hawk beamed and helped himself to more cookies.

Poor Billy, she thought. *I was awful hard on him. . . .*

"Want a ride?"

"What?!" Inside, part of her jumped with excitement, another part felt too old. "You got to be kidding."

"Nope."

She hesitated, then waved him away. "No. Thanks anyway."

"My bike's a monster," he went on as if she had agreed, "but my buddy's got a little 750 with an electric starter and a cozy seat that'd be just right for you. How about I come by tomorrow and take you out?"

"But . . ."

"I'll get you a helmet."

"Won't that be something." She was so thrilled, she giggled.

The next day Minnie was waiting by the road in mud boots, sweatpants, and Sam's old Windbreaker when Hawk drove up in a red Yamaha.

He held her arm while she struggled to get her bad leg over the seat. "Told you I couldn't do it," she said.

"Let me lift you on."

But she didn't want to be picked up and set down like a three-year-old. "If I just had something to stand on."

"How's this?" He stooped and made a step for her with his hands.

It was just the boost she needed. She grabbed hold of the leather seat and swung her leg over it like the horsewoman she once was.

"You look like you belong there." He gave her an approving nod. "Just keep your feet on those pegs and hold onto me. Got it?"

"Got it."

When he was seated, she placed her fingertips gingerly on his hips. He reached back, drew her hands around his waist, and tugged her to him until the whole front of her body leaned into his back and her helmeted head rested between his shoulders.

"Atta girl!"

He switched on the starter and the engine growled. She could feel it in her body.

"You can let me off now," she yelled. "I've had enough excitement." She was only half joking.

"Damn right," he shouted back. "Real exciting."

The bike rocked off the kickstand and took off like a bull out of a chute, roaring as it went. And Minnie roared with it.

They drove down her road, passed the post office, and made a right at the variety store. "How you doing?" Hawk called over his shoulder as they neared the highway.

She shouted into the wind. "Great!"

"Hang on!"

He took the on-ramp. She shut her eyes and tightened her grip. She could feel the power building like a drumbeat in her blood. They went faster and faster. And then they were flying. She'd figured she was too old to ever feel that free again. But she'd been wrong.

They leeeaned right and leeeaned left, scooping out scallops of air. And the wind came rushing at them, no, they *were* the wind, Minnie and Hawk and the bike, there was no separating one from the other. When she opened her eyes, silos and cows and meadows were streams of liquid color.

And then it was over and he was helping her off and her body was still buzzing so much he had to walk her to the porch and help her sit.

"That was really something," she said, feeling giddy like a girl on a date.

"You're a natural," he said. "You ought to get your own wheels."

"But I can't drive, not with this bum leg."

"So ride something like a Vespa—you know, a scooter. The controls are in the handles."

"No. Really?" She pictured waving to Francis as she rode into town and a laugh spilled out of her.

"Sure."

"You mean I could get around again?"

"Why not?"

Bet he could help me buy a real good one, she thought. *And then . . .*

"Well," he said, backing off, "got to go."

"Don't you want to come in or something?" She couldn't hide her disappointment.

"Naw." He stood, looking down at his boots.

"But I made peanut butter puffs."

He took another step back, mumbling about "next time," then turned and walked to the road.

Somehow, she knew there'd never be a next time. "Thanks, Hawk!" she called. "Thanks for everything!"

The rumble of the bike got farther and farther away . . . until it was just a memory.

Minnie sat slumped on her porch swing. She thought of her son. He used to sit like that when she scolded him. Suddenly she perked up: *My Billy likes to shop!* He'd written several times to say he wanted to see her but she was too hurt and angry to have anything to do with him—till now. She pictured him, with that mild way of his, helping her buy a good scooter. *Now* that *would be something,* she thought. *That would be really something.*

May Morning in the Winter of My Life

Rachel Josefowitz Siegel

Gains and losses, joys and sorrows, life is not a financial ledger. At the end there will surely be unfinished business and much that cannot be quantified or even fully understood.

My friend Jane called me this morning. Now that we live far apart, we send each other funny e-mails, loving messages, and we talk once or twice a year by phone. Jane told me that she feels blessed with the people in her life who mean so much to her, some of whom she had known only briefly. I echoed her feelings, for I too feel deeply blessed by our relationship and the many, many individuals who have in some way touched my life, and those who have become so dear to me.

Jane, like me, lives alone. We both proudly acclaim our eightieth birthdays this year. As seasons go, we are both in the winter of our lives. She has survived many hardships, many losses, she lives in a wheelchair, and she feels blessed.

I told her that she is doubly blessed for being able to celebrate and count her blessings. I am not always capable of doing that when the going gets tough, when pains and sorrows accumulate. Sometimes loneliness sets in too deep and the warmest, fullest memories can no longer give me pleasure or relief. I may see my life half empty when I can no longer perform my previous roles or do the things I've loved to do. There are times when even the most caring encounters cannot make up for an overwhelming sense of loss. I have grieved and sorrowed, have fretted over my imperfections. I listen to world news with anger and despair.

But on this beautiful May morning, waking up to my friend's clear voice and loving words, my life feels full and I feel blessed. I rejoice in remembering the challenges and rewards of my work, the wondrous encounters with each of the women and men of all ages who have been and continue to be part of my life, for even the ones who have died will always be present in my soul.

I have shared forty-six years of married life with a dear man who enriched every aspect of my being, even when we quarreled or disagreed and I have learned to live a full life without him. My two sons and my daughter have become responsible and caring adults and we are now more able to show our love and concern for one another without some of the earlier frictions. I relish the bonds I have formed with my young adult grandchildren and the delightful moments or days with my two great-grandsons.

Yes, I feel blessed indeed. I know with certainty that there will be more joys, more sorrows. The gains and losses will not balance out, not now, or ever. But I shall name the blessings while I can.

Crone/ease

Edith A. Cheitman

Caught in the long loose lariat of age
they travel now in pious pairs
or in ferocious flocks—
busloads of white feathered birds
with raptor eyes

In hotel rooms at off-peak rates
they, strangers,
are easy naked
sharing the maps of joy and sorrow
their wounded bodies have become
(caesareans, mastectomies,
tracheotomy's fearful scar
telling of a woman silenced
if only for a while).

"When I die," says one,
body quilted with narrow-gauge trails
left by surgeons armed with staple guns,
"I want a rug made of this pelt."
She pirouettes
bare mirrored in the tile reflected light.
"Let that damned doctor
hang it on his office wall—
my last chance to be a trophy."
Her buddies laugh,
Their white hair crackles fierce.

Enduring confidantes of Chance,
they approach, appraise casinos
without romance.

Mostly they play the slots.

Later, in their rooms, they put up their feet;
split the take;
drink bourbon neat from hotel paper cups.

White Room

Simone Poirier-Bures

Virginia Callan stood before her bathroom mirror twisting a thin blue scarf around her white hair. All day she had fretted over this evening—what to wear, what to bring, what it would be like. She fiddled nervously with a few strands of hair that had escaped from the thick roll at the back of her head. When she reached for the hairbrush resting on the back of the commode, it slipped from her hand and fell into the toilet with a loud plunk.

She leaned against the sink and closed her eyes. Eighty dollars, she had paid. And they had told her the supplies would cost fifty or sixty more. She calculated again the little economies this would require and imagined Kate saying, *"You know, Mother, there are many less expensive hobbies you could take up."* She stiffened a little at the thought, then fished the brush out of the toilet. Maybe she wouldn't tell Kate.

At the front door Virginia took off her slippers and put on her walking shoes. Though the shoes were less than a month old, the heels already showed signs of wear. The walk two weeks ago accounted for that. It had taken eight or nine miles that time to shake the fiery blackness that held her like an iron fist. Each time it came, lodging in her chest like a live thing, clawing at her till her jaws clenched and her limbs jerked, she would walk—walk and walk until the thing tired, lost its grip, fell away. As long as she could remember, the dark thing had lurked there, seizing her at unpredictable intervals. These last few years it had visited her more often. Always, now, she could feel it, waiting in the distance like a circling crow.

Outside, the sky was overcast and the air smelled of rain. She felt for the umbrella in her canvas tote. It would take fifteen or twenty minutes to walk to the community college; she allowed thirty, just in case. She paused at the corner, as she always did, to glance back at her house. She had lived in that small white bungalow with the green door and green roof for forty-six years. Kate and Willy had grown up in its four rooms. She and Jack had grown old there. Then Jack had died.

To the little white house came monthly letters from Kate and Willy. Kate's neatly typed envelope always arrived on the fourth or fifth, and though Willy wrote on the fifteenth, she knew not to expect his letter until close to the end of the month. Today was the twelfth; in three more days Willy would sit down and write. She pictured him bending over a rickety old desk in a mud and straw hut somewhere in the heart of a steamy jungle. She knew it wasn't like that. The photos he sent of the school showed a relatively modern building in a dusty town. Still, she always thought of Willy in the midst of green, sinewy foliage, surrounded by damp, noisy life. Three years had passed since she had seen him. A dull ache began forming in her chest. The last time she had held Willy's arm was when they'd lowered Jack into the black earth.

That was the way things were. Life was a great spinning circle; people and things whirled away, as if pulled by centrifugal force. Everything she had ever loved had spun off into the darkness. Now her life was an empty white room.

"Good evening, Mrs. Callan." It was Mrs. Johnson, standing by her open gate while her dog, a brownish-red rag mop with legs, squatted obscenely at the edge of the curb.

"Good evening," Virginia replied, looking disdainfully at the dog and then at Mrs. Johnson's pink, smiling face. They had lived around the corner from each other for more than thirty years, and until recently had exchanged no more than a few neighborly greetings. This past year, however, since Mr. Johnson had died, Mrs. Johnson had become a pest.

"Not much of an evening for a walk, I'd say," Mrs. Johnson warbled cheerfully.

"No, it's not," Virginia replied, intending neither to stop nor to satisfy Mrs. Johnson's curiosity.

"I hope you're not planning to go very far," Mrs. Johnson persisted. "It looks like rain."

"I've brought my umbrella, just in case."

Virginia kept walking. Mrs. Johnson hurried after her, dragging the dog along behind her. "Oh, Mrs. Callan! Mrs. O'Brian and Mrs. Kopel and I are going to go play bingo tomorrow night. Would you like to come along?"

At least once a month Mrs. Johnson approached Virginia with some invitation. "We're both widows, after all," she would say in a low confidential voice as if she were sharing an intimate secret. But Virginia had never had much in common with Mrs. Johnson and the other neighborhood women her age. All those years they had gathered to drink coffee and play bridge, she had preferred to read or talk with Jack. While they were watching their grown children take their places in the world, she had had Willy to take care of—Willy, the surprise, the blessing of her forty-first year. Whenever she saw Mrs. Johnson walking down the street with her friends, a chattering huddle of gray-haired widows, she thought of clucks, the old brood hens of her childhood.

"No, thank you," she said.

"You really should try it sometime," Mrs. Johnson insisted. "It's so much fun, and they're giving away fifty-dollar prizes. You might win."

"Maybe some other time," Virginia said, hurrying on.

Eighty dollars she had paid for this class. Two nights a week for twelve weeks. *You're no better than an old cluck yourself,* she thought.

After going down the wrong hall twice, Virginia finally arrived at the right room. She was sure the young girl she had stopped for directions had said "Down the hall to your left." In fact, the room was on the right. The girl had barely stopped to hear what she asked, had avoided her eyes, then gestured in the wrong direction.

Virginia had come to the community college only a few times before, once or twice to read in the library and once to watch some travel films on Africa, where Willy was. For years she had seen the newspaper inserts describing evening adult classes and had noted them with mild interest. This time some old yearning had bubbled to the surface and she found herself sending in the registration.

Four young women sat at the front of the room chatting easily among themselves. Virginia recognized two she had seen grocery shopping at Eagle's with their children, though they had never spoken to her. She nodded to them, and took a seat at the back of the class. There were about a dozen students in all, mostly women, all of whom were at least twenty-five years younger than herself. Virginia shrank into her chair.

A young man in his mid-thirties came into the room carrying an assortment of things. The voices in the classroom stopped and all eyes turned to watch him. He busied himself at the table in front of the room arranging a bowl, two small boxes, and a jar of tall brushes. The room crackled with curiosity, but still the man did not speak, did not look at them.

Finally, he turned and said, "Good evening, I'm Dan Frommelt. The first thing we're going to do is talk about how an artist sees things. Take a close look, now. What do you see up here?" After an uncomfortable silence, someone said, "A bunch of old brushes and some boxes." Everyone laughed. Then someone else said, "I see different shapes—rounds, rectangles, squares. The colors are interesting too, and the shadows." After a while, it seemed that everyone had something to say. Everyone except Virginia. She sat forward in her chair and listened carefully. The words around her seemed like little birds, swooping through the room, unpredictable, astonishing. She had never heard *space, form,* and *color* used quite that way before.

Next, the instructor passed out sheets of drawing paper and pieces of charcoal. "Keeping in mind what we've been saying, I want you to draw an impression of what you see on the table." When Willy was small, they often sat together at the kitchen table making simple crayon drawings. They would talk and draw and show each other their pictures. Then Willy got interested in other things and she stopped drawing. She picked up the chalk. It felt awkward, rather like the soft coal she had seen poor country children use for crayons long ago.

Dan Frommelt moved around the class, pausing to comment on each person's work. When he reached Virginia, he leaned over and covered her hand with his own. "Try doing it like this," he said, moving her hand and the charcoal in strong, firm strokes. His hand was large and warm; it had been a long time since anyone had touched her.

A few blocks from the bookstore, Virginia shifted her tote bag from one shoulder to the other. Who would have thought that such small tubes of paint could weigh and cost so much? "They might as well be gold," she muttered. An uneasy feeling was settling on her, as if some great finger in the universe were wagging at her: *all that money wasted on foolishness.*

She thought of Jack, at whom that great finger would never have wagged. She could still see his slim, wiry body bending over an assortment of large plastic bags on the back porch—one for bottles, one for cans and bits of tin foil, one for paper—all destined for recycling centers. In the kitchen by the sink stood an old coffee can for egg shells, coffee grounds, vegetable and fruit scraps—each day Jack had carried it to the compost heap at the edge of the garden.

His gardening had begun during the Great Depression, when they lived in a rural area south of Des Moines. While the whole world was enveloped in sadness and poverty, Jack found he could make almost anything grow. From tiny seeds came tomato and pepper and cabbage plants, sprouting in broken teacups on sunny window sills in February. From the eyes of old potatoes, planted on Good Friday by the light of the moon, came lush green plants that yielded bushels of plump tubers.

There were mountains of vegetables. Throughout those terrible years, Jack left little bundles of potatoes, cabbages, green beans— whatever they had an excess of—at the back doors of the most desperate. So they wouldn't be shamed, he brought his gifts after dark. They themselves had little enough of anything else, but Jack would not hear of selling or trading his vegetables. "It's all a big circle, Ginny," he would tell her, arcing his arms. "What you take is taken from you, but what you give comes back." She had not believed him, though she had loved his earnest, shining face.

After they moved to Clayton and life improved, Jack continued to grow more vegetables than they needed. Somehow, he always managed to find someone grateful for the surplus. He died during planting time—in his sleep, without warning. Virginia finished the planting for him, then found that she couldn't bear to see those neat ordered rows without Jack among them. After that, she let the space go fallow. It was covered with crabgrass and creeping charlie now.

As she often did when she was out, Virginia found herself walking toward the small park by the river. It was out of her way by a few blocks, but she could rest there for a little while and look at the water. She sat on a bench under a large oak tree and looked around. On weekdays, only young mothers and old people came here. Today, there were two of each. The mothers, each with a tot in a stroller, shared a bench and what looked like a pattern book, the contents of which they were discussing thoughtfully. A brown spaniel tugged at a leash tied to one of the arms of the bench. Two old men, sitting at a square cement table painted with a checkerboard design, bent over an elaborate set of chess pieces. One of the men smoked a pipe, and soft rings of smoke hovered over his head like a gauzy halo. She had seen them here before, always playing chess, always silent.

She came to this little park several times a week, drawn by the deep, brooding Mississippi. Each time she saw the river, something stirred within her. Old sediment roiled up, as if the river were running through her. Today the river was quiet, lumbering along like a tired old animal. She knew its fierce mood swings, its cruelty. Every year it dragged some boy or man from the wingdams and swallowed him up.

When the children were little she had brought them here, first Kate, then sixteen years later, Willy. She had shown them this powerful beast of a river and the long barges it carried on its back like a dray animal. Willy had made up stories about the barges, inventing cargoes, romantic destinations, imaginary lives for the people on board. When he was old enough, he had followed those barges—to Europe, South America, Africa. Now she waited for his letters.

She had spent her whole life waiting, it seemed to her now. Waiting for prosperity, waiting for Jack, waiting for Kate to grow up, then Willy. Always watching, always waiting. She felt the dark thing gathering now, thickening in her chest. "You were wrong about the circle, Jack," she said half aloud. "Nothing comes back. It's all carried away like the waters of the river."

A small disturbance drew her eyes to the two women. The dog had come around to the strollers and was licking the face of one of the toddlers who shrieked in protest. One of the women got up and smacked the dog. "Bridgit! Stop that!" Bridgit, her brown head bent, slunk under the bench. "Those are only doggy kisses," the woman cooed to the distraught child.

The mother had long auburn hair—like one of the women in class, Virginia observed. Remembering the class, she thought of how the chalk had felt, once she had become used to it, how it had glided across the paper. She shifted her tote bag. Seven small, firm tubes—primary and secondary colors plus white—and four brushes. She noticed, suddenly, that it was a lovely, warm day, a gift really, for the second week of September. She would go home now with her little bundles, home to her kitchen where she could lay the tubes and brushes on the white enamel table and admire them.

Virginia stood at her kitchen window looking out. The coolness, until lately confined to the evenings, had now seeped into the day, and the Monday morning sky looked as though it were bracing for something. "What do you think, Clem?" The sound of her voice, raspy and thin, startled her. She hadn't spoken to anyone since last Thursday night's class. Clem tiptoed along the counter and rubbed himself against Virginia's arm. His purring filled the room like the low throb of an electric mixer.

A bright white canvas and the paint tubes lay on the kitchen table where she had set them. All weekend she'd been circling the table. They'd spent the last two classes mixing paints, stretching canvasses, and studying various shapes that Dan arranged on the studio desk. But now they had an assignment. On Thursday Dan had told them to take a canvas home and get something started. "There's plenty of time before next Tuesday's class."

All day Friday, the empty canvas, so white, so blank, had paralyzed her with its possibilities. Perhaps she should sketch something first on a piece of paper. But what? Between deliberations, to distract herself, she had answered Willy's letter. "The teacher reminds me of you," she wrote. "He's about your age and size, though your hair is lighter." She thought of the way Dan Frommelt moved among them, commenting and encouraging, the way he had touched her arm, her hand.

On Saturday afternoon she had gone for a long walk. A wind had come up. She had watched the trees jostling the sky like restless children, the river lapping against the shore like a sucking infant. But no pictures came. No shape that she could put on a fourteen-by-eighteen-inch canvas.

Sunday, a sore throat had kept her home. She had spent the day lying on the sofa with a book, Clem and an afghan tucked around her legs. But every time she went into the kitchen to make a cup of tea with lemon and honey for her throat, the empty canvas reproached her. "Tomorrow," she told it.

Now it was tomorrow. Her throat was better, but the canvas was still empty. Through the window she watched a red-winged blackbird skid onto a high branch of the apple tree that Jack had planted. A hard freeze was predicted for tonight. She would have to start putting feed out for the birds soon. Over by the small shed where Jack's rakes and hoses and wheelbarrow were still stored, a clump of wine-colored chrysanthemums caught her eye. They'd freeze tonight for sure if she didn't bring them in. She reached for the kitchen shears hooked beside the stove, and without pausing to put on a jacket, darted out the side door. She cut the blooms quickly and was about to dart back in when she saw a familiar figure approaching.

"Oh, Mrs. Callan!" Mrs. Johnson chirped. "I see you're bringing your flowers in. I brought all mine in yesterday. What a pity we've lost our nice weather!"

"I suppose so," Virginia replied. She began to shiver in her light housedress. "Excuse me, but I've got to get inside," she said. "I had a sore throat yesterday."

"So that's why you weren't in church." Mrs. Johnson said, hugging her heavy tweed coat around her. "You missed our discussion about the fall bazaar. I thought I'd come by and tell you about it."

"Well . . . come in for a moment, then," Virginia said. "I'll get worse than a sore throat if I stay out here much longer."

Mrs. Johnson beamed and followed her in through the side door, all the while talking, talking. The moment she stepped into the kitchen, Virginia remembered the things laid out on the table. She tried to steer Mrs. Johnson past them and into the living room, but Mrs. Johnson's busy eyes had already seen.

"Oh my," she said. "Are you painting?"

Virginia laid the chrysanthemums on the counter and sighed. "I'm trying, anyway."

Mrs. Johnson was at the table now, examining the canvas. "It has no picture on it," she exclaimed. "Did you buy a blank one by mistake?"

"You're supposed to make up your own pictures," Virginia replied, taking the canvas firmly from Mrs. Johnson's hands.

"My Janie used to paint," Mrs. Johnson chattered. "It's much easier if you get one with the picture already on it." She picked up one of the tubes. "All Janie's paints came in little numbered wells with plastic tops so you could see the color. You just had to make a little slit in the top and stick in your brush. Sometimes Janie used different colors than they said, just to see how they would turn out. Her paintings were so lovely! I've framed two of them. You should come by and see them sometime." Mrs. Johnson was almost breathless with talking and smiling.

"I'm sure they're very nice," Virginia said, taking Mrs. Johnson's elbow and steering her toward the living room. "Now tell me about the bazaar."

"It'll be on the first Saturday in November. I'm in charge of the baked goods this year," Mrs. Johnson said. "We can use anything: cakes, pies, fancy breads, even preserves. Can we count on you to help out?"

"Of course you can," Virginia replied. "But I don't want to keep you." She nudged Mrs. Johnson firmly toward the front door. "I'm sure there are other people you have to see as well." Mrs. Johnson opened her mouth in astonishment, and the door closed quickly behind her.

Virginia plopped the chrysanthemums into a quart canning jar and stuck them angrily on the window ledge above the sink. How stupid to have allowed herself to be caught like that! All because of some ridiculous flowers. Paint by number. Really! She looked at the empty canvas, then glared at the shaggy purple heads flopping over the sides of the jar like old women with disheveled hair. They were framed in a windowpane like a painting. *Like a painting!* With a rush of excitement, she began squeezing little worms of color on to a small square of masonite.

One morning, a few weeks later, Virginia felt it as she awoke. It had circled her all night, and now it gripped her in its fiery claw. She got up, made herself a cup of strong tea and toasted an English muffin. The tea hurt her teeth; the muffin tasted like old potatoes.

She had slept badly, dark dreams curling around her. She was lost in a huge cornfield, row upon row of broken brown husks, as far as the eye could see. Dan Frommelt appeared; then he became Willy, but he didn't seem to recognize her. He moved past her, speaking to others she had not even noticed were there, encouraging everyone but her.

It was all the fault of Willy's letter. Here it was, almost the end of October, and still no sign of it. For the past few days she had waited by the door for the mailman, watched him come up the walkway, searched his hands for the familiar blue airmail envelope. But all he'd brought was a Sears catalog, an oil bill, and a flyer from Kmart.

She went into the bathroom to brush her teeth. The face that looked back was ugly—old and lined. Once that face had been smooth, fair. Once her life had stretched before her like a great plain; now it was ending. And what had she gained for living? A daughter and two grown grandchildren she seldom saw, and a son so far away it hardly mattered. She had gathered nothing to her. Nothing had clung. All that remained was a tired old body, flesh falling away from bone. She felt a sudden urge to break the mirror, run through the house and smash them all. She would comb her hair like a blind woman. What did it matter what she looked like anyway? She slammed shut the medicine cabinet.

Nine o'clock. The mail usually came around eleven. She looked out the living room window and *willed* the mailman to appear. The sidewalk was empty; a gray sky glowered overhead.

She picked up a library book that lay on the coffee table. All day yesterday she had found comfort in it. But then the story had ended, and her own life had flooded back over her in all its white nothingness. "Lies!" she hissed, throwing the book down. "Nothing but lies."

She paced the room, her chest full of black fire. What to do? She didn't want to walk this time. She wanted Willy's letter. Two more hours before the mailman would come. If only she could make the time disappear, slice it off like a hunk of superfluous dough. What did a few hours or even a few days matter in *her* life anyway?

Her satchel and an empty canvas lay on the sofa where she had left them. For the past few weeks she had worked on her chrysanthemums; Dan Frommelt had shown her how to layer the color, give it depth. "Now try something bigger," he had said. "And don't be limited by the forms around you. Use your imagination." It sounded like something Willy would say.

How stupid it was to be taking an art class! An old woman like her! What did she expect to gain from it anyway? It was all worthless, worthless! She carried the canvas and satchel into the kitchen and flung them on the table. All that money spent on brushes and tubes of paint! And that new canvas, twice the size of the first one. For a few moments she glared at it. Suddenly, she felt an urgent need to fill that white emptiness. She pulled out the brushes, and began squeezing out large dollops of red, blue, yellow, black on the small palate.

As she stood before the canvas, images began rising in her: Jack's tomatoes, huge and red; the plastic violets Willy brought her for Mother's Day when he was ten; the dark eyes in Kate's five-year-old face, turning away secretively, even then; the wallpaper in her mother's bedroom; the wispy ferns that grew by the old schoolhouse; the limestone cliffs up river. Pictures churned and twisted into one another like an animated cartoon: a giant cabbage became a great gaunt face with huge staring eyes; a spotted fern became a green and red snake slithering in a sea of yellow pigment. Images roiled inside her like a great river, sucking and pulling against one another, separating and converging. Her brush moved with green, red, blue, black. Shapes appeared on the canvas as if by magic.

When she finally stopped, she felt as though she were surfacing after a long swim under water. The dark thing had vanished; she felt washed clean, suffused in light. Strange swirling shapes covered the canvas in brilliant colors. They resembled nothing at all, yet she found them enormously satisfying. She glanced over at the kitchen clock. Just past noon. She plopped her brushes into a jar of turpentine and washed her hands. Where had they come from, all those strange images? She looked again at the dark blue hole, the red swirl, the green ferny thing. They must have been there all along, inside her. Then she remembered: *the mailman!* She had forgotten to watch for the mailman. She hurried to the front door. The red and blue striped edge of an airmail envelope protruded above the black mailbox. She felt as though she were seeing it from a great distance.

At six that evening, Virginia left her house in a state of quiet elation, carrying the canvas in an oversized brown shopping bag. It wasn't finished yet, but she wanted to show it to Dan Frommelt. She was careful not to jostle the bag so the paint wouldn't smear.

The air was fragrant with the musky smell of fallen leaves, and wide streaks of pink and orange lit up the western sky. There was something triumphal about it. The sun had appeared midafternoon, and now perched on the edge of the horizon as if to enjoy the last proud moments of the day. Thin pink clouds were shifting into new configurations, teasing and provocative. It was like her painting. At intervals all afternoon she had gone back to look at it, and each time she had seen something different, something that filled her with wonder and strange little bursts of joy. She had never felt that way before. It was as if she were walking down a wide corridor full of open doors, all leading into colorful, interesting rooms.

"Mrs. Callan! Mrs. Callan!"

Virginia winced. Since their first encounter, she had successfully avoided Mrs. Johnson on class nights. This had meant turning right instead of left whenever she caught a glimpse of her from the corner, and though the detour took her a few blocks out of her way, it was worth it. Tonight, she had forgotten to watch for Mrs. Johnson. Now she saw her plump figure hurrying up the street. Virginia pulled the shopping bag around behind her.

"Mrs. Callan! I'm so glad I ran into you," Mrs. Johnson exclaimed breathlessly. "I haven't seen you in such a long time and I wanted to remind you about the bazaar on Saturday. All the baked goods need to be in the church hall by Friday evening."

"Fine, I'll have my things there," Virginia replied, getting ready to move on. But Mrs. Johnson's eyes had already searched Virginia's person and come to rest on the canvas protruding from the shopping bag.

"My goodness, what have you got there?"

"It's nothing, really."

"Oh my, it's one of your paintings. Let me see!"

Virginia glared at Mrs. Johnson's florid, eager face. *Fine,* she thought with a surge of malice. *Let her see.*

"I'm doing this for a class at the community college," Virginia said with exaggerated sweetness. She pulled out the painting and held it up. "Do you like it?"

Mrs. Johnson stared at the jagged, swirling shapes on the canvas and her mouth dropped open. "I . . . well . . ." she stammered, turning a deep pink.

"Well, what do you think?" Virginia pressed.

Mrs. Johnson's eyes darted back and forth between the canvas and Virginia's face. "I don't know what to say," she mumbled. "I guess I just . . . I don't understand these things."

Mrs. Johnson seemed to shrink like a small wounded animal. Behind her frightened eyes Virginia glimpsed the raw glare of an empty room. She felt suddenly ashamed.

"It's just a study," Virginia said gently, touching Mrs. Johnson's arm. "It's not supposed to look like anything in particular."

They stood there for a long moment. Something between them shifted, rose up, hovered in the air. Virginia kept her hand on Mrs. Johnson's arm, as if to keep her from whirling away.

Dance of Time

Bonnie West

"Just once I wish you'd ask me, and not wait for me to tell you. I mean, just one time you could say, 'Tilly, how was class today?' Is that asking so much?"

Leo looks at his wife of forty-eight years, sitting across from him in the same place she has sat for thousands of meals. Her small, pointed chin is thrust forward, giving her the determined look he admires. Her long, gray hair is piled on top of her head; the Gibson-girl style she had so many hairdos ago has returned and he loves it. He feels they are superbly well-matched but lately she is driving him crazy.

"For your information, class was wonderful," Tilly adds.

"I'm glad," Leo says, reaching for the brown-and-serve dinner rolls while Tilly is still blessing the meal. All he wants is some peace and quiet but she has been at him ever since his retirement, nagging him to join this or that, to go with her here or there.

She begins to tell him about her CPR class at the Y. While talking, she imagines him choking on a chunk of meat loaf . . . imagines administering the Heimlich maneuver . . . saving his life . . . forgoing his $75,000 life insurance. . . .

Leo waves his fork at her. "You like those classes with initials," he says. "Now it's CPR, last week IBM computer class, and let's not forget the IRS and YOU. At least you're too old for a PMS class. Ha ha!" He jabs a potato with the fork and stuffs the whole buttery ball into his mouth.

Tilly wonders why she bothers making parslied new potatoes; they're delicate, even though they are canned, and he is too big a slob to appreciate them. "And what," she asks, "will happen if I have a heart attack and you don't know CPR?"

"I'll have some peace and quiet, that's what!" He grins as he sops up grease and gravy with a piece of bread. "No more crazy ladies in the living room."

Tilly is always holding classes in their house. The last he'd interrupted was a spiritual circle. Tilly had rushed to him, cooing and coaxing him back upstairs. When she got him in their room, she rubbed up against him, and with her lips brushing the white hairs in his ears, whispered, "It's yoga, Leo; we need to concentrate."

"Yoga?" he'd said. "Does that mean no more steaks and chops?"

"Oh Leo, just stay up here a little longer and I'll make it up to you." Tilly rested her hand gently on his chest, slipped her finger between the buttons, and circled her nail around his coarse chest hairs. "I promise." With that she'd raised herself up on her toes and kissed his blushing ear.

Two hours later, when the class was over, she'd kept her promise. He could never stay angry at Tilly for long.

Leo finishes his meal and gulps coffee from his "World's Greatest Grandpa" mug.

"I was thinking," says Tilly, "my ballroom dance class starts tomorrow but afterward maybe I should take something more exciting. I'm in pretty good shape. I could join a swim team, learn scuba diving, even rock climbing. What do you think?"

"Did you make dessert?"

Tilly goes into the kitchen. "I did not," she calls. "I never do."

"My mother always made peach cobbler."

"A lot of good it did her. She should have learned to take care of herself instead of eating all those cobblers. And so should you. You never do anything but watch TV. Why don't you come to the dance class with me tomorrow? It'll be fun. Don't be such a dud, Leo."

Tilly comes back to the table and plops a small dish of Neapolitan ice cream in front of him, and with a flamboyant bow—which she learned at Seniors Onstage, dances back to the kitchen.

Leo shovels all the ice cream onto the spoon and sucks it in and out of his mouth, like he's always done since he was a boy. When it's all gone, he joins Tilly in the kitchen. She is doing the dishes and he snuggles up behind her and wraps his arms around her shoulders. "I'm sorry I don't love classes. But I love *you*, Til."

She twirls and snaps the dishrag at him. "Take that, swine!" The cloth slaps Leo's thigh as he leaps out of the way. "And that!" Tilly catches him on his calf as he scoots out of the kitchen. She laughs, unaware of her anger, and calls after him, "Maybe sky diving."

Tilly returns to the dishes. She is whistling now.

Leo sits in his chair, listening to her off-key rendition of "I'm Just a Girl Who Can't Say No." He looks at the newspaper, but his mind is elsewhere. He is imagining Tilly standing boldly at an open plane door, her hair sweeping circles around her face. . . . She steps calmly into space, plummets down and down. He stands helpless, watching for her chute to open. It gently rocks her back to earth then, unaware of his own anger, he imagines a sudden wind jerks her forward and snaps her neck, leaving him standing alone for the rest of his life. . . .

He goes back to the kitchen, takes her in his arms, and slowly waltzes her around the room. Soap bubbles pop on his neck where Tilly holds him.

The next morning Leo waves from the doorway as Tilly backs her car out of the garage. Specks of dark green paint crumble from the wood frame where he leans his hand.

She turns and calls, "Change your mind and come dancing with me?"

"Not this time, Til."

She blows a kiss and takes off.

Leo stands in the kitchen where the night before they'd danced across the no-wax floor. He goes to the cupboard to get some cereal. What he really wants is poached eggs with cottage cheese and corned-beef hash. He delights in stirring the yellow and white and brown of it together to form a new color. In his mind, it is the color of sand and reminds him of their honeymoon in Arizona. "This is the perfect color to paint the trim on the house," he'd told Tilly. "'Desert Sand.'"

"What does a Swede like you know about the desert?" Tilly disapproved of his habit of mixing food together. "It's not 'Desert Sand,'" she'd insisted. "It's 'Swedish Tan.'"

"She doesn't know the first thing about eating," he says out loud, wishing she were there to cook.

He sets the cereal box on the table and opens the refrigerator. The lightbulb is burned out. Tilly said she'd replace it, but he doesn't want her to. Lightbulbs are his department.

"Today I'll get that bulb," he says, reaching for the milk. Tilly has tricked him again. He had reluctantly agreed to 2 percent, instead of the rich, good kind he likes, and now it's down to 1 percent. "I'll speak to her," he confides to the missing child on the carton.

He carries the bowl to the dining room table, spilling it as he goes, and sits facing the kitchen cupboards. He likes looking at them. He made them himself, but it must be thirty years since he pounded the last nail.

Leo finishes his cereal and switches on a TV talk show he hates. Perverted guests, stupid talk, screaming. At noon he goes to buy the refrigerator bulb.

Tilly is glad to be away from him. She drives off, irritated that he has managed to upset her first-day-of-class excitement. She had misinterpreted last night's intimacy, thinking he would come to the dance class. *I wish he'd take better care of himself,* she thinks. *He used to work so hard. Now all he does is sit in front of the TV.* Some day she intends to take a photography class so she can snap a picture of him napping in front of his favorite soap opera. With the camera she could capture both the title screen, *The Young and the Restless,* and the sleeping Leo.

Tilly pulls into the shopping mall in front of the dance studio. By habit, she smooths the front of her navy blue skirt, brushing away unseen crumbs and wrinkles, and checks her lipstick in the car door mirror. Satisfied, and finally feeling first-day eagerness, she pushes open the pink and gray door—careful not to smudge the shiny brass plate, and enters the room.

She is pleased to see she is not the first to arrive. Several women and a gray-haired, dark-skinned man are milling about, chatting. The man is her type—dark and Latin—and she hopes he will choose her as his partner. She doesn't want to dance with another woman.

The man approaches. "Allow me to introduce myself."

Tilly is amazed; she has never heard anyone say that except in books. She smiles her most gracious smile.

"I'm Frank Giordano, former member of the Minneapolis Symphony, and present participant in the ballroom dance class for beginners. Would it be asking too much to invite you to be my partner . . . for the class?"

"I'd love it." Tilly is suddenly shy. She knows she must say something else and blurts, "What a grand goatee." She wonders if it conceals a weak chin.

The lesson begins and Tilly and Frank are silent, concentrating very hard on their feet. They are not good dancers, but gradually become more confident.

Tilly feels pressure on the small of her back. He is pulling her in. She resists and the effort makes her stumble.

"Forgive me," exclaims Frank. "I'm afraid all my rhythm is in my mouth, and not my feet." He smiles. "Clarinet. That's what I play."

"Ah." Tilly laughs. The man amuses her; however, he has such bad breath she must keep her head turned when he speaks.

"How is it you decided to take ballroom dancing, Mr. Giordano?"

"Please call me Frank," he says in a louder tone than usual. With her ear turned to him, he must think her hard of hearing.

"All right, Frank. Is ballroom dancing an interest of yours?"

"Indeed," he answers, thrusting forward and squeezing her right hand in his. "I used to play for the symphony, but my greatest love was moonlighting with the Mello Tones Dance Band. Perhaps you heard of us?" He continues before Tilly has a chance to lie. "We played all the great spots—Prom on the Midway, Waconia, and the Minnesota State Fair. People loved the big bands in those days. And everybody danced. I always thought I'd love it too, but I was always providing the music and never dancing. So here I am, learning late, but not too late since now I've met you. Tilly. Such an interesting name. Is this your given name?"

"*Non Monsieur,*" answers Tilly with a lilting French accent. "Matilde Marie DuPres, now known as"—and she switches to a heavy Swedish intonation—"Tilly Halvorson."

He laughs.

She wonders, as they box step in silence, *When did I change?*

After class, Frank asks Tilly if she will have lunch with him. They are on the sidewalk outside the studio. He is standing inside her personal space—a term she learned in her Assertiveness for Seniors class—and she keeps edging back. His breath is repulsive. She thinks the foul odor might be garlic, hopes it's not decaying teeth.

Frank cranes toward her. "You're certain you won't change your mind?"

"No, I mean, yes." Tilly backs away another inch or two. "But thank you so much." She is hoping to dance with him in tomorrow's class. He may not be Leo but at least he's a man.

"Well, then," Frank says, "perhaps next time, Matilde." Suddenly, he leans forward.

Tilly sees him coming and turns her face. His lips land on her ear. She scurries to her car, waves, and drives away.

Leo is standing outside the hardware store, not far from Tilly and Frank. The little brown sack, which now contains a shattered refrigerator bulb, lies at his feet. He waits until Tilly drives off, then slowly retrieves the bag and climbs into his old, black Ford pickup. He wraps his hands around the steering wheel, rests his forehead between them, and imagines Tilly in the arms of that oily-looking man, dancing a tango on his grave. After a while, he opens the truck door and reenters the hardware store.

Tilly does not go directly home. It is a beautiful day and she has actually enjoyed the coy exchange. She feels like driving. She heads for Lake of the Isles and follows the one-way road which takes her around Lake Calhoun and Harriet. She loves this ride. She whistles show tunes and makes a second loop. Twenty miles of wasted gas makes her feel like a rebel.

On the way home, she stops at a supermarket where she rarely shops since it is so expensive, but where she knows she will find the fancy, extra-strong English mints she needs for Frank. She browses, finally buying the mints and some pistachio nuts for Leo.

She is worried about Leo's mood, since she missed making his lunch as well as his breakfast. She called from the market and when he didn't answer, she pictured him asleep in front of the television. *My poor old Leo,* she thinks as she pulls into their driveway.

Leo is up on a ladder that is leaning against the house.

"Leo!"

"Just look at this, Til." He dips a brush into a can and splats paint on a spot of freshly scraped wood. "I mixed it myself. 'Desert Sand.' Remember?"

This time she doesn't correct him. "I like it," she says. And for a long time, she stands there, admiring the new paint brightening the old house, and Leo's still attractive body, dancing as he works.

The Inheritance

Joanne Seltzer

I've learned to accept the medical diagnosis:
female pattern alopecia, a hereditary disorder.

If I live to marvel at my eightieth birthday
baby-pink scalp will shine shamelessly
through silky strands of fine white hair.

But if passing years can somehow transform me
into a woman worn bald with wisdom,
dignified and lovable despite eccentricity,
I'll proudly wear my glossy-headed legacy
in memory of my maternal grandmother.

Born to an age of braids and ribbons,
afflicted in every bone of her skull
by the pain of Victorian women,
my grandmother combed and knotted her losses.

Baby Boomer!

Dianalee Velie

This was the year I was sure great things would happen, to be specific, I was turning fifty. I was even looking forward to it. With all the celebrity baby boomers turning fifty, I was in stellar company. Even our president had reached the big 5-0. I must admit though, the year did not turn out exactly as I had expected. Pumped up by the glorious readings of all those celebrities turning fifty, I had approached this year with high expectations. After all, I was vitaminized, supplemented, and exercised. I looked fine and felt great. My poetry and short stories sold well last year, I loved my adjunct positions, and now was the chance to complete my novel and luxuriate in the status of older woman and crone. I was ready to accept my inner beauty and concentrate on spiritual growth. Hey, I knew how to do that. I was, of course, a product of the sixties. But life has a funny way of interfering with our best thought-out plans. I attacked my novel with new gusto and then lightning struck, literally and figuratively. But I'm jumping to the conclusion. All that happened last. Let me start at the beginning of my fiftieth year.

First my daughter divorced her husband and moved back home from Texas. No problem. Our house was big and the nest was empty. For a kid who left for college, it seemed like only a few years ago, with a couple of trunks, I was amazed when the moving van, complete with two cars and a household of furniture, was unloaded at my front door. So, I could deal with two of everything. My attic groaned and said, "Get real." It was her two big dogs, who thought the word "cat" was a four-letter word and terrorized my felines with foamy breath, who sent panic to my heart. I kept serenely telling myself, while taking deep breaths, that all three of my precious kitties died of old age this year, not terror.

As soon as my daughter was nestled all snug in her bed once again, my mom was diagnosed with breast cancer. My sister and I made the decision to bring her from New Jersey to Connecticut for treatment. No problem. She is in a wheelchair. The dining room on the first floor became her bedroom, along with a catchall for my daughter's belongings. Chemotherapy was started and radiation followed. At this point I forgot I was even turning fifty. My friends rallied around and everyone shared in taking mom to her appointments, while I juggled a job, husband, mother, daughter, graduate school applications, and an occasional peek at my novel. Mom's spirits soared, while mine hid somewhere in the basement, determined to find a nonexistent wine cellar. Living with three generations of women in the house can be a very humbling, humiliating experience. Just ask my husband. He tells me it is and I believe him. He would never lie. Oh, he may stay at the office until 9 or 10 p.m. these days, but lie, no, not ever. Unless, of course, you count the whopper when he pats me on the head and says everything's okay. Excuse me!

It was getting to the point where I was afraid to answer the phone. When my son and his wife called from Miami every week, I did reverse Lamaze breathing exercises while cradling the receiver, praying their marriage was wonderful and their jobs fulfilling. Please, no other returns to the womb. I was beginning to think my kids were born with bungee cords where their umbilical cords should have been. I'm hearing from friends that it's the genetic phenomenon of our age.

My writing was taking a backseat. I needed to escape and headed for the hills, to ski of course. I've loved the sport for over thirty years, with never an injury, but fate was full of folly and I came home with a torn knee cartilage. What in God's name enticed me to try snowboarding? I will never know. Hey, dude! I was facing death in the face. Put that on your board and eat it. Racing down the mountain backward on a first-aid sled gives you plenty of time for reflection and high anxiety. How was I to manipulate my crutches and my mother's wheelchair?

Miracles do happen and they are called friends. With therapy, my friends, and a glass of wine here and there, healing went quickly, smoothly, and luckily no surgery was required. My life was starting to sound more like a country-western tune than the poetry that usually slid so easily from my pen.

When my beloved, beautiful, black quarter horse, Andy, my confidant, therapist, and soul mate, died peacefully in his sleep in April, I knew I should buy a ten-gallon hat and start singing. Alas, there was still more to follow. My dog, Spunky, developed allergies, sneezed and broke my nose, so I not only limped, I had a cast on my nose. Terrified of thunder, this same big sweet dog chewed through two kitchen doors and jumped through one basement window. Two surgeries and several thousand dollars later, he is recuperating nicely. I briefly thought about petitioning Hillary Clinton to consider animal health care insurance, but never found the time. But Spunky is easy to take care of considering my other old dog, Mia, picked this moment to have a stroke. No offense to the dead, but walking her now is like walking George Burns. Another letter to Hillary was composed in my mind about long-term animal care benefits, but I let it slide.

The *pièce-de-résistance,* I have saved for last. With just three days to go until my fiftieth birthday. Lightning struck my husband's office where I was happily working on the computer. I got the shock of my life—fingers and neck still tingle—as I watched the roof cave in and the rain pour down. I screamed with fright. It was the last thing to be heard from me for a while. I lost my voice completely. I was silenced and told by the doctor not to speak for at least two weeks while my french-fried vocal cords healed. If I heard one more joke about how lucky my husband was, I was ready to give up my novel, not that I could even remember what I was writing about, and become an axe murderess.

I called out to a Supreme Being and asked her (it must be a her) to cut the theatrics. If she was trying to send me a message, couldn't we work in a more direct medium, say like channeling the message through my computer keyboard? I promised I'd listen.

But, back to my birthday. My mom, sister, aunt, daughter, and best friend gave a great surprise party for me and I was truly speechless. This forced silence had given me time to look inward and observe, not only my own party, but also my own heart. There were many friends there, both old and new, who have touched my life. Each one of them shared a special moment in time with me. Times when I really needed my friends. Times when I reached out and someone was always there. And there they were again. All of us ready to go boom, turn fifty. I know the stories of their lives as well as they know mine. Many of them have put dreams on hold while taking care of those they love. So my visions of finishing my novel by my birthday have gone, but I know it will be finished.

Life has presented me with circumstances that force me to acknowledge what is truly important. The love of family and friends we baby boomers sought in the sixties will sustain us through all the comic and tragic upheavals of middle age, taking us serenely into old age with our arms around one another.

Amanda

Elisavietta Ritchie

Drat, no matter how slowly I pry the screen door, that falsetto click-click-click. But this time it can't wake Mrs. Bromley: my hands—cramped, horrid—managed to dribble *my* morphine into *her* strawberry milkshake. Drop by drop, one, two, three, four, six—

Whose are those slender horses across our field? Foals of my old palominos? I taught children, grandchildren, to ride them. Blue ribbons, shiny under dust, still flutter above the stalls. But didn't I have to sell our horses? How did—?

Deer. Big enough to saddle and bridle. When the farm was fenced, deer stayed in woods and fields. Fences broken, woods thinned, fields up the road manicured into lawns and "housing estates," deer take refuge here. Too early for oaks or apple trees, to produce bounty for them, and though it's already August the vegetable garden lies fallow, so deer are trimming grass that someone, I forget his name, meant to mow. I prefer meadows to lawns, deer to noisy machines.

Careful with these old porch stairs. Hold both iron banisters. . . . Rusted. Keep your balance! And watch you don't talk to yourself aloud: *they* say I do now. But except for the occasional grandchild, no one's left to talk with seriously.

Oh, sorry, osprey, I didn't mean to scare you from your dead sycamore. At least your soprano peep-peep is too feeble to wake Mrs. Bromley, or distract the two brown thrashers cavorting like lovers in a dust puddle, or the great blue heron stalking the shallows, each footstep deliberate, elegant.

How painful my footsteps. Each stabs through my soles. Dear Granny, forgive me that as a child I didn't pay enough homage to your aches.

Careful, a forgotten croquet ball—watch for wickets—No, that was a terrapin I almost tripped on. Football sized. Hello, old girl. You lumber ashore late every year: here's the "X" naughty grandson Noah carved on your dark green shell. Sorry about that. Glad I stuck around through June, when except for laggards like you, most turtles clambered ashore to lay eggs. From the veranda I'd note where they're digging, so I could direct Noah where to find the leathery eggs for transfer to flower pots inside where raccoons can't get them. Sometimes, within weeks, hatchlings are scrambling around. The old turkey roaster is their holding tank until Noah can escort hatchlings to the river. Next June, Noah promises—

Poor Terrapin X, you're exhausted digging, but you've still got to make the river before the tide—wheelbarrow blocks your way. With my cane, I'll nudge you, like a ball, toward the riverbank. We both have journeys ahead.

What, all three piebald cats? Now you, Snowball, and I've got to brush your white angora fur. Left eye blue, right eye green, throwback to nobler ancestry. . . . Winter nights, you fellows warm better than hot water bottles. Today I left you stretched on windowsills, barely stirring to chase katydids. Okay, come along, but don't trip me.

"You're a benevolent witch surrounded by familiars," Judge Reilly said, watching me feed apple cores to raccoons while bantams clucked around. "No wonder you're named Amanda. That's Latin: She who must be loved." Or was it *she who must love?*

Judge Reilly, my last love, now dead as the rest. . . . At least we stayed uncaged, outfoxed officious social workers who think everyone old should be incarcerated. They call my critters another sign of "unhealthy isolation—you should have moved, been moved, into our new state-of-the-art Home surrounded by well-kept lawns and friendly folks your age. And a trained staff."

Not "questionable" women like Mrs. Bromley. Bless you, Judge Reilly, for springing her from jail. Mrs. B's braining her common-law spouse with an iron skillet was unquestioned self-defense. Three half-fried eggs, splattered along with her blood, proved evidence enough. I vouched for her character, and she shows her gratitude by looking after me. Nowadays, others must fetch groceries, help me dress, push that blasted wheelchair. So willy-nilly I'm cared for. . . . But the woman chatters constantly, tidies so nobody can find anything. Why does she stay, when she feels uneasy out here?

"You never know who'll pull down that long dirt road, or row ashore, hide in them woods," Mrs. Bromley warns. Nervous Nelly, checking the umbrella stand in the front hall for old baseball bats. Hockey sticks by the back door. Relics from eras the lawn sported a diamond, and the river froze solid. "A woman alone—"

They can't understand: after an overpopulated life I want solitude. People surrounded me even *in utero:* my fetal brain surely heard clamor around my ballooning mother. Siblings Agatha, Horace, Hammond, twins Edna and Etta, all bossed me till they left the farm for jobs elsewhere. Sad, how the girls ended their lives slowly in "retirement communities," the brothers died quickly on highways. . . . Later, Burt took over the bossing, his bluster, sometimes violence, enough for six men. I tried not to boss Burt Jr. and Madeleine more than necessary.

Dear Granny, like you, I played the piano, sang, and read aloud *The Wind in the Willows, Sea-Beach at Ebb Tide,* poems, to pupils, children, grandchildren. Even before they were born I tuned to Saturday operas and Sunday symphonies on the radio—I've read that fetuses absorb Mozart—though Burt switched to hillbilly. Still, Granny, our children came out all right: Madeleine played piano, granted mostly show tunes, and Burtie Jr.'s trumpet sounded like a wounded bull moose. Madeleine's Sylvie, and Burtie's Noah and Joshua, were almost born singing. What if fetuses hear only heavy metal, rap?

Now Noah's like that heron, tall, thin, graying. Joshua's more osprey: plumper, hunched, fierce glare, retreats with feeble arguments. And Sylvie, too small to dance *Swan Lake,* our wren.

A sagging rainbow of colors dangles like a dead toucan from a pine: abandoned birthday balloons. Dear Sylvie, you love decorating. Remember how, when your pony turned two, you festooned the barn with balloons till they spooked him?

How many winter birthdays, inside snow forts, we ate cakes hot from the oven! Summer birthdays, sticky with ice cream, everyone jumped off the pier, dodging crabs and jellyfish and at night kicking up fireworks of luminescence in the silky river.

The river where I'm heading. Somehow . . . turtle-slow . . .

As for parties you grandchildren give for me, I know each is expected to be my last. Ninety, ninety-one, ninety-two, was the last ninety-seven? Have I fooled everyone, if not myself, long enough? Like those drooping balloons still dancing in the wind . . . a perpetual ring-around-the-rosy.

Like those generations I taught at the schoolhouse. . . . If parents were ill or fighting, I kept their children. Rescued mothers from abusive husbands, tending their bruises as I tended my own.

As one old bruise fades, another purples, but nowadays I blame epidermis aged thin as onionskin, wear long-sleeved blouses Mrs. B calls a disgrace. "Torn! Stained! Rags! What if someone sees you?"

Visitors only appear by mistake. "I've become too much of a hag to entertain," I told that persistent new minister come to determine if I've made my peace with God.

"God is my gardener. I let Him do his job in peace. Now He lets the farm follow its own designs. While it could use human intervention, I don't need any man to intercede between God and myself."

How the minister twitched when wrens swooped through unscreened windows to their nest on the mantel. Then a leopard frog leaped from the sill onto my shoulder.

"Just chasing mosquitoes," I explained.

When the frog landed on his knee, he leapt. "My wife's waiting—"

His sweet mousy wife, cowering under his disapproving eyes.

I never asked those abused wives, *Why stay married?* I myself couldn't have left you, Burt, since on the eve of our marriage, you bought the failing farm from my failing grandmother. She disapproved your smoking—"tobacco leaches the lungs as well as the soil—but at least the homestead stays in the family."

What was it canceled our promised honeymoon in Paris? Was it expanding your hardware store you spent the money on, or the pack of hounds so you could "ride like a proper gentleman?" I didn't argue. I was seventeen, in teacher's college, but began agriculture courses, farmed, bore two babies, taught, gradually saved, and one July took

Burt Jr. and Madeleine to France. During our absence, first you rode my favorite mare too hard after foxes, ruined both forelegs, shot her "mercifully."

Then, arguing for better cash crops than corn or soybeans, you planted tobacco. How could you! Grandmother's ghost was outraged. Shufflings in the bedroom ceiling might be snakes in the attic, but knockings on walls at night when no trees grew close enough to hit the house could only—

After tobacco harvest, we planted winter wheat, and noises diminished. Pots, plates, and paintings still fell on their own whenever you flew into your rages.

Lately, after decades of absence, Granny again visits my dreams. Mother and Father too. Sometimes Edna, Etta, Horace, Hammond, and Agatha. Their ghostly visits aren't scary; everyone's laughing and talking. Welcoming? I've missed you all. And last night—

But Granny, it was Burt, not I, who moved Father and Mother to the ramshackle Institution for the Elderly when their friends were living and dying at home. Father called it "The Wrinkle Factory," others "a fire trap." It was.

Now you are all long in the cemetery. Burt, not long enough. And don't you return.

Granny, when Madeleine died of leukemia, her distraught young husband—what was his name?—joined the merchant marine but sent little Sylvie dolls from distant ports long after she'd outgrown toys. Burtie Jr. died in a noncombat accident in an army jeep after his wife took up with a horny colonel, leaving Noah and Joshua for me to raise along with Sylvie. Natural they'd leave the farm for college and jobs, but bless them, holidays draw them back.

"Oh, Gramanda! Another litter of kittens under your bed!" "Look, a magnificent black snake in the wisteria!" "They'll settle your mice."

Would I could move swiftly as cats, snakes, or mice now.

Yet, finally, I am slipping away . . . as from Burt's parties, loose ends of chatter, music, smells of spilled beer and grilled deer wafting after. The men complimented me on my cabbage salads, apple cakes, and same old blue dress, but under Burt's watchful eye, didn't bother me, not then. Wives complimented me on the salads and cakes, averting their eyes from my same blue dress, rather low cut, but, intimidated by my schoolmarm reputation, didn't bother me either, glad if I walked their kids around the farm.

If I went alone, Burt trailed me, his hawking and coughing preceding him. "Why in hell you sneaking off, woman? My buddies are having great fun after a great hunt! You meeting someone in the woods?"

Though I'd not planned to meet anyone, Burt, first you accused me of self-righteousness, swung so hard I rejoined the party, my face purpling.

Yet Father's words, spoken when as a child I complained of siblings teasing, echo still: *Don't play the victim, darling. Work to become stronger and brighter than everyone else.* Yes, Father, I repeated your advice to Madeleine and Burt Jr., later to Noah, Joshua, and Sylvie, in between, to hundreds of pupils.

Only after you'd all gone your ways, did I emerge from any cocoon of self-righteousness, and sneak off to meet anyone.

Sad, to outlive lovers. . . .

Nowadays caregivers are instructed—I've overheard the social worker—"Keep close watch; the old gal's known to stray. Thinks she can still walk to the mailbox or sail the boat." Finally deeming me incapable of navigation beyond the veranda, Mrs. Bromley relaxes.

This afternoon, I tricked you. While you were napping, collapsed like an old sailbag or spent balloon. You'll sleep for hours. Like the dead, though dead don't snore like chain saws. Bless Roxanol.

It took my magnifying glass to decipher the tiny print. Each ml of Roxanol contains: morphine sulphate 20 mg. What was it I learned long ago when I crammed basic chemistry? My darn eyes gave out before I could unravel the formula and warnings. Sometimes the stuff is tinted or flavored.

Strawberry milkshakes mask additives.

The morality of my actions doesn't trouble me: on occasion, when they thought me asleep, I've watched both Mrs. Bromley and fill-in caregivers filching my medications. One drop-in nurse transferred my morphine to her nasal spray bottle, then when I observed her sniffing it, protested, "Anyone would catch cold in this drafty old house, ma'am."

Is morphine easier on the gastrointestinal track if inhaled?

I suspect you've been increasing my dosage, muddling my mind. Deliberately? So you can turn soap operas high?

"At that modrun convalescent home where I normally work," one nurse insisted through pinched lips, "we're taught television keeps even comatose patients from feeling isolated."

"I *prefer* isolation. Please turn that thing off."

My sewing scissors managed to close on the cord, but someone replaced it. Since then I can't locate any scissors. "Disappeared" in case I, who complain of living too long in pain, take it into my head—?

Today, pains undiminished but limbs unusually flexible, head clear thanks to my holiday from medications, I've made it across the yard. *Made it,* not *walked* or even *limped*. Ungainly, I wobble from tree to tree. . . .

How many have invaded the lawn! First, crabapple saplings, then hawthorns, crepe myrtles, spindly maples; finally pines. Around the perimeter, long-standing cedars and oaks: pin, water, and willow oaks. I keep mental lists of trees the way Burt inventoried his innumerable sizes of bolts and nails, screws, wires, pipes, and ropes.

The cats wander off: mole or shrew here, striped skink there. Bored by my slow pace?

My heart's pounding, like winter waves against the pier. Let's rest a moment—locate the Adirondack chairs I repainted. . . . A flash of white by the berry patch—I'll sit—

What, risk not being able to pull myself up again? No. Or as Burt would say, Hey-ell, no!

The white was the tail of a buck vaulting into the briars. His half snort, half sneeze sounded like Burt when he came.

Drat! I'm wearing not slacks or a skirt, but a bathrobe! Mrs. Bromley, you forgot to dress me! Assumed I'd return to bed after lunch, why bother. Heavens, I'm not bedridden yet! At least when you stuff me into a chair to confront some tasteless pureed mess— Cain killed Abel over porridge like *this*?—my wrists aren't tied to bedrails "to prevent escape."

At least the bathrobe has pockets. And you didn't check them.

But I'm wearing silly slipper socks! No wonder all the pebbles and sticks hurt my feet.

And what a tangle of thorns. Vines keep snatching me, scratching, almost trip—if I fell, could I get up?—what stupidity, forgetting the berry patch! Last month you—no, Mrs. B, you're too portly—a grandchild, Noah? Joshua? Sylvie?—indulged me by wheeling the chair while I filled the colander with blackberries.

"Persons your age," you warned, "should avoid raw fruit, especially what don't come packaged from supermarkets."

"Nonsense. Not my stomach dying on me, just bones. Et cetera." Damn the *et cetera*. I swallowed the berries whole, the only ill-effects my inky clothes. Unfashionable anyway. And wasn't that clever, how I stuffed the last berries into Burt's silver flask with a tablespoon of sugar, and in a later private moment, filled the remaining space with vodka! More palatable than morphine. Also more organic. Noah would approve. What was it he studied? Botany? Or was that Joshua? Biology?

The flask is now in my bathrobe pocket.

Crows! Your alarms could wake the dead, or the drugged. You eye me evilly. Please don't caw! And osprey, back on your dead sycamore, vigilant but silent. And nothing perturbs you, heron? So slender and stately, your head high, dive for a minnow, then—goodness, you've speared an eel! What a tussle! Finally you wangle one end into your beak, raise your head so it slips down your gullet—like Noah eating spaghetti—then stretch to stab the sky. Don't you ever get dizzy?

I'm dizzy. They say I'm losing a half pound a week, refusing that mess of porridge. No wonder I'm hungry. Mrs. B, we'll have fish for supper. I'll drop a line off the pier and catch a catfish, a big whiskered monster. Carrots and tarragon from the garden—

Garden! Reabsorbed by forest. Last hurricane tore the planks from the pier. Noah and Joshua promise to replace them. As for supper— did I forget my itinerary? Onward! Right foot, left foot—or, what Grandfather said soldiers marched to in the Civil War, "Hay foot, straw foot, belly full of bean soup." That's how I taught my pupils right from left. *Let's play Giant Steps. . . .*

Ouch! Help, I've fallen into the underbrush! Lost my balance. . . . Pain spears my left shoulder, might be broken. Same shoulder shattered at age ten, falling off a horse leaping a jump too high. Again I'm cushioned—pincushioned—by blackberry and wild rose thorns. A fakir's bed of nails.

But the flask's intact.

Sun burns through the leaves. Oh, dear, not just berry leaves: poison ivy. A mean joke, to die imprisoned by thorns and breaking into rashes! An ugly corpse I'd make, scratched, blistered, and bloated. If no one found me until winter when foliage dies, I'd resemble that deer skeleton in the marsh. Aesthetically preferable, if not how I envisioned my vaulted solitude.

Madeleine imagined her own—rotting—body "like the pallid innards of the last watermelon in the garden, the one we should have left." Dear Madeleine, you loved metaphors, poetry. I recall one poem we memorized: "O Captain! my captain! our fearful trip—" But I preferred novels in those minutes when I wasn't studying about crops or some newfangled machine Burt brought home to test but he refused to read directions.

"Yet with poetry," Madeleine claimed, "I devour much more in a short time." Foreseeing you'd have only a short time? You read to little Sylvie "The Owl and the Pussycat" and all Granny's old favorites I'd read to you. . . . You chose poems you wanted, at the end. Yes, Maddy, I read them to you, and to Sylvie. Did it help either of us feel less alone?

Earlier, I wouldn't have dreamed of dying alone. After all the crowded occasions of others' passings, that claptrap of bedside vigils, long faces, forced smiles or forced tears, all those congenital—or do I mean congenial—rituals in which one automatically participates. Some of my tears were very real indeed. . . .

How brittle, dry, are—stiffs. As a child, seeing Grandfather laid out, I asked Granny: "If he could stay soft, would he somehow keep alive?"

And Burt, your funeral comes to mind. More dignified than deserved, but I kept up the farce. Including regarding the demise, attributed to coronary thrombosis. You yourself downed all those peculiar pills with a bottle of Jim Beam, you'd sent me out to feed your yapping hounds. When you expired, no hound howled, as a dying master's dogs do in books. Neither did they complain when I parceled them out among your old buddies, on condition nobody bring them back to chase my critters. Gave away your dead stag heads from every wall. Several of those buddies kept showing up at odd hours offering help around the farm: *Such a pretty widow. Isn't she lonely?*

She is not, thanks, and she drives the tractor, and the grandchildren handle chores. Corn, wheat, and soybeans green as ever. No tobacco.

Did I become captain of my own ship?

Oh, Burt, how people smiled at that huge granite stone you'd ordered with bas-reliefs of hounds! "Blessed hounds of heaven," the old minister said, wryly. Rather, *hounds of hell*. Carved beneath your name: "and his wife Amanda." Only dates needed chiseling in.

Ha! I *will* escape lying beside you for eternity. Listening to your bones rattle as you cough.

But I *must* get up! Yet if I stay still, it hurts less. I'll rest just a moment.

After the wake, I learned of your last business deal: selling our fields across the road to a developer. I admit, some of that money later helped the grandchildren through college. After your funeral expenses.

"Fireworks, firewater, and all the venison a body could eat," your buddies kept recounting. "The old fart's wake was a blast!"

And a blessing. So might mine be, even absent a body to bless.

Every blessed possession—generations' legacies of pictures, books, china, silver, and jewelry—I've given the grandchildren already because, as Mrs. Bromley warned, "You no longer know everyone in town."

"Kitchen stainless feeds you good as silver," she says. "So what pots are dented, plates chipped, *you* don't notice."

I do notice bared walls and shelves, but pretend to prefer less clutter. Isn't accustoming myself to space—Outer Space—wise?

That real estate agent we discovered nosing around, urged someone phone Goodwill to collect the creaking beds, sagging sofas, threadbare sheets, tattered towels, dented canning cauldrons, wood stove, even the tone-deaf piano, "before your heirs sell the place."

Granny, I've other plans than let developers grind up your land, lucrative though this might be for them.

A decade ago, though Motor Vehicles wouldn't renew my license, I drove the battered pickup into the village. I should say now, *town*. Bob Reilly, that bright young lawyer unaware his grandfather had been more than "just a family friend," notarized my will designating the land as a wildlife preserve, the house a shelter for battered women. Always some in need. Those dusty canning cauldrons feed thirty. Piano and furniture *are* repairable. The cats are provided for with sacks of kibbles which they guard against mice. My "immediate survivors" already enjoy their specified shares of cash that little by little I've withdrawn from the bank to spare them that meddling mess of accountants. Any money leftover will support the place. Despite travails, my life has frequently been happy; now let others jumpstart their lives.

Appropriate that Granny's Farm, never considered Burt's, serve this purpose.

Granny, you'd also approve of that young lawyer who comes around whenever Sylvie visits. Age ten, Sylvie confided, "Bobbie Reilly promised to marry me when we grow up." Now they are grown, do they think I don't know he sneaks into her bedroom?

My beloved Judge Reilly, you too would approve. Sad, finally this morning I thrust your letters in the woodstove. You insisted long ago I burn them, but you wrote so eloquently. To Mrs. B's consternation, charred bits litter the kitchen. Like the ashes I'd become if I listened to those people advocating cremation.

Does anyone advocate death by blackberry barbs and poison ivy? Fire *is* cleaner. . . .

Selfish to hang on so long, just for Noah, Josh, and Sylvie. If only Madeleine, and yes, little Burtie with his trumpet. . . .

This morning Madeleine waved from the vegetable garden while picking peas. Naturally a dream, no peas left by August.

No more time to mourn those departed, or stick around to see how the living turn out. I've overheard enough prognostications: first, "a year, at best," then "a month," now a whispered, "just a few days. . . ."

I've tried to follow Father's advice to "seize the day." Perhaps despite everyday responsibilities, problems, and now these darned infirmities, I *have* lived every day to the full, even those that left bruises and scars, figurative, literal. And pain reassures: you are alive.

Seize this hour—as if these ruined hands could seize anything.

Can't remain splat in the brambles. Was that the screen door creaking? And here come the cats. As if sensing my dilemma, you fellows cluster on my chest, in this heat—Stop licking my face! You, Snowball, especially furry—and especially visible, might betray—

Go home! Scat! Move!

I can't move. Must move. *Must* stretch my better hand, grab that thick vine sprouting—leaves glistening poison. Terribly slowly, muscle by bone. . . . Up, get up, pull myself up. . . . Cradle the arm, which outweighs old pains. Finally I can resume—my crazy pace.

Why must you cats—Mrs. Bromley knows you always follow me—

Pity the dinghy is beached high above the tide line. I'd drag it to the water, push off as if to meet you, my beloved Judge, once more. . . .

How many sunsets I've sailed or rowed to your duck blind on stilts, trailing lines so my excursions appeared purposeful. . . . Perch or bluefish did indeed bite: we'd scale and gut them, cooking on your Coleman stove. *After* a languid hour on the faded quilts. Granny's handiwork. Autumns and winters, strings of decoys floated from the blind. We never shot a bird. After tonging the waters below the pilings, we feasted on oysters and each other. I was your "Venus on a half shell."

Last night, dear Judge, you visited my dreams. Something about a boat.

That dinghy. On closer inspection: eelgrass spikes through the hull, wasps unfurl from under the bow. Mice tatted the sails into lace.

I'm a shipless, shiftless captain now. Can't take any cat to sea in a pea-green boat. Even without an owl.

Too early for owls. But last night a pair of them were *who-who-whoing* back and forth for an hour. Scared the daylights out of Mrs. B.

The riverbank is steep. I always knew where muskrat and otter hid their dens, though after the hurricane, they burrowed elsewhere. Just offshore, flotillas of turtles thrust periscope heads above greenish brown ripples. Minnows are schooling. Crabs patrol below. In deeper water, bluefish. So even leaving, I'll have critters, "familiars," dear dead Judge Reilly.

To die while making love! Rather, after.

We loved enough times to curl Snowball's fur, or that minister's bald head. . . .

Who will brush you now, my cats? But stop hovering! Darn sticktights. . . .

Or am I the sticktight?

I remember: Noah studied ecology, will run the refuge. Joshua's degree was in agriculture. And Sylvie, still crazy about horses, is a social worker, trained to run shelters. Mrs. Bromley can fuss over everyone, including cats.

I can disengage myself with serenity. Almost too perfect.

Suddenly I want to stick around to see how it all turns out! Like losing a good book before you've finished it. I'll resume my morphine, concoct cocktails of Percodan and OxyContin, let my zombied mind wander like that albatross it is becoming—

Then what, sleep my way to death? Hey-ell no!

"Lord help me! Where—"

That's Mrs. Bromley howling! Lord help her indeed, not enough drops of Roxanol in that milkshake. The woman will waddle like a huge snapper into the yard. Or up the drive, her charge escaped before—"Might fall—break everything—how could the old gal have fled wheelchair, house, yard—crawled the entire way to the road? Cars might strike her, someone might rob, kidnap, demand ransom— Sun setting already, Lord, help, we'll have to phone nine-one-one, launch a search—" You remember, Judge, how Mrs. B dislikes dealings with the law.

But as Burt said after a stag had wandered into his sights off-season and the police started inquiring, "There ain't no way those mother-fuckers are gonna find any carcass around here. *Hey-ell no!*"

The breeze is chilly for August. Yes, nights I am glad for cats.

The water will be warm. Damn, I can't bend to test it, or pull off these ridiculous slipper socks! Useless against oyster shells underfoot, jellyfish, crabs. Scratches bleeding so much, sharks would swim all the way upriver.

I'll float above them all.

First, blackberry vodka. . . . Wriggle it and me free of this blasted bathrobe. Venus again naked on her oyster shells—I'm laughing be-fore the first sip!

Sorry, heron, I didn't mean you to flap off croaking your disap-proval. Please don't attract any trackers.

Hey-ell, yes, down the vodka. . . . Slide down the bank. How light—no, clumsy—what silky water. . . . What strange joy!

Silver minnows tickle my thighs.

Beyond the river, out in the bay, beyond that, in the ocean, I'll nourish the fish that long nourished me. If they notice a trace of li-quor, how much tastier their catch.

JOYS

Pushing Sixty

Rina Ferrarelli

Pushing sixty in a fifty-five-mile per hour zone,
humming with the tires that roll on the pavement,
bouncing as the car bounces over cracks and potholes,
she moves away from what she knows so well,
and leaves the Dark Tunnel behind and the River of No Return,
she crosses bridge after bridge,
flowing with the current toward places unknown.
Trusting the spare legends of a map
and what wisdom she's gathered along the way,
she no longer makes excuses not to go,
afraid of getting lost, afraid of what she'll find,
as if surprises could never be good. She's no longer anxious,
hugging the rail, stuck in the right lane, and then worrying
about those Right Lane Must Turn Right signs
that could take her across a deep ravine, or a large
body of water to other places where she's never been.
She moves steadily and without hurry
In tune with the road humming under her, turning
and switching, and keeping with the flow.

A Different Woman

Joan Kip

> . . . Untwisting all the chains that tie
> The hidden soul of harmony.

> John Milton, *L'Allegro*

"Would you want Leo back?" I asked Marta. Widows for almost five years, Marta and I were drinking tea at the table in my dining room. Along the wall behind the table, photos of Art reside in proprietary grace, his lively, amused gaze following me around the house he built. After posing my question, though, I felt I'd uttered an unforgivable blasphemy. I wanted to bow apologetically in front of each of Art's photos, in the hope that public repentance might obliterate the heresy of my thoughts. Deep inside, I knew it was myself I was questioning.

Marta's reply was ambivalent. Her marriage to Leo knew profound love and loyalty and fierce disagreement. Both Latin American by birth, and impassioned by nature, Marta and Leo's in-house battles centered around the issue of control; the males of their generation assumed a dominance that did not sit gently with Marta. Since Leo's death, however, with no vetoes to trouble a long-held dream, Marta transformed the gloomy living space of her house into a wide-open, sun-catching studio, and replaced the concrete backyard with an exotic flowering garden. Her voice held no equivocation as she confessed that, for the first time in thirty-five years, she felt a sense of unparalleled freedom. I sat back—the attentive listener—happy this was Marta's exposé, not mine. Awed by her honesty, I poured myself more tea and felt smug with complacency at my own more perfect marriage.

For weeks after sharing tea with Marta though, the word *freedom* kept lighting up my brain, flashing on and off like the security light that illuminates the outside of my house at night, a warning to intruders to stay away. Freedom hammered at my heart and I could no longer hide what I have long known: I am a different person since Art has died. Though he brought a sublime serenity to my life—without him I have known raw grief which all but destroyed me—the freedom I'm now living is one I'd find hard to surrender. It's as if the cocoon of marital comfort in which I was happily indulged for so many years burst asunder, catapulting me into a new world where I might fly to a star or sink to a waiting grave. Flying, however, is not without its terror.

Uneasiness began to haunt my days and wreck my nights. The light that once flashed *freedom* stopped turning on and *guilt* moved in, holding high a banner marked *disloyal*. Unable to face my pursuing nemesis, I continued to deviously question my women friends about the freedom in their own marriages. Rosie, in her sixties, whose second marriage is proving as troublesome as her first, had no hesitation in describing the institution of marriage as a prison. Elizabeth and Ann, friends in their eighties, were both perplexed by my question and mentioned in reproachful tones the word *compromise*. The screw turned another notch deeper in my psychic guilt, and I wondered if it's possible for love and freedom to coexist within a marriage. Perhaps this is simply a philosophical abstraction, but it has become less so since Art has died. Paradoxically, his death has forced me to face the cobwebs in my closet, and it was precisely these cobwebs which led me to visit Amos, a Buddhist therapist I occasionally see, whose quiet observations invariably move me out of confusion and back into understanding.

Feelings of profound guilt and disloyalty toward Art overwhelmed me that Wednesday afternoon as I sat across from Amos and wept. Did my present feelings of freedom imply a past entrapment? Were my fifty-two years with Art merely the fantasy of a needy imagination?

"You are talking about two entirely separate issues, Joan. Your guilt, and your marriage," Amos asserted.

Slowly I began to understand that my guilt had nothing at all to do with Art and the quality of our marriage. It was the guilt of self-deception, of denying what is mine. The reason I feel free is simply because I am. It is a freedom conceived in love and made viable through loss.

My life with Art was one in which we fostered each other's needs, smoothed one another's rough spots and lived our subscribed roles. Helpless when faced with an appliance, a stuck typewriter ribbon, or a recalcitrant car that refused to start, I'd simply call Art who would unerringly fix the problem. Likewise, in social situations where I knew Art might wish he were elsewhere, I'd see his face as he searched for me to rescue him, and I would immediately be there. Neither of us intruded across party lines. It worked for us. But, at the same time, we protected each other from pushing against our growing edges, and part of me willingly relaxed into an extended gestation and would only be born after Art died.

Now, the canvas of my life has stretched to fit a broader frame. Since I no longer have conflicting loyalties, I have moved closer to my children, who have enlarged their roles to include an element of protection toward me. In an intimacy fashioned out of our individual grieving, the three of us flow together more gently now. I handle my own finances, maintain the house, and visit friends with no time constraints calling me home. I fly to Los Angeles when I feel like seeing my granddaughter, Megan. My grandson, Adam, frequently stays for dinner and sleeps over to escape the clatter of his fraternity. I wouldn't want to give any of it up.

The other day, nervously cutting down invasive bamboo trees in the garden, I felt Art there, keeping a watchful eye on me. The stems varied in length from twenty to thirty feet and, as they fell, I prayed they wouldn't decapitate a rose bush. Then I heard Art's encouraging voice: *See, I told you you could do it.* And I stood there wondering at my assumed helplessness when we were together.

It was not like I was held in servitude to a system devised by Art during our marriage. On the contrary, he was a scientist endowed with Godlike patience, while I, his most recalcitrant student, wondered about the nature of the world around us—how it all started, how the planets were formed—the questions an inquisitive child would ask. But rarely had I listened to his answers.

As a child, danger lurked in the dark underbelly of knowledge in my raveled home, where my father's affairs and my mother's unhappy desperation hovered like a simmering volcano over my days and nights. I learned never to ask questions of my parents since, if I did, they might confirm my worst fears and disappear, leaving me with no forwarding address. And then who would be there for me? Better not to know anything, I reasoned.

Later, every learning situation became a tug-of-war between my desire to know and my intractable gut fighting to remain ignorant. Ironically, though, the battleground changed after Art died. Blind grief shocked me out of my habitual rut and my mind jump-started to a different rhythm. As I took hold of life again in a world less shuttered, I began to ask questions of those around me and to wait for a response. Soon, I found I was hearing the answers with a more open, receptive heart. I found, too, that there was nothing to fear since the worst had happened, and I was still alive.

Two weeks after Art died, a colleague of his named Seth telephoned to offer me comfort and suggest that we meet for coffee. Art had known and admired Seth, and I recalled the odd attraction I'd felt toward him the one time he came to our house for dinner, about ten years earlier. It was then I realized that what held me enthralled was Seth's resemblance to my father. My love affairs during my teens and early twenties invariably involved charismatic older men who, given the slimmest evidence, I'd fit into a projection of my idealized father, the father who would sustain and never leave me.

Meeting Seth in a café felt too formal, so I suggested we have tea at my house instead. Together, we sat at the dining room table talking about Art and, as I studied Seth's face, I felt the old attraction—coupled with an uneasy excitement—stir within me. The conversation turned to Seth's concern about my life without Art and how I would manage living alone. Would I remain in the house? Were my children around and supportive? As we talked, my despair, as though by design, moved silently into the shadows and, in its place, I found an old theme being replayed. No longer hidden in ambiguity, I came face-to-face with my sexual longing for this man alongside me.

During the next six months Seth came for tea a couple of times, and each time I lost more of my initial uneasiness. In September, I invited him to dinner. As I stood preparing hors d'oeuvres in the kitchen, waiting for his arrival, a mix of aloneness and excitement fluttered through me, and I longed for Art to protect me from myself. Sensing the dynamics of the evening would be different, I opened the door to Seth with some trepidation. I knew I was sailing into uncharted waters. A glass of red wine steadied my fears and, as Seth and I chatted over dessert, I had the distinct physical sensation of expanding into a looser space, of tossing overboard a layer of baggage which had outlived its time. Later, listening to music upstairs in the living room, our conversation more intimate, Seth spoke about his two brief, unhappy marriages and his pleasure in the company of women. In turn, I emphasized the blessedness of my years with Art, adding that I had no intention of ever marrying again, though perhaps I'd take a lover sometime. It was a calculated remark, and Seth's quick rejoinder was to the point. "Let's take off our clothes," he ventured.

Caught in a web of my own design, my mind sounding its familiar warnings, I panicked. Hoping to find an easy exit, I looked into Seth's face, but saw only impassivity and his lingering question. Playing for time, I got up from the couch, walked across the room and switched off the music. Then my heart moved to my rescue. "Let's," I replied, turning back to Seth.

Downstairs in the bedroom it was more than my clothes I took off. I also let go of a script written by a triad of enforcers: twentieth century middle-class England, where sex was a blushingly dirty word; my parents, whose sexual war games bruised my innocence; and finally, but perhaps most importantly, my conforming self who had learned to bury her sexuality under a colossus of shame.

Art and I had loved and trusted each other for fifty-two years and our lovemaking was a shared delight, yet we both knew part of me was hiding and still feared my mother's mantra. "To trust your love to a man is the quickest path to abandonment," she used to say. After I lost Art, the terrible grief that burst through all of my withholdings liberated parts of myself I'd never known. At the age of eighty, I met them.

My relationship with Seth is, I tell him, my great experiment. He calls me on every one of my tightly held protections, and his pleasure in meeting my body is matched by my own freedom to respond. Ours is a relationship with no hidden agenda, no commitments. Our occasional evenings of uncomplicated delight are the intertwining of two desires who touch down and embrace each other, knowing they will meet again, sometime, somewhere. And although sex is not absent from our meetings, it is, rather, my compelling ache to be touched and held and to touch and hold that pulls me back each time to Seth. Like the newly born whose being depends upon the enfolding presence of a parent, those of us who are now so old, glow more warmly when we, too, may share our tenderness.

Though my life is still a solitary one, my imagination gifts the empty spaces with a fantasy I cling to. It is that one day, returning home from the market, I will open the front door and find Art waiting for me upstairs in the living room, lounging in his favorite leather chair, wearing the green velour jacket we bought together.

"There she is," he says, as he swivels the chair in my direction, the way he always did.

I leave the groceries in the kitchen, walk the six steps up to the living room and, as Art stands to greet me, I take his face in my hands and speak his name. Holding each other, we stroke the familiar bodies, our natures merging, breathing in eternity as a little bit of heaven returns.

Yes, I want him back, with every cell of my being. But it would be different.

At Seventy, Mom Finally Goes Camping

Bill Sherwonit

Mom's friends back east thought she must be crazy. "You're doing WHAT?" they asked when told of her summer plans.

"I'm going camping," she would calmly repeat. "Finally."

Even more outrageous was the destination Mom had picked for her first-ever tent-camping trip: Alaska. And the Brooks River of all places, home to one of the world's largest gatherings of brown bears, the coastal cousins of grizzlies. A little crazy? Perhaps. But unquestionably a courageous act, too, for seventy-year-old Torie Sherwonit. My mother had come to Alaska twice before, in 1983 and 1990. But this was her first trip without her husband and my father, Ed, who died from complications of cancer in December 1990.

After forty-four-and-a-half years of marriage, Mom began the painful readjustment of learning to live alone. It was also the start of an often frightening, yet sometimes joyful, voyage of self-discovery. She began doing things never imagined possible. Driving long distances alone. Buying a brand-new car. Doing yard landscape work and home repairs. Planning cross-country trips.

"I was married so young, I didn't have a chance to experience myself as an individual until I was much older," she explained as we discussed her visit to Alaska. "In part, it was my generation. My greatest joy was taking care of Dad and you kids. Going back to work at age thirty-nine was a big step for me. Doing that and becoming active in the PTL (Parent-Teacher League) helped expand my horizons."

"Still," she said, "up until Dad died, I was much more of a follower. I often hid behind my husband. I never thought I could be this independent."

It was such newfound independence—and a growing sense of adventure—that led Mom to Katmai National Park's Brooks River and Camp. Given the option of staying in Brooks Lodge or the National Park Service campground, Mom decided a compromise might be best: two nights in a tent, followed by three nights in a cabin. This was probably something she would have tried when younger, if things had been different. But as a child growing up in Connecticut, her home for sixty-seven years, she was plagued by allergies and asthma so bad that camping was out of the question. And later, when married, her occasional suggestions of a family campout were inevitably vetoed by my father.

"Dad liked his comforts," Mom recalled. "He said he'd done enough camping during World War II. His idea of a campout was to go to a motel."

And Mom had neither the experience, nor the confidence, to lead her own camping expedition.

To prepare for the Katmai campout, we spent a weekend at Nancy Lake State Recreation Area. There, in the relative luxury of a stove-heated public-use cabin, Mom spent her first night ever in a sleeping bag. After hours of fidgeting and sliding and tossing about, she finally fell into a restless sleep sometime after midnight, only to be awakened a couple of hours later by a "call of nature." Her trip to the outhouse was repeated every hour or two, until 9 a.m. Frequent bathroom trips were nothing new, she explained. It had something to do with her medication. Still, "It's a little more inconvenient when you have to go outside to the john."

Plagued by an assortment of maladies, from arthritis to ulcers, Mom had come to Alaska equipped for almost any medical emergency. Her personal survival gear included a half-dozen pill bottles, with medicine for allergies, asthma, stomach, and head. Despite her first-night difficulties, she later wrote in the cabin's log book, "My first camping experience (at seventy) and I sure enjoyed it."

The Nancy Lake weekend was followed, five days later, by Mom's venture into uncharted territory. Foremost in her mind wasn't the camping, but the bears. "Are you sure I'm going to see bears?" she asked for the umpteenth time upon our arrival at Katmai. "I'm so looking forward to that." Any final doubts disappeared that evening as Mom watched a dozen of Katmai's brown bears fish for salmon at Brooks Falls.

On returning to our campsite, Mom and I retired into the tent shortly before midnight and snuggled into our sleeping bags. Then she proceeded to wriggle and squirm until 3:30 a.m. The next morning, still groggy from her largely sleepless night, she confided, "It's probably an experience I could have done without—but I don't regret it. It's just that my body ached so. And I think the dampness bothered me. Plus I had 'restless legs.' I don't know how people do this for days at a time."

Despite some apprehensions about meeting a bear in the twilight of an Alaskan summer night, Mom insisted on going alone to the outhouse, without even taking a flashlight to brighten her way. More intimidating than any bear was the thought of another night of tent camping, but night number two went much more smoothly. So smoothly, in fact, that Mom decided she could take more of it. She had no trouble falling asleep. No claustrophobia. No restless legs or aches. "Pretty good, huh?" she asked.

I nodded my agreement. It was, indeed, an impressive performance. But despite her newfound enthusiasm for tent camping, Mom reluctantly—well, not too reluctantly—agreed we should move to the lodge. We did, after all, have reservations. We made the switch and celebrated my mother's successful campout in the luxury of a cabin complete with sink, shower, oil-heated stove, and beds with mattresses and blankets.

For three more days we walked among the bears—from an appropriately safe distance, of course—and ate sockeye salmon fresh from the Brooks River. Another first for Mom. Almost inevitably, we had a few close encounters with bears along the trails. Despite assurances that they were used to people's presence, Mom experienced a few moments of high anxiety; perfectly natural for someone still getting used to Alaska's ursine residents. Though admitting "sometimes it's a little scary," Mom kept emphasizing that she "wouldn't have missed it for the world. This is such an incredible experience. All of these things I wouldn't have done alone, if Dad were still alive."

In some ways, then, my father's death, though sorrowful, has been a blessing for my mother (though she might never say so). She's found parts of herself, including an adventurer's spirit, she never knew existed. At age seventy, Torie Sherwonit has mingled with the bears. And she's experienced the joys and trials of sleeping in a tent. What a gift to come out of hiding. Even if it means acting a little crazy at times.

Cane

Katharyn Howd Machan

for jackie, as we continue

In sparkling velvet, blue a hint throughout,
she takes the stage, her hip a thrust of knife
through bread and bone as drumbeat brings about
rich transformation only fullest life
can make real breath and truest reach. No young
embrace of this long art can give so much,
however dexterous and deft among
applauding crowds; it takes a seasoned touch
to ripple through the air of time and move
an audience to know the why and when
of how they've come to live and deeply love
the yes of saying yes despite again.
She carries us in arc of curving gold
as music celebrates a new word: *old.*

The Further Adventures of the Crackpot Crones: The Dance Class

SuzAnne C. Cole

> Laughing Out Loud is the Virtue of Crackpot Crones who know we have nothing to lose.
>
> Mary Daly, *Outercourse*

Once again, my friend Sally and I have released our inner crackpot crones. (Although I must record here Sally's objection to the word "crone." Five years younger than I, she prefers to be known as a "cronette.") Three weeks ago she called with news of a Japanese modern dance troupe, *Buto-Sha Tenkei,* coming to Houston for two performances. She couldn't attend either one, but she had learned that the company's dance master would conduct a master class for interested students.

"Wanna go?" she asked.

"A master class?" I demurred. "We're not dancers."

"Oh, come on," she said. "You talked me into joining your Neuromuscular Integrative Movement class; that's dance exercise—and we love it. Besides, the class is for theater majors too."

"Okay," I said, "sign us up." Too late it occurred to me that the closest we came to being drama majors was our mutual talent for hyperbole. So be it. There had been other crone adventures—a sweat lodge one cold January, eighteen women crammed into a sweltering teepee, praying and singing "Amazing Grace" for hours. Backpacking in the Sierra Nevadas with me, a devotee of spas, carrying a forty-pound pack, digging holes for latrines, drinking water from a lake—and loving it.

So today Sally and I waltz into the community center, confirm our enrollment, leave our shoes at the door, and enter a large gymnasium lined with mirrors—and folding chairs. *Oh goody,* I think, *we get to sit and watch a demonstration.*

But she heads confidently for the middle of the floor, where hordes of long-limbed young people as supple as snakes stretch their bodies into shapes I couldn't have duplicated in utero. Sally and I must be the oldest students by a score of years. She at least looks like a dancer—thin, small-breasted, long strong legs—while I could model for *matryushka,* the Russian nesting dolls. She's also wearing black, definitely the color of the day, while I have on pastel floral Danskin leggings and matching oversized T-shirt.

I gravitate toward a corner in the back—right in front of the folding chairs just as dozens of junior high kids pour into the gym and fill them. No time to worry about our proximity as we rise to honor the dance master. A frail man, black beret slipping down a bald head, he wears a cocoon of clothing. After brief introductions through an interpreter, we move into a warm-up—making figure eights with our arms, swaying our bodies like trees, stretching our faces by pretending to chew gum. Repressing giggles, I carefully imitate the solemn-faced dance master.

Then we are passengers on a bus bumping down a country road. In irregular rows we hang onto imaginary straps, heads, shoulders, and knees bobbing as we pantomime our ride. Next we become seaweed on the ocean floor. I close my eyes as we drift along with the current, the better not to see myself in the mirrors—or the snickering students watching us with bored faces, this clearly not the field trip they had envisioned.

We become passengers on a space shuttle, blasting off the earth with explosions of energy, then space walking with giant deliberate steps, children playing *Simon says take three giant steps.* The twenty-something man in front of me, bleached blond crewcut, displays multiple nipple rings under his loose tank top. My concentration wavers. What does it feel like to have those installed? Dance Master, could we portray the emotion of this young man as he decided to pierce his body? Could we dance the insertion of the rings?

In a new scenario, we are balloons filling with air. As I sail along, a photographer, vest bulging with film and lenses, kneels for shot after shot, covering the room, even lying down to get a coveted angle. I consider pulling my T-shirt over my face until I envision that potential picture.

Next to me Sally blissfully dances on, eyes closed in a trance. She looks disappointed when we are told to sit for question/answer time, but I sink gratefully, if not gracefully, to the floor. Someone asks if the dance master knows the history of *butoh.* *"Hai,"* he replies, "yes." His interlocutor ventures another question; could he tell us then? Briefly he explains that *butoh* developed as a spiritual response to Hiroshima and Nagasaki. I wonder if he considers watching me dance seaweed sufficient revenge. I wonder if I do.

A teacher risks another request; since her junior high students will be unable to attend a performance, will the master demonstrate a brief routine? She apparently doesn't consider our class performance an adequate representation of a dance form described by its devotees as physical, spiritual, and intensely moving, but that doesn't matter. "No," he says, "come tonight." The only performance her students will view is ours.

Dismissed, we find our shoes and straggle out as the photographer asks those whom he photographed to sign releases. Sally and I are not asked. I pick up a brochure from the table as we leave and discover that the English translation of *Buto-Sha Tenkei* is "Chickens from the Sky." Crackpot crone and cronette, we two heavenly chickens leave laughing. Too Westernized to absorb a Japanese spiritual climate in one dose, we have not found nirvana in our dance class. On the other hand, we've lost nothing but a morning.

Fare Well

Maureen T. Porter

It was over. She turned the key and wearily stepped into the cozy nest she had shared with her husband for fifteen years. Her *late* husband. The sharing time was over. He'd gone quickly. No chance for farewells.

She hadn't known what to expect. Certainly not this overpowering sense of freedom. *Is there something wrong with me?* she wondered. *Shouldn't I feel bereft?*

The anguish of formal grieving was lifting, replaced by long suppressed energy and elation welling up from deep inside. She missed him. She wanted him back. But not as much as everyone had warned.

Isabel sank into the easy chair by the window overlooking the bay. No need to prepare an evening meal. In fact, no need to do anything. She smiled to herself. *Unless I feel like it.*

Maybe she would just sit there—watch the sailboats race, gaze at scudding clouds and swooping gulls, or read her book. Or maybe she would write in her journal, or play piano, or put on some favorite recordings, or . . . suddenly possibilities seemed unlimited.

This is terrible, she thought. *I'm a widow. In mourning.* She had seen women almost throw themselves into the open grave when they buried their beloved. She had sobbed too and felt her insides torn out of her as Sherman's coffin was lowered into the cold earth—but that was nearly two weeks ago.

The children had begged her over and over to stay with them. "Ma," they'd all said, "this is no time for you to be alone."

"I'll be perfectly fine," she'd insisted, and pulled herself away.

They'd meant well but she needed to come here, to come home. Every time she returned to it, the house wrapped her in a warm, welcoming hug. Besides, this cottage had been their retirement dream; she'd felt closer to Sherman here than anywhere else.

A can of tomato soup and a handful of crackers seemed like a good idea. She sat at the table by the window, opened her book, and ate and read until the setting sun put on a glorious display behind the oak trees. Sherman would always run for the camera when he saw a beautiful sunset, had always planned to produce a calendar for their friends.

Well, maybe I'll just do that in his memory, she thought. *But not tonight.*

The raucous yakking of birds woke her at five the next morning. Isabel turned, flung her arm, as usual, over Sherman's shoulder. . . . She bolted upright. *He's not here!*

Where was he, her other half? But there was no longer another half. Just her. Alone yes, but also somehow whole.

The sun was just rising across the water, a big orange balloon on an invisible string. She never tired of witnessing the miracle.

Okay, Independent Self, what's next? The closet? Cleaning always centered her. She could pull everything out and strew it around while she scrubbed and polished inside. And if she didn't finish today, she could leave the mess for tomorrow.

But maybe that wasn't such a good idea. Sherman's side of the closet was full. Could she gather the courage to remove his things and dispose of them so soon? *Yes. Let's just do it and get it over with.*

After coffee and a bagel, she plunged in and didn't come up for air until three in the afternoon when hunger pangs suddenly hit. The huge walk-in closet smelled of lemon oil and freshness. Good time to take a break.

A sardine and onion sandwich, a pickle, a can of Pepsi and she was in business. It was fairly warm outside, so armed with a book and lunch, Isabel headed for the deck. No need to jump up. Dishes could wait. Closets could wait. Even worrisome thoughts like, *Why was I so constricted with Sherman?* could wait.

Bliss. . . . She lost all track of time.

When the book ended, she laid it down with a sigh. She had always been a pushover for a happy ending. A contented smile lingered as she thought about the new chapter in her own life. Maybe a happy ending was in store for her too.

She pulled the old lavender shawl closer as the evening chill drifted in from the water. The sun was setting on her second week as a widow.

That night the loneliness started—real loneliness, like a dull ache. She and Sherman had been each other's best friend for so many years that their comfortable togetherness had been taken for granted. She was used to sharing thoughts, talking, sometimes flat out gabbing with him. Now there was only silence, a silence so loud, it moaned.

Maybe a walk on the beach before bedtime would soothe her. They had strolled together many a night, the closest of companions, sharing the beauty of the shore.

An almost full moon was rising slowly over the horizon, obscured at times by drifting clouds. She started to stroll along the water's edge, picked up the pace to jog, . . . then to run, . . . and finally raced madly until she could go no farther.

Her slacks were sopping, her sneakers, soggy. She dropped to her knees, a supplicant to grief. Sobs wracked her body. A wailing took control, choking and wrenching her until she capitulated.

It felt good to let it all out, to be physically and emotionally spent.

Time passed. She found the strength to sit up, shook her silvery, sand-heavy hair, then lay back down, staring at the sky.

That's when she remembered Sherman's belief about stars. He always used to say that when a person dies he becomes a new star. Isabel stared intently at the heavens, trying to figure out which of all the stars was her Sherman.

Out of the corner of her eye, she noticed a blinking light. It was just like Sherman—flirting, playful, shamelessly trying to get her attention. "Is that you?"

She turned her face to the light and felt her heart smile.

"Well, Sherman, I hope you're getting along with the rest of the folks in heaven. I know that's where you are. You were too good to be sentenced to hellfire and brimstone." Isabel wasn't sure there was an afterlife; it seemed so far-fetched. But maybe, just maybe. . . . "Can you see me, Sherman? Do you know my thoughts?"

Well, if he did, he wouldn't have to worry about her. He would know she was content and confident and able to handle life without him. And he would know that she missed him with all her soul. *"Sherman, dearest, . . . dearest Sherman. . . ."*

The night chill snapped her to attention. "Sorry, my love, I have to leave; the kids are waiting for my call." She reached out, as if to give the twinkling light a farewell touch, then jumped up, took a deep, full breath, and briskly trotted home.

New Grandmother

June Sutz Brott

My two-year-old granddaughter, Abby, is sitting in the highchair in my kitchen, singing about Mary and the little lamb. I am making her a vegetable omelet. Suddenly a man—a big brute—bursts through my kitchen door, which I thought I had locked. He heads menacingly toward the child.

"Stop!" I scream. "You lay a hand on that child and I'll kill you."

The beast scornfully looks me over from head to foot. "Yeah? You and who else?"

He reaches for the child.

Without hesitation I grab my big French knife—the one I was using to chop celery and carrots. I rush toward him and plunge the long blade into his back. He moans and falls. I gather Abby in my arms, soothing her fright, and feel no remorse for the limp body on my kitchen floor.

Or maybe I don't use the knife. Maybe I grab the small revolver which I had secretly hidden in the back of my spice cupboard. I aim at him, holding it with two hands like Susan Sarandon in *Thelma and Louise.* He keeps coming. I shoot. He falls to the ground. I stare—icily and triumphant—into his shocked, drug-crazed eyes.

At first these fantasies of violence shocked me. After all, I am a, middle-class, nonviolent, older woman. I have never even held a gun in my hand. In the past, when I theoretically speculated about murder, I concluded that I was more likely to be killed than to kill someone else. But all that changed after my first grandchild was born. I suppose I felt similar powerful urges to protect my own children when they were small, but that was long ago and perhaps I have forgotten.

The whole grandmother business started one evening over dinner when my son and his wife announced they were expecting a child. I was appalled, speechless. The words chilled my heart. I thought of Shirley MacLaine in the movie *Terms of Endearment*. She exploded at the dinner table when her daughter told her she was pregnant.

"WHAT? Are you crazy? You can't do that to me! I'm too young to be a grandmother!" I screamed at my son. Well, I wanted to scream. But I didn't.

Being a grandmother didn't fit my self-image. Here I was bursting with postmenopausal energy, switching gears at midlife, starting a new path, going back to school, working on a master's degree, competing with students the age of my children, and covering my salt and pepper hair with Clairol Golden Brown. It was bad enough admitting (only when asked) that I was old enough to have a married son. I usually avoided telling anyone my age and those few who learned I was in my fifties appeared genuinely surprised. I loved it when they exclaimed, "You really have grownup children? Wow, you must have married young!"

Then my granddaughter arrived. I wasn't particularly excited the first time I picked up Abby. In fact, I was scared. I had to remind myself that since I hadn't dropped any of my own three on their heads, I probably wouldn't drop this new, tiny, pink, utterly helpless bundle.

The first time I babysat for infant Abby, I heard a sudden noise at the door while I was giving her a bottle. My imagination took off. *What if something happens to Abby while she is in my care? What if she is hurt?* Of course there would be no choice. Of course I'd have to kill myself. *Wait just a minute,* I told my galloping panic. *What would I really do if she were really in danger?* That's when I started to realize that I was capable of—yes—killing someone—or was willing to be killed attempting to protect that baby.

After acknowledging this unsettling insight, I felt calmer. And stronger. Gradually, the negative shock of being a grandmother faded, and I started buying things. First a portacrib. "Now she can stay overnight with us," I told my husband.

Then I bought a car seat. Abby used it only every few weeks but it gave me great pleasure just to look at it. While driving, I astonished myself by constantly talking to her, slanting down the rear view mirror so I could beam at her reflection.

"See that stoplight, Abby? Watch it turn green. That means we can go. Pretty soon we'll be at my house. Then you'll come in and sit in your highchair and I'll make you an omelet. Would you like that?"

Abby would gurgle and nod and I would sigh, utterly content.

I rarely used pet names for my own children. And "sweetie pie" and "darling" sounded saccharine. So I was amazed at what spilled out of my mouth, expressions whose origins are a mystery. Abby Dabby-lollipop. Or Miss Sweetiepumpkin. Miss Peanut or Miss Apricot. ("You're my favorite girl so I call you all my favorite things," I explained to her.)

Sometimes I want to be asked to babysit and often I volunteer, marveling at the miracle of Abby, her velvety skin, fine hair, and perfect little fingers. Sometimes I think of children who grow up in homes without books or anyone to read to them. "Read-uh-book" was Abby's first sentence.

Whatever I offer Abby to eat she takes, totally, innocently trusting. When she cries, I whisper gently and sometimes she becomes calm. When Abby dumps juice over the floor or rubs pudding in her hair, I tell her it's okay, and she's okay. Then I understand how a child could be wounded by critical, punishing words, and how a downcast face could conceal lifelong scars on a child's heart.

I am lucky to be a grandparent. No matter what personal or professional matters bother me, Abby is the best medicine. With her, I am happy, smiley, and other-centered. Once, when I had to take an MRI, I shook off my claustrophobia by concentrating on a mental visit with her.

When my son knocks, I drop what I am doing, run to the door, open it partway very slowly, peek outside, then suddenly fling it wide open. Feigning surprise, I swoop giggling Abby up in my arms.

"Hello, Abby. I'm so happy to see you."

"Huh-yo, Gah-ma. I happy see you too."

We hug.

She squeezes her arms around my neck and delivers a damp kiss. Bliss. I melt.

What more could I possibly want?

Declaration of Independence

Phyllis Wendt Hines

In the days of my youth
I accepted as truth
That the law and the church made a pair,
And that openly bedding
While minus a wedding
Was sinful and shocking and rare.
In no way could I handle
The hot breath of scandal
If I were to try an affair.
But there's something so nifty
In being past fifty
Without all those kids in your hair.
No one to impose on,
A door you can close on
The creeps you no longer can bear.
And the tangled finances
In late-age romances
Can reach the absurd. I declare
If that old hocus-pocus
Should come into focus,
I think I'll just have an affair!

Delta Currents

Davi Walders

Leaving crusts of *beignets* buried in powdered sugar, the steam of chicory coffee circling toward ceiling fans, we take to the streets again, wandering. Our faces press against store windows as we peer at pottery, price tags, a summer blazer's watery blue. We need nothing; our legs maintain their desultory pace.

At this confluence, careers, like closets and houses, have been sorted, revised, and refilled. Children graduate and begin elsewhere; husbands and history of long marriages anchor us. Our Rolodexes have been emptied of the extraneous; we need only time and space and the Mississippi.

Mapless, we keep walking, relying on the direction of the cooling breeze, the distant music, and well-worn Reeboks to deliver us to a grassy destination along the great river's banks. It is hot and humid as we climb stairs, cross footbridges, pass the cracked brick of deserted warehouses. We have come east and west to rest by this mouth of waters. The current of our words carries us.

Suddenly, the landscape turns green and soft. Banks swell with leafy oaks and shiny magnolias. The Mississippi stretches beyond, curving and gray, yawning with barges and paddle wheelers. Filled by streams and tributaries, patient with the pull of tides and levees, the river glides lazily toward the waiting Gulf. Under a white gazebo, trombones slide; the sax responds. With a trumpet's glitter, saints and sun skitter across the water.

We forsake the benches for the grass, tossing shoes aside. Flat on our backs, knees angled up in homage to aging spines, we let the sun paint Rothkos on our eyelids, splash color on our cheeks. Turning fifty is a time for lying and listening, for words and silence, for the tickle of thick green on bare feet. Ants crawl the damp waves of our hair, bite our thighs. Oblivious to the glare, the changing rhythms of the band, we stare into the kaleidoscope of lashes and closed lids.

"Remember, . . ." she says. "Remember, . . ." I respond. Words flip the pages of college scrapbooks. Chairs in dorm rooms too stacked with clothes for sitting, beds buried in books and notecards, toilet stalls where we held each other's heads until we gave up grasshoppers and Black Russians, learning to stick with Scotch. Nō Dōz nights cramming olives into our mouths until our brains swallowed Western Civ. Regurgitating it all into blue books before sleeping it off on wrinkled sheets.

Standing guard in dyed-to-match pumps as we took new names, tossed the last petals of budding identities. Waiting for the lift of a receiver, the click of a Watts line while lying in hospital rooms, standing at airports, holding on, on hold.

Worries about daughters, degrees, speeches, and silences, opening offices and options, closing chapters and caskets. Nervous or numb, through laughter and tears, just being there. Eighteen, twenty-five, thirty-two, forty, fifty. "Thank you," she says. "Thank you," I echo, changing the stress.

The trombone teases the trumpet; the Cotton Belle shrieks and pulls out, loaded with tourists. We lie a moment longer, silent, drifting. Stiff but standing, we brush wrinkles, ants, grass, and amble toward the snow cone stand. Crunching watermelon and kiwi, we lean on the railing as the still-hot sun sinks into the river. Red and green drip down our chins, staining our hands. Syrup spills on our skirts, on the bank. Napkins stick to our fingers. We are a mess, giggling, watching the current, listening to the Mississippi lecture us on growing up.

Full Circle

Margaret Karmazin

1955:

The water in the creek is glassy clear and stinging cold. Vida can see rounded river pebbles lying magnified on the bottom. She is stretched out on the bank dragging one hand in and out of the water, her eyes fastened on a tiny silvery fish. She is alone. Terry and Susan are off looking for good springy sticks to make bows. Vida has already made her bow and it lies on the ground beside her with a collection of sticks that will be her arrows. When the others return, there will be a quick argument over who gets to be Indian chief. Afterward, with no hard feelings, the girls will race through the woods.

In the meantime, Vida enjoys her solitude. She can study the tiny fish and the insects gliding on the water's surface. She can slit her eyes and enjoy the sensation of running her fingertips back and forth over the smooth round stones. She becomes so engrossed, she does not notice the ants traveling over her ankles and wouldn't care if she did. Sun dapples her back; she can feel its scattered heat. From downstream come random shouts of her friends, but they seem so far away. Soft bliss seeps over her and, for only God knows how long, she slips into eternity.

1970:

Four young women sit Indian-style in a circle on the floor. They are using a room in the Student Union. The spring semester is in full swing and, being seniors, they feel competent and in control. Unworried about grades, they luxuriate in being outraged. All of them have abundant hair and are wearing raggedy bell-bottom jeans.

Vida speaks first. "We can try the examining of our vagina thing or just continue working on consciousness raising." Anyone who knows her can tell she hopes everyone will opt for the second suggestion. Her cheeks are flushed, her eyes wary.

"I don't care what we do," says Brenda, a chubby, buxom girl with freckles and carrot hair. "Just something to get my mind off that bastard I helped get through biochem."

"You're the kind of woman they use," Melissa tells her. Melissa is skinny and black and wears an Afro that glistens under the lights. "You just lay down like a welcome mat and say, 'Hey boys, why don't you wipe your feet on me?' You ask for it! You think I'd spend my spare time cracking the books for some guy who forgets I exist as soon as he leaves my room? Yeah, right. You ask for it, honey!"

Brenda says, "But it's easy for me to help people with biology. I'm good at it. And he needed—"

"So?" says Vida. "So you have it to give and he needs it. So what? I have a great record collection. Does that mean I have to give my records to anybody off the street who happens to want them?"

Melissa is torn. "Well in that case, maybe you should. Maybe instead of joining the establishment's false materialistic values, you should refuse to play and just hand out those records to anyone who wants them!"

"Well, that makes a lot of sense!" says Vida. "Why then shouldn't Brenda hand out her talents and time to anyone who demands them? What's the difference?"

"The difference is," says Melissa as if talking to a particularly obtuse child, "that one concerns objects and the other personal abilities! Records are replaceable but abilities are unique!"

"I don't see the difference," snaps Vida. "I say we shouldn't give anything to anyone that we don't feel like giving! For eons, women have been milk machines in the physical, emotional, and intellectual sense. Males and children simply use us to feed on!"

The young women, all angry in their own ways, are unconscious of their beauty. They are unaware of how firm their flesh is or how smooth and flawless their skins. Instead, they each believe they are flawed.

June, who has been quiet until now dimly realizes this. "You know, we've all been trained to worry constantly about how we look!" she says. "Don't you see? They keep us distracted by setting things up so we'll be dissatisfied with how we look!"

"So we don't think," says Vida. "You can't keep a thinking woman barefoot and pregnant and a milk machine!"

There is a silence, then Brenda says, "I can't help it, I still want to get married."

"Oh Goddess," moans Melissa. "She just doesn't get it."

"No, she doesn't," says June.

Vida slides closer to the stubborn redhead. "Listen, Brenda. It's our duty to change the world. If we don't take a stand, we'll end up like our mothers. Do you want to be used up at forty, all helpless and weak and dependent?"

"She's right," says Melissa, scooting to Brenda's other side. June is still sitting across from them but she shakes a fist in agreement.

"We have to stand firm," continues Vida. She squats, looking wiry and tough, like a soldier in the jungle. "The thing is we need to hold ourselves aloof from men and not get married. Ever. If we want sex, we can just do it, like men have done, just for pleasure or to fulfill our needs. But never, ever should it be connected with being dependent on them. The last thing on earth we want is to go all mushy, to yield, to need anyone. Do you hear me, Brenda? We have to change everything."

1974:

Vida stops to marvel at the incredible antique gold color of Trish's curls after she has tucked her in bed. She pauses, speechless, enjoying her sense of fitting in with the wholeness of nature. The tiny tot pops her thumb into her mouth and her fat little cheeks bounce as she sucks it. Vida groans in a bliss that is almost sexual.

In the living room, Rick has sunk into the sofa and spread his long legs out in a wide V under the glass-topped coffee table. *"All in the Family*'s coming on," he says.

"Before it starts, go look at Trish. She's an angel from heaven. I mean it. How did we get so lucky? She's better looking than either of us."

"Speak for yourself!" says Rick, laughing. "Make some popcorn, okay?" He disentangles his legs from under the table and jumps up to go take a look at their two-year-old daughter. Vida heads for the kitchen and gets out a pan and the oil.

This is the way life is supposed to be. A man, a woman, and a dimpled child in a cozy apartment, passing the evening in front of the TV with salty, butter-coated fingers. She has put on a bit of weight from these salty, buttered evenings, but it all feels so wonderful, she almost doesn't care. This is what being a female really is about. It's definitely true what they say about biology being destiny. How sorry she is for those poor women who don't get the opportunity to be a wife and mother. How empty their lives must be.

Just when the program is starting, the telephone rings. "Damn it, let it go," says Rick with exasperation. "Archie's gonna—"

"I'd better get it," she says, knocking popcorn onto the sofa as she struggles to get up. "Could be Debbie. She was seeing the specialist today."

Rick rolls his eyes. He has never shown sympathy for Vida's friend who is something of a hypochondriac, although she does have irritable bowel syndrome, eczema, and migraines. That's a fact.

It *is* Debbie and she's terrified. Apparently, the doctor wants a slew of tests including a lower GI, which is hell on earth. "They give you this endless enema and make you hold it 'til you burst and then you shit all over the table," she says on the phone.

Vida has one eye on the television and brings the telephone over to behind the couch so she can watch it. She knows it annoys Rick when she carries on telephone conversations while a show is on, but to Vida this is pleasure multiplied. Warm cozy atmosphere, a good program on, and her best friend on the phone. Happily, she listens to Debbie's despair and when she hangs up, rejoins Rick who drapes his arm around her shoulder and slips his hand down onto her breast.

When their program is over, he says, "Wanna do it?" and they run giggling to the bedroom where he strips down in seconds and eagerly flings himself onto the bed in a stiff beach boy pose. She jumps on top the way he likes it and it's over in about five minutes. "Love you," he murmurs, then his mouth hangs open and lets out a shattering snore.

Vida quickly walks to the bathroom, shuts the door, and masturbates. *You can't have everything,* she assures herself. Then wonders, *Or maybe there's something wrong with me?*

1984:

"Why don't you hire a detective if you really think he's doing something?" Joanne sits next to Vida at the long brass-trimmed bar while they both struggle to find someplace comfortable to put their feet. It's 6 p.m., happy hour in the Red Lizard Lounge. "Why the hell are we sitting here anyway? Why do men like this? Let's get a table."

"No," says Vida. Her mouth is tense. Her eyes dart around the room. "This gives us a better view of the place. Lisa said he comes in here. Like when he says he has to stay late for plant club after school. I thought I smelled booze on his breath one of those times but I didn't think anything of it then."

"What are you going to say if he does come in? 'Hi Rick? How ya doin'?'"

"I'll say whatever comes to mind," says Vida as she draws hard on her cigarette and stares in the direction of the bartender.

"That bartender has a really nice ass," says Joanne.

"Yeah," says Vida automatically.

"If it's any consolation, you're looking really good yourself. I mean you could pass for twenty-eight, maybe even twenty-seven. No way do you look thirty-eight."

"Thanks," says Vida, turning to regard her friend. She stubs out her Merit and fishes in her purse for a stick of gum. "You look younger than your age too."

"Yeah, right," says Joanne. "After three babies, I look like shit. If Greg ever leaves me, I'll have to find a blind guy cause once anyone sees my saggy stomach with all the stretch marks, he'll lose his erection."

"I think you're exaggerating," says Vida. "You have beautiful hair and really good boobs. Men overlook anything for good boobs."

But what does she really know about men? All she's sure of is that she's miserable with Rick. All she knows is the gnawing, hollow sensation in her stomach and the fact that the other day she found herself standing in Waldenbooks with chills running down her back reading *The Seven Signs of Infidelity.* Of the seven signs, she has six.

"Whatever the case," sighs Joanne, "I'm too tired for sex. By afternoon I'm like day-old spaghetti. The only reason I have enough energy to sit on this bar stool is because my sister took Mathew for the day."

Vida signals the muscular bartender for another gin and tonic. "This is the horrible part," she tells Joanne. "I think he's fooling around with Karen Hightower. He's always acted kind of funny around her. And lately, he's been avoiding sex with me when he used to be a maniac. The weird thing is, *I'm* horny now. I don't know why but I think about sex all the time. Like a seventeen-year-old boy or something."

Joanne smiles knowingly. "It's your age. I read that in her thirties, a woman thinks about sex every six minutes. It's her peak."

"What happened to you then?" asks Vida.

"Too many kids. I think they're referring to people with a life."

Vida snorts. "Like I have one?"

"You don't know for sure he's cheating."

Vida turns on her stool to look at Joanne. "He's coming home later and later. He doesn't even spend any time with Trish. He and Karen have been working on that curriculum project for months now. When I happened to walk into the faculty room at the Spring-Sing concert, just the two of them were in there and I had this intense feeling that I was the outsider, that I was the one infringing on their privacy. I could just tell they'd been discussing me. You know how Rick blushes. Well he blushed. Then there was his gas tank. He filled it before dropping me off at Nancy's baby shower and supposedly went to volleyball one block over. He got all discombobulated when he picked me up a couple of hours later and I asked how come his tank was down a full fourth. And of course, there's the sex. For the first time in thirteen years, he can't get it all the way up."

Joanne murmurs but says nothing.

"I feel it in my gut, Joanne." Then, "Why are you so quiet? Do you know something?"

"Not really," says Joanne, but she is looking away.

Vida panics. Her eyes are like a tiger's. "You know something! You'd better tell me! You better tell me right now!"

"Oh God," says Joanne, her eyes filling with tears. "Please, please don't end our friendship, Vida. You're my best friend, please—"

Vida stands up and looks a foot taller. "You tell me now, Joanne. Or I will never speak to you again! How dare you keep something from me. For crying out loud, I can't trust anybody!"

Joanne is crying. "I love you, Vida, believe me. I didn't say anything because I didn't know if it was important or not and didn't want to—"

Vida is red-faced and hard. "Just tell it, Joanne."

Joanne sniffs and wipes her nose. "Greg saw Rick at the library with some woman. He—"

"The *library*?"

"Yeah, I know it doesn't sound like Rick, but there he was. Greg swears."

"What did she look like?"

Joanne looks down at the floor. "I think it was Judy Kessle."

It was like a kick in the gut. "Judy Kessle!" Something clicked inside Vida. Suddenly an incident at the faculty Christmas party flashed into her mind. She'd come around a corner and seen Judy remove her hand from Rick's arm. There'd been something strangely intimate about it, something not quite right. Now it all slammed together into one perfectly assembled jigsaw puzzle. Not Karen Hightower at all.

She jams her cigarettes into her purse and shoves her arms into her jacket.

"Vida," pleads Joanne, scrambling from her stool, her face like a begging puppy.

Vida flames past her and out to the car. When she shoots out of the parking lot, she has no idea where she is going. That expression she's heard her mother use—"the carpet was pulled out from under her"— well, that's just how she feels. It's as if her car is shooting through space. Nothing over her, nothing under her.

1994:

Vida clicks the computer to screen saver and lays her head on her arms. It is 5:25 p.m. and another day done. Well, "done" is an illusion; nothing is ever done. The fourteen folders stacked in front of her are cases in point: all hopeless people who never lift a finger to help themselves, people who have sucked on the system year after year. Amazing, the energy these individuals are able to devote to being such parasites when they're all too tired to get jobs.

She raises her head and glances around at the paraphernalia in her office cubicle, crammed with books and files. Her eyes rest on the commercial photo of her grandson, taken with both parents, even though Trish no longer lives with Scott.

All of this infuriates her—her daughter's penchant for taking up with flunkies, the cluttered office and everything about her job. "I'm forty-eight and this is it," she says to her reflection in the glass of her cheaply framed college diploma. "Look at me, double chin, undereye circles and overdyed hair. Look at me."

The next day Susan Blannard from a neighboring cubicle takes Vida to lunch at T.G.I.Friday's. Vida hates the noise there, but Susan loves the place and she's buying. "Listen, Vida," Susan says after they have ordered their pita sandwiches, "anyone can see you're burned out."

"Wow, it shows?" says Vida. "You mean people notice I've gained fifteen pounds, my hair looks like straw, and that I have the energy of a sloth?" She smiles through her sarcasm.

"Yeah, they notice," says Susan. "You want to talk about it?"

The sandwiches are delicious and the french fries crispy and perfect. In the old days, Vida wouldn't have let them add the fries but who gives a crap now? What is there to starve for? No man has seen her naked for over four years.

"What's there to talk about? My life sucks. There's no way out I can see, other than suicide, but I don't have the guts. I'll just grit my teeth and stand it 'til I'm dead. If aliens came down in a spaceship right now and offered me the chance to leave forever, I'd do it. Without a second thought I'd climb on that ship."

Susan is silent, chewing.

"And this whole liberal bullshit about helping people. Susan, by now you know it's bullshit, don't you? People are the way they are. They're born into a dumpy life and they stay there. You can't lift them out. You can pull and pull and pull and as soon as you let go for one second, they fall back down. You know that, Susan." Vida's face is red.

"Well, I don't believe it. I can't if I'm going to stay in this line of work. It's our job to pull them out, Vida!"

"You're what, thirty, give or take?" She laughs. "Wait 'til you're forty-eight! Just wait. All that airy-fairy stuff, by then it's trampled, honey." She looks at her friend's smooth face, wide open to the world like a pansy turned to the sun. *I used to be like that too,* she thinks but does not permit herself to sink into melancholy. Instead she chooses to be enraged. "Everything lets you down."

"You're still young and attractive, Vida."

"Oh bull. You can say that because you're feeling generous. You can afford to feel generous because you're pretty and young and have a husband who loves you. You still believe people are good. You still think that underneath it all, they'll treat you nice. You believe everyone is worth saving and that you can rescue them if you're given enough time. You see, I don't believe that anymore and I'm not pretty and young."

Vida pauses, then adds, "When you're young and healthy and life responds in a friendly manner to every little crook of your finger, you're in a blind spot. You actually believe it's going to stay that way."

Susan closes her mouth and sets her jaw. There is a pause and then she says, "You don't want dessert, do you?"

Vida snorts. "Hell, yeah. I think I'll get that fudge pie the guy over there is digging into. Why not?"

"I think I'll just have coffee," says Susan.

Vida laughs again. "Watching the figure, huh?"

They finish the meal in silence.

2005:

Vida stands on the veranda of her new home, which was built exactly to her specifications. It resembles an Australian outback house with its wraparound porch and overhung roof. But this is not Australia; it is Colorado and Vida cannot get over her joy in living where she can sit in a back-porch rocker after dinner and watch the sun set behind the Rockies. Where she can observe the mountains turn from blue and violet to black jutting giants, rimmed in red and pink.

It has been two years since they installed stents in her arteries, since she was rushed to the hospital with a hippopotamus sitting on her chest while visiting her cousin in Denver. All she remembers is being flat on the stretcher with lights flashing past her as the ambulance screamed through endless unfamiliar streets, as if she were inside a terrifying kaleidoscope. Everyone was kind; they were so much friendlier than back East. She decided then in the emergency ward, that if she survived she was going to make the West her home even if she had to wait tables and live in a trailer park.

She never imagined she would experience this again—this giddiness with a delicious thump in the pit of her stomach when Karl walks in the back door, stomping his feet to shake the dust off. Big old bald Karl with the wrinkled red neck; she loves him so much she could squeeze the juice out of him. You'd never know to look at him that he was a cancer survivor.

"How come that gravel isn't here yet?" he asks. "Didn't Lenny call?"

Vida almost runs to meet him, buoyed by her rapture. "He didn't call," she says, "but you know Lenny—always late. Remember the stones for the terrace? He delivered them a day after he said he would."

"Yeah," says Karl, "I remember. You feel like some tea?"

She smiles and nuzzles her nose into his warm rough cheek, sucking in the sweet outdoors odor. "You want a bran nut muffin? I just made some."

"Anything," says Karl, and she races to the kitchen like a girl. Indeed she looks younger than she did ten years before. Her skin is rosy clear and she tucks her shirts into her Levis, can actually see her ribs in the mirror, she is so slim. The two of them walk every evening after their meal of fish or lean meat with stir-fried veggies. She sleeps like a child snuggled against him.

"You want to ask the Crowels over for cards tonight?" he asks as he downs half his tea in one swig.

"Sounds all right," she says, surprised that she means it.

The Crowels are the sort of people she would have hated when younger—rednecks, not too bright, the wife reads Harlequin Romances, the man's language is peppered with prejudice. But lately she's been able to see through that kind of thing to the underlying substance. It seems that hiding in everyone's interior is an innocent child, light as a spring morning. How had she missed this for so long? How had she passed all those years inside various cocoons of despair, not knowing how good the wind feels against her face? Or how light hits a porch railing at sunrise, how it causes a geranium petal to glow as if lit from within?

She knows death is possible every moment—maybe that's why so many moments seem delicious. Before she sets out the muffins, she opens the window over the sink and sucks in air so deep it almost hurts.

When Less Is More

Christine Swanberg

Today an amazing machine
says my body needs 1,447 calories
per day to run efficiently.
Any more turns to fat
which makes me look
like a koala bear. Of course
I love koala bears
and one could do worse,
but that's not the point.
At fifty-two, my body needs
   less. I need
      less. Mostly I love
the elegant simplicity
this time can bring if you
remove the clutter.
   Yes, Postmenopausal zeal
     is real.
I am a woman glad
the last Modess box gathers dust
like the Monopoly game
with missing pieces. Glad
to dance off the clanky, hardscrabble
festival of desire and striving,
striving,
like a spider who can't stop
spinning webs

where they're sure to be
unwanted. Happy, yes,
for a life pared
to the succulent essentials
and time around each one
    to savor. Like
radio jazz on a cold, February night
beneath a blue comforter,
    listening
with no worry of morning's rush,
no panty hose to bind you,
no boss to defer to.
    Like that
And the watermelon relish
of a life pointed toward exquisite
    freedom, O.
Choosing less to have more.
Debt free. Unencumbered
by mortgage, greed,
    the need to please.
My suitcase is small and worn

Bent—Not Broken

Cherise Wyneken

Ethel put her hands on the arms of the chair and pushed down—trying to raise her weak knees and answer the phone. After three tries she made it. "Hold on," she said—feeling her way to the desk.

"Hi, Grammie," came a familiar voice. "This is Jeanine—calling about Christmas. The gang will all be here Christmas Eve and that means you, too. Ted will come and get you. Plan on staying over and spending Christmas Day with us."

"Stay over? What about Spunky? I know you don't like dogs."

"Can't you get your neighbor to look after him? It's just one night. You can't spend Christmas alone."

And so it was arranged. Arranged—like most things seemed to be now. Ethel had been fighting the battle for independence ever since she was pronounced legally blind. Although her body was wearing out, her spirit and mind were going strong. She had hoped to remain in her little yellow house at the end of Mulberry Lane for the rest of her life. Having gone from total sight to macular degeneration, the growing patch of black was slowly enveloping even her peripheral sight—making daily living harder. Each year that passed had brought its glitches and resolutions. From cataracts to operations, from thick-lensed glasses to a white-tipped cane. From keeping house and crocheting afghans to hiring housekeepers and watching the evening news with her ears.

Hints from the Blind Society—like how to manage the stove, connect the right shoe to the right foot, measure liquid being poured into a glass, find utensils at the table, or use her cane—along with help from relatives and friends had extended her independent living. Now eighty-seven and arthritic, she found herself struggling to win the fight.

"Come live with us," her son urged from Southern California.

"I'd just be a bother."

"They have such wonderful retirement places now," her daughter said. "Why not move to one of them?"

Her fear of being trapped on an upper floor during a fire or an earthquake loomed large in her resistance to that idea (along with "What to do with Spunky?"). As she packed her overnight bag she began to wonder if she was doing right by staying on her own. Like now—with Ted coming to pick her up—she was growing more and more dependent on others. Was it fair to them? *Everyone does for me. I seem to do nothing for others.*

And frustrations were multiplying. Well-meaning people, who straightened out her house, left her unable to find things or discern which pills were in which bottle. Her clothes collected spots until her daughter came from out of state and cleaned them. Someone had to place her finger on the line so she could sign her checks. Were there ants on the kitchen counter where she spilled the orange juice?

But it was Christmas. She put aside her problems and went to join her grandchildren. After warm greetings and hands that helped her down the stairs, they led her to the corner of the living room. Set her in a soft beige chair. Though her back was to the view of San Francisco Bay, the sun shone down and warmed her. The others drifted off to do their chores or play. She felt more alone than by herself at home. At least there she had Spunky. *Wonder how he's doing without me? And I miss going to church for the Christmas service.* At last she heard footsteps and the clink of ice.

"Here, Grammie. How about a bit of Christmas cheer?"

Next came the doorbell, greetings, footsteps on the stairs. She saw each family enter—eyes fastened to her ears.

"Who is standing near me? Move a little to my side so I can see your face." After hugs all around, Ethel stretched out her hands in search. "Someone's missing. Where's that handsome husband of yours, Trish?"

Silence. Someone cleared his throat.

"They're not together anymore," said Connie. "She kicked him out."

"Kicked him out? But why?" She felt around for Trish. "I thought you two were so in love."

Trish took Ethel's glass. "Things happen, Grammie. Let me get you a refill."

The others drifted off. Jeanine and Connie to the kitchen—chatting, fixing food. Kids down to the den playing Nintendo. Greg at the piano, Diana with her flute—playing Christmas music. Cold crept in with the setting sun and whiffs of roasting quail. Ethel sang along to the music until she heard footsteps once again. Trish coming with her refill.

"Thank you, dear," said Ethel. "Now sit down a bit with me. Tell me all about it."

"Oh, Grammie. I was *afraid* you'd ask. I'm too ashamed to tell."

"Well, do it anyway. It can't be all that bad."

"Oh yes it is—he's been untrue to me. You know—with another woman."

Ethel reached for Trish's hand and brought it to her lap—squeezing it warmly. "It's not the first time a man's done something like that."

"Well it's the first time for me—and I hate it. He wants to make up and vows he'll never be untrue again. But Grammie—how can I ever trust him now?"

"You have a point. But it's what you've got to do. Take him back—let him prove himself. Even the cops don't always press charges on a first offense. Then if he strays again, you'll know what you are dealing with and can take steps. There is no marriage without trust and forgiveness."

"I can't do that. It hurts too much."

Ethel moved Trish's hand up to her cheek. "See this scar? You should have seen me when I fell. All red and oozing. It was hard for me to appear in public—it looked like I'd been beaten. But gradually the red turned to a scab. Then the scab came off and left a fiery scar. Now you can barely see it. Your wound is still fresh. Give it time."

"That's not the same. My wound is on the inside."

"Those kind heal, too. I know. Your granddad was unfaithful, too. But look at all the good years we had together as we healed. I really loved that man. I would have been so lonely without him."

Ethel let go of Trish's hand and gave her a gentle shove. "Go on, child. Call him. Tell him to come join us. What's Christmas without Jeff—and his bass viol?"

Later, after dinner was served and their gifts exchanged, Jeff came and sat beside Ethel.

"How can I ever thank you, Grammie? She says that she will talk."

A Sign of Life

Lucille Gang Shulklapper

The makeshift sign read, LADY'S LOCKER ROOM IN USE BY *MEN*. At first, Ashley noticed the misspelling with the eye of an elementary schoolteacher. For a time, she had collected amusing notes and signs with spelling errors but last week in Savannah for the walled city garden tour, she had walked right into the sign blocking the entrance to the hotel where she stayed: USE ANOTHER ENTRINSE. Then, the s had been crossed out and replaced with a c. Finally, a thick black line almost obliterated the words. Underneath the first two lines, the writer had printed, EXIT ONLY.

She had paused then, a bit bewildered by the unexpectedness of the sign flapping in the warm breeze. Somewhat embarrassed, she backed away, chiding herself for not walking around the broken cement path to the door. *After all,* she said to herself, *if people can exit, why couldn't they enter?*

But in the end, she straightened her rounded shoulders in the pink cardigan the saleswoman insisted would make her feel like spring despite the chill in the air, and circled the hotel until she found a rear entrance. Her feet hurt from wearing leather pumps. She looked with disdain at other women on the tour wearing sneakers or sensible walking shoes. Even the younger women on the street going heaven knows where in sneakers looked like they were about to play basketball or tennis.

What would Everett have thought if I wore sneakers, she wondered, hesitating to lie down on top of one of the double beds in the hotel room until she had removed the bedspread and folded it neatly over the back of a chair. *I have to do things by myself. . . . I have to do things by my-*

self. . . . No tears. . . . ran through her head like one of those stupid rap tunes she despised. The seven-word refrain played itself out when Everett died and started again when rain fell on the scarlet impatiens he had planted in large pots along their driveway.

Well, he's not here, she thought, rolling the spread down to the end of the bed. She poked at wispy gray hairs escaping from their hairpins onto the hard pillow beneath her head and smoothed her suit skirt. The beginning of a headache nagged the vein over her right eye. She would have to shower and hang up her clothing in the closet before she could rest. And every time she opened the closet door she came face-to-face with an ironing board some well-intentioned person in hotel management had placed there for her convenience. As it was, she hated ironing. After all, hadn't she done enough of it when the children were little? All those little dresses with those stupid ruffles and collared school shirts for the boys.

None of those sneakered young women ever ironed or even cooked. A lot of them ordered in. The way to a man's heart is through his stomach. Her mother had told her that and she'd been right, too. You'd think the whole world hinged upon supper being served at six o'clock: the children hungry and impatient; Everett reading his newspaper, quizzing her about politics, shaking his head when she couldn't answer, gulping his food without a word.

Now the refrain ran through her head again. She suddenly hated the thought of another walled garden, the torn ticket stubs in her worn but still good crocodile purse that some environmental activist might attack her for carrying though she'd bought it in a time when no one gave a fig. The new trendy material was called microfiber. Micro, maxi, super, all new words. And computer words, dongles and bytes. Well, she'd go to one more garden. *I have to do things by myself . . . I have to do things by myself . . . No tears.* She'd pretend interest in potted plants and creepy vines, oohing and ahing like the other women.

She'd done that oohing and ahing as long as she could remember. Way back in kindergarten, the teacher had removed her from the block corner and put her in the doll corner. "Young ladies play with dolls," Miss Jockert had said, "not blocks."

Thick air choked her when she awoke from her nap. No fire bells or alarms went off, no sirens. She must have had that dream again, that terrible stupid dream she couldn't figure out for the life of her. She was a little girl having to take a nap. The window was open, a breeze was blowing the lace curtains, but she couldn't breathe. She tried so hard to get up from her bed to go to the window, tried and tried and. . . .

"Why, Ashley Harris," she told herself, coughing and speaking aloud, "there's nothing wrong with you. It's just that stupid old dream. Water under the bridge." She studied the room, the oh-so-cheerful wine-colored flowers growing on the green chintz, the fake Edwardian desk with room for a computer, and the telephone, which hadn't rung once in her five days in Savannah. A business suite, the clerk had told her, looking down at his papers. And she had nodded as though she was supposed to understand something. Men liked it when you agreed with them.

In the days following her return to Orlando, she decided to take up golf. For some reason, she liked the idea of swinging a golf club through the air. Everett had a set of clubs in the garage and he had already paid the initiation fees and the dues. It wasn't right to let good money go to waste. The fresh air would do her good. Besides, that new young woman from the pro shop, Terri Chalk, kept calling her, wanting so much to get women to play.

She knew it was Terri when the phone rang because no one else called during the day; the children made dutiful calls at the same time on Sunday nights. Yes, she told them, I'm fine, just fine, hoping she laughed at the right time, and clucked if something were wrong. When she hung up, she felt as though she'd never said a word. On Sunday nights her dream always recurred and once she coughed so hard she hoped she'd die and they'd find her the following Sunday. They knew where Everett was buried and what to write on her gravestone. She kept the name of the funeral home taped above her kitchen counter, along with the numbers to shut off the electricity and the mail. Ashley chuckled, thinking about the mail. Nothing but flyers and people trying to sell her things.

She had been surprised by Terri's youth when she met her but more so by her authoritative manner. In fact, she'd been a bit taken aback when Terri called her by her first name. And the young man in the golf shop had complimented her about how good she looked in her new golf clothes. . . . She really was a fool to have bought that purple outfit.

She was wearing it when she read the sign: LADY'S LOCKER ROOM IN USE BY *MEN*. She badly needed to go to the bathroom. Taking lessons made her nervous—although she was certain Terri didn't know how she felt, what with all her smiling and acting so polite and all. Two men brushed past her in the hallway without so much as a polite, "excuse me," as if she weren't standing there, plain as day in her purple outfit with matching visor.

Ashley pushed open the door to the ladies' locker room. Heavy cigar smoke almost obscured the five men playing cards. A greasy looking man with a slight build and curly gray hair looked up. "Can't you read?"

"Yes, I can read, thank you." Ashley could taste the smoke as though she'd eaten it with a soupspoon.

"You're welcome," he said with a smirk.

The men continued to play cards. Ashley couldn't breathe, nor could she move. A fat man with huge square shoulders, like an ex–football player, glanced at her, then emptied his beer mug and belched.

Deep anger burst through Ashly and she dashed out of the room and yanked the sign from the door. She felt as though someone had lit a match to her fingers.

Fury, flaming and crackling like a firecracker, propelled her back into the locker room. "Yes, I can read," she screamed, ripping the paper sign into shreds and throwing them at the men.

They just sat and looked at her.

Seconds later in the pro shop, Ashley howled, "I can't even go to the bathroom in private!"

The manager had been trained to listen. All he said was, "I'm sorry," and continued to tally the day's receipts.

A young woman approached Ashley. "I've got to shower and change my clothes. This is ridiculous. I'm going in there. You coming?"

Ashley nodded.

"Tough shit," the girl told the men after they asked her if *she* could read. "Get out of here."

Not one made a move.

Ashley screeched, "Get out of here!" And a great wall of air rushed into her lungs, filling her with an energy she had never known. Or could not remember.

"What a bitch," one of the men said.

Ashley made no effort to stem her anger. "Bitch?! I'll show you a bitch." She kicked over the card table and stomped it with the spikes on her golf shoes. Then watched with satisfaction as the men scrambled to leave the locker room.

"I warned those men," Ashley told her children that Sunday evening. "I could have started a discrimination suit, you know. The manager apologized to me over and over.

"No, you don't need to come down. All I have to do is yell 'fore' and you should see them get out of my way.

"What am I laughing about? Don't you know a good joke when you hear one?"

For a long while, she sat by the phone, part of her still laughing. But when she finally stood she was amazed by the tear stains on her purple outfit.

Fresh Air

Dolores Landy Bentham

"What are they?" he asked. It was obvious what they were. His real question was were they alive.

"Are they alive?" he asked.

They were human brains in large jars with fitted lids on shelves over the soapstone sink in the neuropathology lab of the medical school.

"No, they are not alive. The brains here are all dead. The repetitive nature of the work does that. Our brains have been dying for years in this lab. Mine is as dead as those in the jars."

"Sorry, ma'am, I didn't need to know all that. I'm just delivering this envelope and I saw those brains and I didn't know."

"Well, now you know," she said as she stuck her head into the chief's office for the lunch order. She knew the answer, of course; it had been the same for seven years. Sometimes lean corned beef was substituted for lean pastrami. Make sure it's lean on rye with mustard and the cigar—Cuban of course. You could get them then.

He hesitated a moment at the door. "I may be just a delivery boy, but my work is never the same. Each day I have to find places I've never been to and read addresses I can barely make out. It's not much, but it's challenging. And I get to walk around outside and smell the clean air. This place stinks. How can you breathe?"

"I can't and that's the trouble. I can't breathe. It is stifling in here. I would like to go out and walk around the city under the bright sky and smell the sweet odor of flowering trees instead of the formalin in those jars. Maybe I would rather deliver things to hard-to-read addresses and if I couldn't make out one I'd leave it at the next place and let them sort things out for themselves."

Encouraged by this, he went on. "I will someday buy a rig and deliver long distances over highways and turnpikes and watch the trees fly by. I'm saving up to buy a rig. But that's down the line. I have to prepare myself first."

"What do you mean prepare yourself? What do you have to do?"

Warming to the subject, he went on. "I have to get the proper driver's license. Then I can work for someone who has a rig and I'll make enough money to buy my own."

"Prepare yourself," she said. "Prepare yourself. I wish you a good life."

With that he turned toward the door, but cast one last look at the dead brains in the jars. And, sniffing the formalin-laden air, escaped.

"What's the matter with you?" asked Lee, her workmate. "Come on. The course starts tomorrow and the class sets are not ready."

"No," she said, "I will not clean the class sets. I will not do the H & E's, the tols, the Weigert's. I will not cut the celloidins or check the bibliography for his book. I am going to lunch now and I probably won't be back." She grabbed her bag and went out the door.

How rash she had been. What would she do? She stopped at the deli. From behind the counter the man asked, "The usual?"

"Yes," she said automatically. The usual was the lean pastrami on rye with mustard. "Make it lean," she added. She picked up the bagged sandwich. Her feet, on their own, took her to the cigar store where she purchased the double Corona.

She stopped at the luncheonette for a peanut butter and bacon sandwich on toast and a coffee. She sat at the counter. As she was downing the last of the coffee, the deliver boy took the seat next to her. "It's you," she said. "Is this how you prepare yourself? The price of a sandwich is high here."

"Yes, but the sandwiches are good and I like the way the people look who come in here. They look good in their white coats. Where is yours?"

"I left it back in the lab," she said. "It holds odors. I've told them I probably won't come back, but I guess I will. You see, I haven't prepared myself for the next thing, as you are doing. I don't have the courage to go. That smelly place is like my home. I'm afraid to leave."

"What would you like to do?" he asked. He seemed oblivious to her gray hair. He might as well have been asking a child what she wanted to do when she grew up.

"I want to do science. My own—not somebody else's. I want to discover things. I want to know how things work, what causes what. I want to publish papers under my own name. I want to be one of the names in the bibliographies I check for the chief." With head and voice lowered she added, "But it's too late."

"Look at me," he said, "and say, 'It's not too late.'"

She didn't want to do that. She was embarrassed. The waitress was there.

"Say it," he insisted.

"It's not too late," she murmured.

"No, like you mean it." And in a loud voice he repeated, "'It's not too late.' Say it."

She jumped off the stool and said it louder this time. "It's not too late." And even louder. "It's not too late."

"Now say, 'I just have to prepare.'"

"I just have to prepare."

"No, louder."

"I just have to prepare." Then she shouted, "It's not too late. I just have to prepare." And in a low voice, "Don't order. Do you like pastrami—lean with mustard on rye? Here, have a sandwich. And take this cigar too. It's the best, a double Corona."

He smiled, picked up the bag with the sandwich, and slipped the cigar in his pocket.

As she flew out the door she called back, "I'm gone. I've got phone calls to make. I'm on my way." And she walked out into the clean air, smelling flowering trees under a bright sky.

Noah's Wife and the Change of Life

Prartho M. Sereno

No one ever talks about
what happens to Noah's wife
after the boat lands.

Her life on the ark is no secret—
day in and out adrift in that huge
wooden pod oozing with musk,
all manner of lovers
all over the place.
Long necks, curling feathers,
and those terrible innocent eyes.

What happens to Noah's wife
when the rain stops and the dove
returns, olive branch in her mouth?
When the boat sighs and settles
on a sun-baked rock?

I'll tell you: she leaves.

She wakes one day and can no longer
live with the smell of her past.
She walks out into the newly hatched
mountains, and there,
she joyfully loses herself.

Why Vermont

Elayne Clift

In the Vermont village where I live, there is a sign in someone's front yard that says "Experience Deceleration." At first I thought it was funny, but now, as they say in New England, I think it's a "wicked good sign."

I've changed my lifestyle completely since moving here two years ago, and it might look as though the transition was easy. It wasn't. For years, I lived in a town where identity is everything: In Washington, DC, who you know and what you do is paramount and if you lean too far left of center, you are suspect. Before moving to rural Vermont I felt marginal because I am a feminist, a journalist, a truth teller. People weren't exactly beating my door down to offer me work. My career had floundered because of choices I made when I decided to write. I grieved and thought about where else I'd like to live and what I would do without the plethora of meetings and conferences at which to see and be seen. I traveled to various women's fora, got involved volunteering for a shelter, went to writers' conferences. And all the while I held onto the will to write, the belief that I was a writer, even when my depressed psyche argued otherwise.

Years ago, when my first book was published (*Telling It Like It Is: Reflections of a Not So Radical Feminist,* KIT, 1991), I *knew* I was a writer. That meant carving out time for my craft, which implied reconciling a few things: First, I had to accept the fact that I was never going to be on Gloria Steinem's Rolodex despite my years of feminist activism. Bella Abzug (may she rest in peace) was not going to ask for my help, and Betty Friedan would not be quoting me. This realization made me reflect on the whole of my life and my career—which began when I moved to New York in 1963 at the age of twenty. This is an important reference point because the 1960s were a volatile time, and most young adults with brains were dropping out like flies. But I hung in, doing the establishment thing, insofar as you could without a college degree. Outside of privately intense compassion, I was not a civil rights activist, and I did not engage in fierce debates on the Vietnam War. I simply enjoyed my freedom, and avoided mob scenes and marijuana.

Reflecting back upon this stage of my life, I realized that for the first time since 1979, when I finished my college degree and embraced feminism, I was no longer involved, committed, attached—no longer a real organizational maven in charge of this or leading that. I was a dropout. In a town like Washington, that is a terrifying reality.

For a while it seemed courageous to defy convention. My work was getting published enough to make me feel like a serious and successful, if poverty stricken, writer. But then, feminist publications went under, liberal publications found my work too conservative while conservative publications found it too liberal, and Anna Quindlen was already at *The New York Times*.

At about this time, my fifties snuck up on me, and I found myself curiously disinterested in power, politics, and polemics. I was deinvesting, perhaps growing lazy. Striving had subsided, bureaucracy no longer beckoned. If I died tomorrow, I reasoned, I'd still have a pretty impressive obituary. At the same time, however, because this ennui was so out of character, it became a source of psychic conflict. My struggle, if written as an equation, might have read:

$$A = \frac{P - M}{ML}$$

or Angst = Personality minus Motivation over Modern Life. One problem was that a weird sort of déjà vu, all-over-again quality invaded events, and my life seemed suddenly redundant. I longed for something truly original to occur, for some AHA! Experience. Instead, I felt like people do when they say, "If you live long enough, all faces look the same." I wondered: Did women con themselves about the fifties Power Surge, or was it me?

Then I saw the upside. It was great not to be driven by achievement. I was learning the art of laid-back living. Spending a day writing, or reading, was heavenly and I was reminded of my freedom whenever a friend said, "I'd give anything to be doing that!" "The Great Transition" was also enhanced by my Crones—the group of friends who had bonded with one another at my fiftieth birthday. Most people think of crones as haggard, old women who have nothing to offer but evil spirits. But in prepatriarchal times, crones enjoyed special status as intellectual and spiritual leaders. Many women now reclaim their power during this important transition time and have revived Croning Celebrations.

By the time my group's Sixth Annual Cronefest occurred, my life had changed dramatically. My children were grown, my husband had retired, I had published five books and was seeing more of my work in print. I was teaching in universities, and had adjusted to a lifestyle without business suits or bravado. "Power City," a toxic venue for creativity, was no longer the place to be if I wanted to nurture my muse.

When people ask me why I chose Vermont, I wax eloquent about the friendly people, community life, the state's egalitarianism, the safety, the charm of the place. I tell them I have always wanted to live in a state so exquisitely beautiful that no matter where you point your feet or your car, there is a breathtaking sight to behold. And I've always wanted to live in a place where you had to "beware of moose!"

But the real reason is this: Here, away from the "madding crowds," I can think. I can be. I write. And when I write, I am. Here, life is real, I am real. I am not an image trying to fit into a mirage. What I say is valued, and when poetically put, appreciated. Here, amid artists and carpenters and teachers and women who play in the snow with their children, I am at home. I am comfortable. I speak comfortably. I have a voice. And when I watch the mist rising off our pond in the early light of day like steam floating up from a cup of tea, or listen to the rustle of leaves like a little symphony of wind instruments, or drive a country lane in the periwinkle glow of dusk, that voice is clear. When it speaks, people listen. When it sings, it is heard. When it mourns, it is comforted. When it jokes, there is laughter. When silent, there is safety.

That is why I am in Vermont as I begin the third stage of my journey, having voyaged from maiden to mother to crone. Finally, and at last, I have jettisoned expectation, rejected competition, turned down the blinding city lights. In their place I welcome the genuine goodness of my neighbors, the beauty of the landscape, the gentleness of the muse.

I experience deceleration, and it is indeed wicked good.

Out of Time

Nancy Kline

My eighty-seven-year-old mother is singing me off-color French songs.

It is almost noon. We two are seated on my parents' deck in the late June sun.

"Ah, *vous dirai-je, Maman*—?" she sings, her slim voice as quavery as the oriole's, her feathery hair a fragile shade lighter than the sunlight, palest yellow, white.

"*Au clair de la lune, mon ami Pierrot*—" sings my mother. "Or there was one, how did it go? In Italian. They always asked me to sing it at parties." She hums a few bars, then sings: "*Viva la figa, viva la figa!*" She pauses. "I don't speak Italian, I never knew what it meant, exactly. It was a real crowd-pleaser."

I smile at her. "What a character you are."

"Yes," she says, and looks pleased with herself. "I'm so old. People don't know what to make of me."

I laugh and turn my face up into the warmth of the summer day. "Wasn't there one about a fortune hunter?"

"The one who marries the rich old maid!"

And my mother launches into the ballad of their wedding night. She takes off her clothes. She turns off her hearing aid. She takes out her teeth. She takes off her wig. She takes out her eyeball and puts it in a glass of water.

"I'm becoming her," my mother says.

"No you're not."

"Well, my parts are certainly wearing out. And your father's."

Daddy has driven into town, despite his cataracts, to get the Sunday papers. This late morning moment is my mother's and my own.

"How is he?" I ask. His heart stopped three years ago, for a full two minutes, before they brought him back.

She doesn't answer me right away. Then says, "I'm furious at him."

"For dying?"

"I worry about him all the time."

"I'd like to punch him in the nose," I say.

"Yes."

How can somebody you love so much cease to exist?

Despite the doctors' dark prognosis, he seems to be amazingly himself these days, just slower and slower. What isn't the same, what will never recover, is how we think about time.

We stop to listen to it now, slipping in and out between the shimmering aspen leaves, around the dark green holly bush whose branches click on one another, out beyond us, at the edge of the yellow field.

"So," my mother says, "are you still—sitting down?"

I've been meditating, recently. "Yes. Every morning."

Just the slightest whiff of disapproval floats in my direction. Mother is a Marxist, has always been. As such, she lifts her skirts instinctively away from anything that might smack in the least of mysticism.

"I lift weights every morning," she says. She pauses, reconsiders. "Well. One weight. A two-pounder."

She flexes her left arm. Sure enough, a bump is visible beneath the poignant falling folds of wrinkled skin.

"A powerhouse!"

"Do you remember," she says, "the time we were on our way to Albany and Ben got lost—"

Daddy always gets lost on the way to Albany, it is inevitable.

"—and drove by accident into the Buddhist monastery? How appalled we all were by that lady who was bald?" She gives me a long penetrating look. "You're not planning to shave your head?"

"Not today. But Buddhism makes sense to me. I don't know why. I'm an agnostic. At best."

"You and your father," she says. Like some bad gene we share.

"He's agnostic?" I look at her speculatively.

"Actually, now that you mention it, he told me recently that he talks to God."

"He does?!"

"He was on his third Rob Roy when he told me."

"What does he say to God?"

"According to him, he says—" she pauses, then says in my father's diffident, friendly, optimistic voice, "'I hope you're there!'"

We laugh, the two of us. The tears spring to my eyes. And I'll bet to hers. But we look away from each other so as not to see. Somewhere down the road the dogs are barking.

"Would you like more coffee?" she asks.

"Sure."

She gets up and leans for a moment against the wooden railing of the deck, gazing out at the fragile green mountains that rise in the distance.

"Daddy and I are both getting smaller," she remarks, scientifically. "Have you noticed?" She sounds genuinely interested in the discovery.

"I have." They are both shrinking, growing down, before my very eyes.

My internist tells me you can lose as much as an inch a decade after the age of thirty. A daunting thought, especially when your full height measures four feet eleven and three-quarter inches, as my mother's does.

Did.

Once, she turned to me with fire in her eyes and said, "My whole life would have been different if I'd been five feet tall!"

Now she remarks, "I have a fantasy these days."

"Oh?"

"Wouldn't it be nice," my mother says, "if we could all just get smaller and smaller until we simply, finally, disappeared?"

Fifty is coming, my fifty, I am living out my fiftieth year right now, and though I struggle not to feel this as a desert, I do. I feel it as a loss, a starkness: I have lived more than half my life, it's gone, how is that possible? Where is everybody going so fast? Running out of time.

I have no patience with this feeling, but it gusts around the edges of my life, like driving across the desert, buffeted abruptly by high winds you cannot see. The car swerves suddenly, unnervingly. I take hold of the steering wheel so hard my knuckles whiten.

One of the knuckles on my right hand is arthritic. I have my mother's arthritis, as she had her father's at my age.

My son asks am I going through a midlife crisis. Well yes. But what is that?

He called me on the phone last night.

He is driving across the country this week, back to the East Coast from the West Coast, where he goes to college. He is heading to his grandparents' house, to spend the weekend. By prior agreement, he telephones every two days. On my nickel, of course.

"Hi, Mom," Gabriel said, last night. "The Rockies were awesome."

"Where are you now, Sweetie Pie?"

"Missouri," he said.

"How's Missouri?"

"Endless."

"Don't fall asleep at the wheel!"

"Be cool," he said.

I took a deep breath. "Oh all right. I'll let you be a grown-up."

Gabriel said, in my voice, my cadence, he didn't miss a beat, "But. Who will worry? If I don't."

I laughed. "I'm glad we understand each other."

We have the same hair too. At a certain crisis moment in the hair-cut cycle, our dark curls abruptly spring out away from our heads in exactly the same wild shape and pattern, like a formal hedge gone haywire. We are both known for this. His best friend calls him Fuzzy; mine calls me something even worse. The last time Gabriel came home, before visiting his father's barber, he put on my eyeglasses and smiled a middle-aged smile for the camera. If he'd flashed my pass-port at the frequent flyer desk, they'd have awarded him my miles.

This isn't always easy. Gabriel is majoring in psych and feels the need to tell me, every time he calls, about his need to separate.

"I'm very angry at you," he explains, in a neutral psychoanalytic tone of voice. "I love you enough to tell you that. I'm really furious at you, for the divorce."

His father and I were divorced ten years ago.

"Still?" I say.

"There's no time in the unconscious."

"How about Henry?" I inquire. "Are you mad at him?"

"No, Dad and I don't have enough of a relationship yet. The day I know he loves me, I'll get angry at him. I'm working on it right now. That's why I have to spend more time with him than you this summer."

"Because you and I like each other."

"Yes."

"That's why we can't spend more time together and you're mad at me."

"You got it."

"Great."

After conversations like this one, I seek my parents out to apologize for having been so irritating all these years.

"Mom?" said Gabriel, last night.

"Yes?"

"Where's the Mississippi River?"

"Somewhere along in there," I said.

Geography has never been my strong suit, or his.

He will have found it—crossed it—by this afternoon.

Imagine. My firstborn child is driving a car, all by himself, across the United States of America. So he'll have time to think, as he explains it.

It wasn't till we'd hung up that I suddenly remembered I was his age when I sailed for France. I crossed the ocean, I had a life at twenty.

He has a life, my son. Astonishing.

I found myself singing Woody Guthrie:

> Passing through, passing through!
> Sometimes happy, sometimes blue,
> Glad that I ran into you!
> I'm so happy that I met you passing through!

Then burst into tears.

Because it turns out our children are just houseguests, visitors in our lives. When they arrive, and for a long time after that, they seem so permanent, all interwoven. An illusion. They prove themselves to be the man who came to dinner. One day, years after we've forgotten how to have a private life, they graduate from high school and they're gone. The population shifts, another room becomes available.

It felt to me last night as though my son had driven through my life and out the other side—like that tunnel you can take straight through the Alps—as though the whole time I was under the illusion he was stationary, he was really moving.

And right on his heels my seventeen-year-old. Lovely Miranda. Watch her dust.

In another year my daughter will go away to college. This year, she is taking her SATs, and dieting.

"I'm so fat!" she is always lamenting, and believing it. "Just look at me!" She is gorgeous. She has the breasts I've always wanted, she is tall and slim, her wavy blonde hair falls in a cascade around her shoulders.

"Disgusting," she says belligerently, into the full-length mirror.

Just last week, she managed, one night, right after we'd gone out for Chinese food, to get into the dress she'd worn three years before, to her eighth grade graduation dance.

The dress was a little tight.

"Mom?"

The problem is that I'm her mother. There's not one thing I can say to her that won't misfire. So I try to keep my mouth shut.

"Mom?"

Good luck.

"What?"

"Am I fat?"

I was lying on my bed, attempting to digest my moo shoo pork.

"No."

"Are you sure?"

"You look great."

"I can hardly close this zipper."

"Maybe that's because you were a child when you bought that dress."

"So?"

"So you're not, now. You're four inches taller. You've changed shape. In addition to which, you've just eaten 'Special Diet Steamed Vegetables with Rice.'"

"But I have such fat thighs! They're disgusting—look at them!"

"They're not," I said, and tried to banish the image from my mind's eye of my wavery own. I never thought that I'd be jealous of such things, not me. I'm not that kind of mother.

I'm green with envy.

"And my butt!" Miranda said.

"It's just right," I said.

"You're just saying that. Look at it! It's fat!"

"It's not."

"And my calves!"

"They're beautiful."

"They're not!"

And then I blew it. "Go for a run, if you feel that way."

"See!" My daughter whirled around to face me. "I knew it. I am fat; you were lying all the time. I'm going on a diet; I'm fasting. I won't eat anything ever again!"

"Miranda," I said, "could you do this in your own room for a while?"

Sometimes, of course, we go shopping together. We stop for a salad and iced coffee. We cross the park to look at the impressionists. "Cézanne," I say. "Monet," she says. We rendezvous at van Gogh's sunflowers.

On the other hand, I am sometimes the most embarrassing mother in the East:

"How could you call me 'Snooky' in front of my friends?!"

Slamming out of the kitchen.

"Mother. You're not going to wear those pants. Are you? They're practically bell-bottoms!"

Then there are more complicated moments still, when looking at me she sees some distorted, funhouse image of herself, and she strikes out to smash the both of us. She calls me names, she judges my life. We are both raging, shouting, hurt. We hate each other.

Half an hour later, Dr. Jekyll is back.

She makes a batch of popcorn in her hot-air popcorn popper, sans butter, sans salt, sans everything, and we watch a rerun of *The Brady Bunch* together.

And vice versa.

Sometimes I find myself in such a fury of dislike for her—her narcissism, her impatience, her opinions—that I want to pummel her out of existence. Until I suddenly realize it is myself I am looking at, unmediated. Excruciating.

I hope when this part is through that Miranda and I will choose to be friends. Already she knows things that I don't know. Like her brother before her, she is outdistancing me. Impassioned about the structures of government, she reads me essays I don't understand about the Constitution, then explains them. I expect she'll be a lawyer. Or an opera singer. She will not be me, that much is clear. Sometimes.

Sometimes, despite our twin confusion, it is obvious to both of us that we are not identical. Then we forgive each other.

What a roller-coaster ride, and the two of us hanging on by our fingernails.

A door slams somewhere in my mother's house.

"Your granddaughter must be up," I say.

It is now high noon, which seems to register as early morning on her internal adolescent clock.

My mother turns toward me. "Miranda's very tall," she says, accusingly.

"Don't look at me," I say.

I'm five feet one, my mother's daughter. And shrinking.

"She has her father's height," I say. "But she's really not, you know. Very tall. Her generation is huge. She's only five feet seven."

Out onto the sunlit deck steps a blinking Miranda, still fluffy and bewildered with sleep. She is wearing orange boxer shorts with Princeton Princeton Princeton written all over them and a maroon Wisconsin T-shirt featuring a vicious badger.

"Good morning," we say.

"Hi," she says, and plops into a chair.

My mother's pale blonde skin has leapt me like a forest fire, treetop to treetop, to settle on my blonde fair daughter. I have my father's darker skin, but they look alike, my mother and my daughter, except for the disparity in their heights. Two blue-eyed blondes whose chromosomes have floated to the surface in that dreamy milky complexion.

Not that I covet such skin, which has caused my mother such grief.

"Did you put on fifteen?" I say to Miranda, who groans in response.

The damage was done to my mother in her early childhood, when her family lived for four years out in Colorado. There was no fifteen then. The sun burned down around her daily, monthly, four years' worth of fire to make her skin blaze, incandescent, unprotected. And then, at the other end of her life, to make the cancers bloom. Small growths, nothing to write home about, they appeared when she was in her fifties—two on her back, one a few years later on the back of her left hand, then two at five-year intervals on her arms. These were removed each time without fanfare, to leave white scars not nearly so dramatic as the other colorful benign bumps she'd begun to sprout, with age.

One day, when she was seventy, she saw a spot that didn't look right, midway up the fine firm bridge of what she called her Alcott nose. My daughter has inherited that too.

"I'll have to have this spot removed," my mother said, but refused to be accompanied to the hospital. "He told me it would take an hour," she explained. "Then I get in a cab and come home."

Had she foreseen the truth, she would still have objected to company. She does not ask for help. Her blood is too proud for that, too Puritan. Her mother, my grandmother, moved out to the frontier in a covered wagon as a child. When she was my daughter's age, she taught in a one-room schoolhouse, where her older students, great big frontiersmen, ruffians, all chewed tobacco in class and spat the juice out on the floor. To protect her long skirts, my grandmother drew a huge chalk circle around herself, into which her pupils were forbidden to spit. Then she taught them how to read.

On the day my mother reported for the operation that she didn't call an operation no one came along.

"Are you okay?" I asked on the phone that night.

Her voice was changed, unrecognizable. "No," she said.

"What do you mean?"

My mother had never told me before, not ever in my life, that anything was wrong with her.

"Mother, what's the matter?"

I heard her in the silence struggling to regain control.

She said, "My nose is gone."

"What?"

"Half of it. Half of my nose is gone," she said. "They have destroyed my Alcott nose."

They had kept her ten hours in the hospital, then finally released her. In the recovery room, the nurse in charge of home care took her bandage off and had her look in the mirror: "I want you to see what it looks like, so you won't be surprised when you change the dressing."

My mother looked.

"Now, honey, you were just operated on," said the nurse. "It will heal real quick. Here's how you bandage it."

Then she told my mother she was free to go.

"Sue the bastards!" I said. "I'll be right there."

"My nose is gone," she said, dazed, incoherent.

In fact, it remained, but twisted. Violence had occurred, visible as a twisted scar with a small red puncture at its center.

She joked, "When I get the flu, it's double trouble."

Small children asked her what was wrong.

She always answered them with careful courtesy: "I had an operation," and explained, so they wouldn't be afraid.

But she was.

When we suggested reconstructive surgery she refused. And though she said, "I'm too old to care about my looks," it wasn't indifference we saw in her eyes.

And it was more than skin that was restored when finally, at eighty-two, she obeyed her family doctor when he ordered her to mend her ways—"It's affecting your sinuses," he said—and permitted a plastic surgeon to take a tiny piece of her left cheek and graft it over her scar. When the bandages came off, she telephoned to tell me that her Alcott nose had risen from the dead.

"Hurray!" I said. "That's wonderful."

"Isn't it?!"

"Although I thought you were too old to care."

She laughed.

"At least I'll be intact for my funeral," she said.

I am always asking her look-alike grandchild if she has put on her fifteen, all over.

"Oh, Mom," my daughter's always sighing. "It takes forever!"

I tell her she might try wearing a bigger bathing suit.

Because today more of her surface area is covered than usual and the pale June sun seems mild enough, I do not press the point. Warmth filters down around the three of us, the distaff side. The men are out driving their cars.

"Guess what?" my mother says. "I discovered the meaning of second childhood last week!"

"Oh?" I say. "Uh-oh."

"What do you mean?" says Miranda, lazily. Her eyes are closed against the sun.

"It's like this," my mother says. "You see and hear and smell and feel the world around you, and in you—without relation to time. There's no past, there's no future."

The Buddhists have a name for this; it isn't second childhood.

"It was the Library Fair," she says. "Last weekend. We were walking up Tinker Street. Beautiful—late afternoon, everything sparkling and moving. Throngs, you know. Everybody in shorts: fat ladies, skinny ladies, men with knobby knees. I've never seen so many knees. Kids standing sideways in the walk, transfixed at the sight of other kids' balloons." She pauses. "One little boy stopped right in front of me and said, 'I'm almost as big as you are!'"

Miranda opens her eyes to take a look, blinks, puts a hand across her forehead like a visor.

"Then I saw," my mother says. She looks at me. "How many Library Fairs have I been to—fifty? Suddenly, last week, I saw it was the first Fair I had ever felt, and the last one I would see."

"What do you mean?!" I say.

"It wasn't that I wouldn't live to see next year," she says, putting out a hand in my direction. "There was no sense of doom—it was entirely joyful. I see! I will not see like this again. The sudden sense that all of it was beautiful. And new. And would never be duplicated."

A breeze comes up, to ruffle us.

"The point is," she says, "that the beginning of life can happen even to someone at the end of it. That's the second childhood part."

"Enlightenment," I say.

"What?"

"That's what the Buddhists call it."

"Sounds very grand," she says, and shrugs it away, then takes the gesture and transforms it into the neck exercise she has been trained to do throughout the day for her arthritis.

Miranda, who is an exercise neurotic, watches her with interest. "How do you do that?" she asks. And the two of them launch into a joint training session.

Beyond them suddenly I see a lithe brown deer as silent as a shadow come nibbling into view, at the edge of the woods above us.

"Look!" I say.

The lovely creature raises its head to look—sees us—a frozen instant—bolts. White tail like a handkerchief. Gone.

"That was Florabelle," my mother says. "Have you met her twins yet, Miranda? Deerlet A and Deerlet B?"

Miranda laughs and stretches.

"They are the most charming, tiny replicas. You'll see. They're teaching themselves to bound. We both talk to them, when they come out of the woods for lunch."

"Aren't they scared of you?" asks Miranda.

"Not a bit. They don't have the good sense of their mother. I expect to meet them on the screened-in porch any day now."

"How about the wild turkeys?" I say. "Have they come back?"

"Oh yes! As extraordinary-looking as ever."

And abruptly, my mother is up and out of her chair, all four feet six of her, and into her world-class impersonation of the passing flock, the male, pinheaded, fatly feathered, magnificent, a-strut, puffed up with wild turkey testosterone, and then the brood of docile, self-effacing, browny wives, who trail behind him at a distance, coughing every now and then like courtiers.

My daughter and I fall back against our chairs, filled up with laughter.

"Such bounty," Mother says, and straightens out her pale blue blouse.

In the silence that follows, we can hear the brook running over stones. It is not the season yet when all the water has dried up.

Mother says, "Our books are another bounty." She pauses. "Do you know what I found last weekend, at the '3-for-10¢-Table?' A first edition of *Stuart Little*."

That was my favorite book when I was very young and it was our ritual for her to read me a story every night.

Every night, when I was just beginning, when the dark had fallen, Mommy came and sat down on the edge of the itchy brown plaid blanket I had pulled up to my chin, and when she opened the book and began to read to me, she took me to some other place. Wherever it was that Stuart Little slept in his matchbox and got lowered down the drain on a string to salvage Mrs. Little's wedding band. Wherever it was that Pooh ate too much honey and Peter Rabbit too much lettuce, wherever Captain Hook terrorized the neighborhood and fled in terror himself from the ticking of a clock.

This place my mother took me when she read to me was out of time.

She turns to her grandchild now and says, "How would you like a poached egg on toast?" As if the idea had just occurred to her.

Miranda smiles and nods.

This is their ritual. For two decades now, whenever the children have come to visit, this is the ritual food their grandmother has offered them.

"Orange juice?" she says.

It occurs to me that she has lived on this planet seventy years longer than my daughter. I have been here nearly fifty. My daughter will outstay me and my mother by who knows how many years. Will Miranda remember us, the three of us, out on the deck together in this suspended instant, in the quiet country noon?

I marvel at our intersection.

I wonder will it last, if I record it here.

Acknowledgments

Grateful thanks to the friends who gave feedback, especially Dennis Quinn and Margaret Karmazin; to the authors who contributed their inspiring view of aging; and to all the great older women who have led the way.

Copyrights and Permissions

"Year End Villanelle" was originally published in *Electric City,* January 2, 2004. Available online at http://www.zwire.com/site/news .asp?brd=2228. Reprinted with permission of the author.

"Ride" was originally published in *Reader's Break,* Volume IX (1999). New York: Pine Grove Press. Reprinted with permission of the author.

"White Room" was originally published in *Veritales: Beyond the Norm* (1993), Helen Wirth (Ed.) (pp. 75-98). Fall Creek, OR: Fall Creek Press. Reprinted with permission of the author.

"Baby Boomer!" was originally published in the *Darien Times,* January 9 (1997). Reprinted with permission of the author.

"Pushing Sixty" was originally published in the *Chariton Review,* vol. 26, no. 2 (2000) (Truman State University, Kirksville, MO). Reprinted with permission of the author.

"At Seventy, Mom Finally Goes Camping" was adapted from a story in the *Anchorage Daily News,* December 20 (1992), p. E2. Reprinted with permission of the author.

"Cane" was originally published in Katharyn Howd Machan, *Delilah's Veils* (1991). Ithaca, NY: Sometimes Y Publishing. Reprinted with permission of the publisher.

"The Further Adventures of the Crackpot Crones: The Dance Class" was originally published in *It's a Chick Thing* (2000), Amy Beanland and Emily Terry (Eds.). York Beach, ME: Red Wheel/ Weisser. Reprinted with permission of the publisher.

"Declaration of Independence" was originally published in *Step Into My Metaphor: Poetry by Group 10* (2003). Stuart, FL: Wensel Enterprises, Back Yard Publisher. Reprinted with permission of the author.

"Delta Currents" was originally published in *Ms. Magazine,* May/ June (1994). Reprinted with permission of the author.

"Full Circle" was originally published in a different form in *Concho River Review,* Fall 2001, under the title "Before." Reprinted with permission of the author.

"Bent—Not Broken" originally appeared in *Dialogue,* Winter 2000, published by Blindskills, Inc., P.O. Box 5181, Salem, OR 97304. (503) 581-4224, Toll Free: 800-860-4224. Web site: www.blind

ABOUT THE EDITOR

Janet Amalia Weinberg, PhD, MS, BA, is a founding member of one of the first feminist therapy collectives and has moved beyond her psychology practice to focus on other important challenges. Her short stories have appeared in numerous publications, including *Potato Eyes, Reader's Break,* and *West Wind Review.* At sixty, after ending a seventeen-year relationship and helping her mother through her final illness, Dr. Weinberg moved from her secluded mountain home to Ithaca, New York, to start a new life and to begin work on this anthology.

CONTRIBUTORS

Dolores Landy Bentham at seventy-five is hitting her stride. She's painting watercolor landscapes of the Catskills, playing Mozart better than last year and, of course, writing. But she, like her character in "Fresh Air," had an unfulfilled ambition. That ambition to call herself "scientist" was realized two years ago when she presented her "Evolution as a Learning Process" at the poster session of the meetings of the American Association for the Advancement of Science in Denver.

June Rossbach Bingham Birge is listed in *Who's Who of America* as a biographer, playwright, essayist, and writer of books on psychology. She was born near, and lives in, New York City. Having attended Vassar, she graduated from Barnard College ('40), and has an honorary LittD from Lehman College. For forty-six years she was married to Jonathan Bingham, a Member of Congress (D-NY). After his death, she married Robert B. Birge, a publisher. She has four children, ten grandchildren, and ten great-grandchildren.

Karen Blomain is a novelist *(A Trick Of Light)*, poet, and professor of creative writing at Kutztown University in Pennsylvania. She and her husband have nine children and are awaiting their twelfth grandchild.

June Sutz Brott, after working in the public relations field and after raising three children, earned her MA from San Francisco State University, where for ten years she taught business writing. June wrote a biography *(Needle and Thread: A Tale of Survival from Bialystok to Paris)* about her family's sole Holocaust survivor. Because she herself never had grandparents (two were Nazi Holocaust victims), she realizes how lucky both she and her grandchildren are.

Mary M. Brown, fifty-four, is a writer and a college professor at Indiana Wesleyan University, where she has taught American literature and creative writing for almost twenty years. Though she was born in Missouri and lived in California, Texas, and Illinois, she's firmly affixed to Indiana and working on a book about living there as a fine, deliberate choice. Speaking of good choices, she's also been married thirty-five years—two children, five grandchildren.

Ruth Cash-Smith, who hails from the Illinois cornfields, lives in "Down East" Maine. Her articles and essays have appeared in over seventy publications, including *The Writer, Family Digest, Good Old Days, Down East, College Monthly,* and *San Diego Family Press,* as well as in five anthologies. She has received a Pushcart nomination in fiction. In her late forties, she began to travel to Singapore, Hong Kong, and Malaysia to present intensive business communications courses for managers.

Edith A. Cheitman learned language from pigeons, has been writing poetry for fifty years, been awarded fellowships, published in and/or read at a variety of magazines and galleries, and published her first collection, *Dream Swimmer,* in 1981. She has made her way as a psychotherapist, seller of encyclopedias, bartender, and ice cream truck driver. She is currently attempting to reclaim language for use by people who have met time clocks in person. She makes excellent corn chowder.

Elayne Clift is a writer in Saxtons River, Vermont, who turned sixty-two this year and is proud to call herself a Crone. A Vermont Humanities Council Scholar, she teaches women's studies at several New England colleges and universities. Her latest book is *The Limits of Love* (Xlibris, 2003), a collection of short stories. It follows *Croning Tales* (OGN, 1996), short fiction about wise women's "ways of knowing."

SuzAnne C. Cole, sixty-four, former college English instructor, wrote *To Our Heart's Content: Meditations for Women Turning 50.* She's also published more than 200 works in a wide range of anthologies and commercial and literary publications including *Newsweek,* the *Houston Chronicle,* the *Baltimore Sun, Writer's Digest,* and *New Texas 2002.* She fervently believes in aging positively; family and the support of great women friends help make that possible.

Marsha Dubrow earned her MFA in fiction writing and literature at Bennington College, which published her chapbook, *Single Blessedness.* In 1969 she established one of the first "women's issues" beats for Reuters News Agency where she became a North American Correspondent after winning her sex discrimination suit. Her women's image-related stories have run on the covers of *New York* and Britain's *Punch,* also in *Harper's Bazaar, Vogue, Washingtonian,* and the University of Chicago's *The Awakenings Review,* and her short story "Pearls" appears in the anthology *Looking Back.*

Rina Ferrarelli is an award-winning poet and translator who emigrated to the United States from Italy at age fifteen. She taught college English and translation studies, and has three grown children. Her latest books are *Home Is a Foreign Country* (Eadmer Press, 1996), a collection of original poetry, and *I Saw the Muses* (Guernica, 1997), translations from the lyrics of Leonardo Sinisgalli. Her work has been published in numerous journals and has been included in dozens of anthologies and textbooks.

Sarah Getty's first book of poems appeared when she was fifty-three. Titled *The Land of Milk and Honey* (University of South Carolina Press, 1996), it was part of the James Dickey Contemporary Poetry Series and won the Cambridge Poetry Award. Her poetry has appeared in *The Paris Review, The Western Humanities Review,* and *The New Republic,* and is included in the anthology *Birds in the Hand* (Spring 2004, North Point Press/Farrar, Straus, Giroux). She lives in Bedford, Massachusetts.

Jo Ann Heydron, who lives in Palo Alto, California, just turned fifty-two. Her first story was published in 1982 and her next, after the *sturm und drang* of raising three children, was published in 1999, when she was forty-six. She is currently working on her first novel, tentatively titled *After Christmas.* Her fiction, poetry, and articles have appeared in *The Nebraska Review, Puerto del Sol, Sojourners: Faith, Politics, Culture, Prairie Schooner,* and elsewhere.

Phyllis Wendt Hines was editor of *Sketch,* the creative writing publication of Iowa State College. In 1946 her first short story was given honorable mention by *The Atlantic Monthly* and in 1947 it was included in a college textbook. Now, at the freewheeling age of eighty-three, she has chosen to speak her truth in poetry, light verse, and short essays.

Ruth Harriet Jacobs, PhD, at eighty, is still working as a gerontologist and sociologist. She is the author of *Be an Outrageous Older Woman* (Harper Collins, 1997) in addition to eight other books. She is a researcher at the Wellesley College Center for Research on Women, teaches part-time at several other colleges, speaks on aging issues to many audiences, and leads memoir and creative writing workshops at senior centers and elsewhere. She got her BS at forty, and her PhD at forty-five.

Sonja Johansen, PhD, is a college professor who served as a Peace Corps volunteer from 2000 to 2002 after her retirement at age sixty-five. Three months of language, cultural, health, and safety training in Nepal was followed by a year of teaching high school math and a year of conducting biostatistics seminars for physicians. Now in the States, she has renewed acquaintances with her granddaughter, garden, and computer, and is writing about Nepal.

Margaret Karmazin's writing has appeared in over sixty national and international publications, including *Playboy, North Atlantic Review,* and *Weber Studies.* She has published a novel *(Bones)* and a chapbook of science fiction stories *(Millenium Women, Pipers' Ash Ltd, '02),* and was nominated for a Pushcart Prize *(Eureka Literary Magazine).* She is also an artist with paintings exhibited in numerous galleries and has illustrations in *SageWoman, We'Moon,* and *A Summer's Readings.* She is fifty-eight and lives beside a lake in rural Pennsylvania with her husband and two cats.

Joan Kip, a hospice counselor for many years, writes about aging and matters of the heart and is currently finishing her memoirs. Her work has been published in the *San Jose Mercury News* and in the *Bellevue Literary Review.* She is eighty-eight years old and makes her home in Berkeley, California.

Nancy Kline has published widely, both fiction and nonfiction. The prototype for the mother in "Out of Time" lasted, all her marbles intact, until December of 2004, one week short of her 101st birthday. As for the narrator and her daughter, whenever possible they still sit and talk to one another on the deck, while deer and wild turkeys eat lunch beyond them in the field.

Janice Levy is the author of the children's books *Totally Uncool, Abuelito Eats with His Fingers, The Spirit of Tio Fernando, The Man Who Lived in a Hat, Alley Oops!* and *Finding the Right Spot.* "Life is full of possibilities," Janice observes. "When one door closes, another opens, but it can be hell in the hallway." To her sisters in spirit, she says, "Let's get out of the hallway."

Mike Lipstock's work has probably appeared in 150 or so magazines and fifteen anthologies (including the *Chicken Soup* series, five times). He has also been nominated three times for a Pushcart Prize, has received many first prizes here and there and a ton of rejections. Prior to retirement, he was an optical executive and began writing as a hobby, which, he is thankful, has been successful.

Melissa Lugo has studied literature and creative writing at Harvard University and Manhattanville College. She has published short fiction and poetry in *The Caribbean Writer, The Mochila Review,* and *Poetry Motel.* Her first novel, represented by Writers' House, is under consideration with publishers. She has worked as editor of the literary magazine *Inkwell,* and as a writing teacher. Currently, she is hard at work on her second novel. Besides writing, she enjoys Latin dancing and belting out Broadway show tunes.

Katharyn Howd Machan, born in 1952, Associate Professor of Writing and Women's Studies at Ithaca College and the author of twenty-two published collections of poems, was named Tompkins County's (New York) first poet laureate in 2002. She directs the national Feminist Women's Writing Workshops, Inc., which offers an annual summer retreat on the shore of Cayuga Lake, New York. Under the stage name Zajal, she is also a professional belly dance performer and teacher, with an emphasis on feminist spirituality and history.

Nell Coburn Medcalfe's nonfiction has appeared in *Ocular Surgery News, Crescendo, Passager* (University of Baltimore), and several issues of *Tropic,* the *Miami Herald*'s Sunday magazine. In 1996, she received the First Place Award for Nonfiction in the South Florida chapter of the National Writers Association competition. A native Floridan, she earned both her bachelor's and master's degrees at Florida International University, and lives with her husband, Pete, in the Coconut Grove section of Miami.

Valerie Miner is the author of ten books including the novels *Range of Light, A Walking Fire, Blood Sisters, All Good Women,* and *Winter's Edge.* Her work has appeared in *The Gettysburg Review, Ploughshares, Salmagundi, Prairie Schooner, The Village Voice,* and many other journals. She has won awards from the Fulbright Program, the NEA, The Rockefeller Foundation, and other sources. She is Professor of English and Creative Writing at the University of Minnesota and travels widely giving readings and lectures.

Simone Poirier-Bures began writing seriously in her late thirties and had her first novel, *Candyman,* published on her fiftieth birthday. Since then she has published two more books, *That Shining Place,* an award-winning memoir of Crete, and *Nicole,* a collection of short fiction and memoirs. Her work has been included in more than thirty journals in the United States, Canada, Australia, and England, and included in eleven anthologies. She teaches creative writing at Virginia Tech.

Maureen T. Porter went from high school, to work, to marriage and motherhood. After her three children had grown, it was finally *her* turn. She graduated from the University of Rhode Island and loved every minute of it! Now, reading, playing piano, quilting, writing, and playing with her great-grandchildren are her joys. At seventy-nine, she realizes there's not much time left, but she still has so much to do and learn that the days are not long enough.

Elisavietta Ritchie's books include *In Haste I Write You This Note* and *Raking the Snow* (both winners, Washington Writers' Publishing House); *Flying Time* (includes four PEN Syndicated Fiction winners); *The Spirit of the Walrus; Arc of the Storm; Elegy for the Other Woman;* and *Tightening the Circle Over Eel Country* (Great Lakes Colleges Association's "New Writer's Award"). *Awaiting Permission to Land* (published by World Tech Communications) won the Anamnesis Poetry Award.

Edythe Haendel Schwartz, at age sixty-six, is a teacher, poet, visual artist, and athlete. As a member of the Davis Aquatic Masters, she swims a daily workout from 6 a.m. to 7 a.m. every day. She is also a wife, mother, daughter, and grandma. Her poems have appeared in the journals *Calyx, California Quarterly, Earth's Daughters, Poet Lore, The Higginsville Reader, Poetalk, Pearl,* and others.

Joanne Seltzer is a late bloomer who started writing seriously in 1973 at the age of forty-three. She has since published more than 600 poems in a variety of journals and anthologies, including *When I Am an Old Woman I Shall Wear Purple.* Joanne has also published short fiction, literary essays, translations of French poetry, and three poetry chapbooks. Mother of four and grandmother of four, she lives with husband and cat in Schenectady, New York.

Prartho M. Sereno is now a full-time poet in the schools in Marin County, California, after sojourns into various worlds—four years in India, farming and teaching yoga in Maine, cooking in an international restaurant in Oregon, exhibiting and selling watercolors in Southern California, and teaching at Cornell University. She has published a book of poetic essays, *Everyday Miracles: An A to Z Guide to the Simple Wonders of Life* (Kensington, 1998), and her poems have appeared in numerous journals and anthologies.

Bill Sherwonit, a nature writer, was born in Bridgeport, Connecticut, but has called Alaska home since 1982. He has contributed essays to a wide variety of newspapers, magazines, journals, and anthologies and is the author of ten books about Alaska. Most recently he is co-editor of *Travelers' Tales Alaska.* Sherwonit lives on Anchorage's Hillside, where he writes about the wildness to be found in Alaska's urban center as well as in the state's far reaches. His Web site is www.billsherwonit.alaskawriters.com.

Lucille Gang Shulklapper is a workshop leader for The Center for the Book, an affiliate of the Library of Congress. Her fiction and poetry appear in anthologies, magazines, and in a book of poems, *What*

You Cannot Have. Living up to traditional expectations led to work as a salesperson, model, realtor, and teacher, throughout schooling, marriage, children, and grandchildren. In her late sixties, she rejoices in a voice and a room of her own.

Rachel Josefowitz Siegel, MSW, was born in 1924 in Germany, of Lithuanian Jewish parents, and lives in Ithaca, New York. She has published numerous articles on women and aging and co-edited four anthologies by and about women, including *Women Changing Therapy* (The Haworth Press, 1983) and *Jewish Mothers Tell Their Stories* (The Haworth Press, 2000). She lectures and conducts workshops on aging as a creative process. Mother, grandmother, and great-grandmother, her many roles give her much joy.

Christine Swanberg's books of poetry include *Tonight on This Late Road, Invisible String, Bread Upon the Water, Slow Miracle, The Tenderness of Memory,* and *The Red Lacquer Room.* Her work appears in anthologies such as *Knowing Stones, I Am Becoming the Woman I've Wanted, Jane's Stories, Key West,* and *Pride and Joy.* Over 250 of her poems have been published in seventy journals such as *The Beloit Poetry Journal, Spoon River Quarterly, Amelia, Chiron,* and others.

Sylvia Topp, after writing fitfully while working full-time as her two children were growing up, is finally able to seriously pursue this vocation. When not working part-time in the copy department of *Vanity Fair,* she travels to under-explored parts of the world, collecting material for articles. She is currently working on a short story about her first summer in New York City in 1958, and a book centered on her Scottish great-great-grandmother's diary, written while crossing the Atlantic in 1844.

Pamela Uschuk's prize-winning work has appeared in over 200 journals and anthologies worldwide and has been translated into ten languages. In 2000, Wings Press released her book of poems, *Finding Peaches in the Desert,* followed in 2002 by a second book, *One-Legged Dancer.* Her third book, *Scattered Risks,* is due out in October 2005. Uschuk is the director of the Salem College Center for Women Writers in Winston-Salem, North Carolina, and is just over fifty.

Dianalee Velie is an award-winning poet/author/playwright who started publishing in her forties and continues today at age fifty-seven to make writing and the teaching of writing her much-loved career. Her poems have appeared in hundreds of journals worldwide, most recently in *The Connecticut River Review* and *Peregrine,* and her short stories have been included in numerous anthologies. She conducts poetry workshops throughout the country and has taught poetry/writing at numerous colleges.

Davi Walders is a writer and education consultant whose poetry and prose have appeared in more than 150 magazines, newspapers, and anthologies. Her third poetry collection, *Gifts,* was commissioned by the Milton Murray Foundation for Philanthropy. She developed and directs the Vital Signs Poetry Project of The Children's Inn and NIH (National Institutes of Health in Bethesda, Maryland) which serves patients and families of those in treatment for life-threatening illness.

Bonnie West is a freelance writer whose stories and essays have appeared in *Woman's Day, Redbook,* and many other magazines. She is fifty-nine years old and has recently produced the first two of several Yoga CDs: *Yoga for Writers* and *Yoga at Work and at Play.* Contact her about her writing or her CDs at yogabonnie@yahoo.com.

Cherise Wyneken is a seventy-six-year-old freelance writer who found joy late in life through writing prose and poetry. Selections of her work have appeared in a variety of journals, periodicals, and anthologies, as well as in her book of poetry, *Seeded Puffs,* (Dry Bones Press, Inc.) and her memoir *Round Trip* (PublishAmerica). She is the mother of four, grandmother of seven, and lives with her husband of fifty-three years in Albany, California.

Order a copy of this book with this form or online at:
http://www.haworthpress.com/store/product.asp?sku=5591

STILL GOING STRONG
Memoirs, Stories, and Poems About Great Older Women

_____in hardbound at $49.95 (ISBN-13: 978-0-7890-2870-9; ISBN-10: 0-7890-2870-0)

_____in softbound at $22.95 (ISBN-13: 978-0-7890-2871-6; ISBN-10: 0-7890-2871-9)

Or order online and use special offer code HEC25 in the shopping cart.

COST OF BOOKS_____

POSTAGE & HANDLING_____
*(US: $4.00 for first book & $1.50
for each additional book)*
*(Outside US: $5.00 for first book
& $2.00 for each additional book)*

SUBTOTAL_____

IN CANADA: ADD 7% GST_____

STATE TAX_____
(NJ, NY, OH, MN, CA, IL, IN, PA, & SD
residents, *add appropriate local sales tax)*

FINAL TOTAL_____
*(If paying in Canadian funds,
convert using the current
exchange rate, UNESCO
coupons welcome)*

☐ **BILL ME LATER:** (Bill-me option is good on
US/Canada/Mexico orders only; not good to
jobbers, wholesalers, or subscription agencies.)
☐ Check here if billing address is different from
shipping address and attach purchase order and
billing address information.

Signature_____

☐ **PAYMENT ENCLOSED: $_____**

☐ **PLEASE CHARGE TO MY CREDIT CARD.**

☐ Visa ☐ MasterCard ☐ AmEx ☐ Discover
☐ Diner's Club ☐ Eurocard ☐ JCB

Account # _____

Exp. Date_____

Signature_____

Prices in US dollars and subject to change without notice.

NAME_____

INSTITUTION_____

ADDRESS_____

CITY_____

STATE/ZIP_____

COUNTRY_____ COUNTY (NY residents only)_____

TEL_____ FAX_____

E-MAIL_____

May we use your e-mail address for confirmations and other types of information? ☐ Yes ☐ No
We appreciate receiving your e-mail address and fax number. Haworth would like to e-mail or fax special
discount offers to you, as a preferred customer. **We will never share, rent, or exchange your e-mail address
or fax number.** We regard such actions as an invasion of your privacy.

Order From Your Local Bookstore or Directly From
The Haworth Press, Inc.
10 Alice Street, Binghamton, New York 13904-1580 • USA
TELEPHONE: 1-800-HAWORTH (1-800-429-6784) / Outside US/Canada: (607) 722-5857
FAX: 1-800-895-0582 / Outside US/Canada: (607) 771-0012
E-mail to: orders@haworthpress.com

For orders outside US and Canada, you may wish to order through your local
sales representative, distributor, or bookseller.
For information, see http://haworthpress.com/distributors

(Discounts are available for individual orders in US and Canada only, not booksellers/distributors.)

PLEASE PHOTOCOPY THIS FORM FOR YOUR PERSONAL USE.
http://www.HaworthPress.com   BOF04